The Mystical

Initiations

of Peace

The Path to Self-Mastery, vol 8

The Mystical

Initiations

of Peace

KIM MICHAELS

Copyright © 2018 Kim Michaels. All rights reserved. No part of this book may be used, reproduced, translated, electronically stored or transmitted by any means except by written permission from the publisher. A reviewer may quote brief passages in a review.

MORE TO LIFE PUBLISHING

www.morepublish.com

For foreign and translation rights,

contact info@ morepublish.com

ISBN: 978-87-93297-46-3

The information and insights in this book should not be considered as a form of therapy, advice, direction, diagnosis, and/or treatment of any kind. This information is not a substitute for medical, psychological, or other professional advice, counseling and care. All matters pertaining to your individual health should be supervised by a physician or appropriate health-care practitioner. No guarantee is made by the author or the publisher that the practices described in this book will yield successful results for anyone at any time. They are presented for informational purposes only, as the practice and proof rests with the individual.

For more information: *www.ascendedmasterlight.com* and *www.transcendencetoolbox.com*

CONTENTS

Introduction 7
1 | Introducing the Sixth Ray 9
2 | Introducing Nada 11
3 | Becoming Peace Is the Highest Level of Service 15
4 | How to Live Without Making Karma 23
5 | Invoking the Skill to Live Without Making Karma 41
6 | All Conditions on Earth Are Opportunities 67
7 | Invoking the Vision that all Conditions Are Opportunities 89
8 | How to Stop Blaming Yourself 117
9 | Invoking Freedom from Blame 139
10 | The Illusion of Perfectionism 167
11 | Invoking Freedom from Perfectionism 185
12 | Overcoming a False Sense of Responsibility 213
13 | Invoking Freedom from False Responsibility 239
14 | Finding Peace in Relationships 267
15 | Invoking Peace in Relationships 289
16 | An Escape from Escapism 317
17 | Invoking Freedom from Escapism 341
18 | Self-Actualizing by Self-Emptying 369

INTRODUCTION

This book is part of the series *The Path to Self-Mastery*. The purpose of the series is to give you a complete course for knowing and passing the mystical initiations of the seven spiritual rays. The books in the series form a progression, and it is recommended that you start by working through the books to the First Ray of God Power, the Second Ray of God Wisdom, the Third Ray of God Love, the Fourth Ray of God Purity and the Fifth Ray of God Vision before progressing to this book.

The purpose of this book is to teach you about the characteristics of the Sixth Ray, which will show you how to be at peace with yourself and your life on earth. If you are new to ascended master teachings, you will benefit greatly from reading the first book in the series, *The Power of Self,* because it gives a general introduction to the spiritual path as it is taught by the ascended masters. This will give you a good foundation for taking greater advantage of the teachings in this book.

This book is designed as a workbook in order to help you better integrate and apply the teachings. You will get the best results if you give the invocation that corresponds to the chapter you are studying. It is recommended that you give a specific invocation once a day for nine days and then study part of the corresponding dictation before or after giving the invocation. Each evening, make calls to be taken to Nada's retreat in the etheric realm over Saudi Arabia.

You give an invocation by reading it aloud, thereby invoking high-frequency spiritual energy. For more information about invocations and how to give them, please see the website: *www.transcendencetoolbox.com*. You can also purchase a recording of the invocations and give them along with the recording. The recording is available on *www.morepublish.com*.

In order to learn more about the ascended masters and how they give dictations, see the website *www.ascendedmasterlight.com*. If you are not familiar with the concepts of the fall and of fallen beings, please read *Cosmology of Evil*. That book gives a profound yet easily understood explanation of why there are some beings who have no respect for the free will (or lives) of human beings. It explains why they are willing to do anything in order to control us or destroy those who will not be controlled.

1 | INTRODUCING THE SIXTH RAY

Color of the Sixth Ray: Purple and gold
Corresponding chakra: Solar Plexus chakra
Elohim of the Sixth Ray: Peace and Aloha
Archangel and Archeia of the Sixth Ray: Uriel and Aurora
Chohan of the Sixth Ray: Lady Master Nada
Decrees for the Sixth Ray: 6.01 Decree to Elohim Peace, 6.02 Decree to Archangel Uriel, 6.03 Decree to Master Nada.

Pure qualities of the Sixth Ray

Traditionally, the primary Sixth Ray quality is seen as peace but it is a "peace that passeth understanding." It is an inner sense of being unmoved by the dualistic appearances that are pulling at one from all sides. It is the ability to stand in the midst of a raging conflict and feel the stillness within. It is the ability to feel the pull that seeks to draw you into an unbalanced expression of anger, yet you can remain centered and decide that you do not want to go there.

When you have this peace, you can then give truly selfless service because you will intuitively work to bring harmony into every situation. Harmony is the key to helping people see beyond the dualistic struggle and find common ground. A person with developed Sixth Ray qualities is always looking for common ground and has an ability (especially when the upper chakras are also pure) to draw people towards common ground.

Perversions of the Sixth Ray

The immediate perversions of the Sixth Ray qualities are anger and agitation, expressed as a very aggressive drive to force others to change or to punish those who resist. It is a non-peace that also passeth understanding because there is no way to reason with a person who has perverted the Sixth Ray qualities. They act blindly on their feelings of rage and they will time and time again do or say things they regret later. They will even do things that everyone knows is wrong, yet be completely blind to it at the moment.

Another perversion is what some see as peace, but it is truly passivity, the unwillingness to take a stand for anything. People with this perversion tend to act as victims who can only react to external forces and refuse to take responsibility for their lives. There are also people who lose individuality and become part of a "mob mind" that acts blindly or blindly follows a strong leader. Another perversion is a blind sense that violence and warfare can provide viable solutions or that in some situations they are the only way to react, even justified ways to react.

2 | INTRODUCING NADA

Lady Master Nada ascended during the last days of Atlantis, almost 10,000 years ago, and she has long ago reached the level of Buddhic attainment. In her last embodiment she was born into an important family, and her father and her brothers and sisters were all engaged in government, law or higher business management. Naturally, they were all very much engaged in the process of trying to prevent the sinking of this entire continent, which had a civilization that was in many ways more sophisticated than our own.

Despite the fact that Nada had the intelligence and opportunity to have taken up a position in society, she chose to stay in the background and silently held the spiritual balance for her family members and indeed for society as a whole. The reason for this was that she had already balanced her karma in her previous lifetime. She could see the truth explained in the description of Hilarion, namely that the problems created through the duality consciousness truly have no solutions.

Her family members were still at the level of consciousness typical of many spiritual students today. They felt the need to fight in an epic battle in order to serve an ultimate cause. Nada had transcended this level, and she knew that the highest way to work for the raising of the planet was to raise her own consciousness and stay out of the dualistic struggle. Given that so many people at the time were completely absorbed in the dualistic struggle, the true spiritual adepts could not prevent the sinking of Atlantis, as free will must be allowed to outplay itself. What happens at the physical level is more like a theater performance where nothing has permanence. By holding the spiritual balance, Nada made it possible for many lifestreams to move on and learn from the Atlantean experience, instead of becoming stuck in repeating old patterns. It was through this truly unselfish service that Nada qualified for her ascension.

Today, Nada teaches in the retreat of Jesus, located in the etheric realm over Saudi Arabia. She teaches the exact same lesson that she herself demonstrated. The first step under Nada's guidance is to attain true inner peace, which can come only from unconditionally surrendering all the conditions that pull your mind away from the Middle Way of the Buddha.

For many students this can be a highly frustrating experience. Despite the tutoring under the previous Chohans, many students still retain the desire to engage in an epic struggle. They might desire to free the planet from dark forces or to eradicate false ideas. They are all on fire for *doing* something, yet Nada puts them in an environment where there is nothing to do. She even has rooms where those who will not stop doing can directly see that the more they *do*, the more chaotic things become.

For some students it can take a long time to realize that you will never bring peace – neither to your own mind nor to the world – through *doing*. It is only by surrendering all desire to *do,* that you can begin to feel the Flame of Peace shining through you. It is only this flame that can bring peace on earth, good will among men.

Only when you surrender the desire to *do* and the belief that you know what to do, will you pass the initiations of peace. Only when you have attained this inner peace, will you be allowed to move on in Nada's retreat to where you can actually begin to give service to life. The service you give from the Sixth Ray is *not* that you *do* something for others or force them to do what is for their own good. The service you give is that you hold the spiritual balance whereby people have the greatest opportunity for making better choices.

You will then begin to learn how Jesus gave his service, and you will see how he never sought to force anyone. Instead, he gave people a frame of reference by shining his light. Then, he allowed people to react to the light, even to persecute and kill him. Service on the Sixth Ray truly means that you are the open door for the Christ light that makes everything more visible.

This can have two effects. One is that it makes it easier for people to see what is real, and this gives them a foundation for making better choices. The other is that if people deny the Christ light, they will have to live out their own unrecognized negativity and project it upon the light and the person radiating it. Even in this way do people receive a greater opportunity to discern between the dualistic illusions and the reality of Christ. Giving people this opportunity – with complete non-attachment to how they make use of it – is the highest form of service.

When you come to this level, you will begin to receive direct, personal tutoring from Nada. She will show you any remnants of false peace and false service in your being. When you follow her guidance and free yourself from it, Nada will take you to meet Jesus who will then take you through a set of concentrated initiations that are designed to help you work through and transcend the Piscean mindset. When you have passed these – and you will only get them when you are ready to pass them – Jesus and Nada will lovingly take you to the next level of initiation under the illustrious master of Aquarius.

3 | BECOMING PEACE IS THE HIGHEST LEVEL OF SERVICE

Nada, I AM. The Chohan of the Sixth Ray is the office I hold, not out of necessity but out of love. Some of us who are Chohans could long ago have ascended to higher offices in the spiritual realm. We have chosen to remain with earth out of love for the lifestreams on earth, for the planet itself, for Saint Germain and his Golden Age, for Jesus to see the fulfillment of his mission, and for many other reasons. One of these is that earth truly is an experimental planet where (if we are successful in raising the planet and its inhabitants to a higher level), we will create a matrix that can be used to raise other planets that are also lagging behind the acceleration rate of the material realm as a whole.

How many planets are there in the entire material universe, how many planets with life where there are self-aware beings who, although very different in physical appearance, are indeed similar to humans in the sense that they have used their free will to descend below the 48th level of consciousness? Well, my beloved, we are not talking millions of planets, but we are talking multiple tens of thousands of planets. Of course, there are billions of planets where the inhabitants have chosen to raise their consciousness and follow the acceleration rate (in fact, co-create the acceleration rate) of the entire universe.

What is peace?

The Sixth Ray has often been called the ray of peace and the ray of service. What then is peace? It is not the absence of conflict, as many among human beings think. They think that if they can just remove conflict or remove the causes of conflict, or remove the people who are in conflict, then there will be peace. There will not necessarily be peace, although, certainly, it takes human beings and dark forces to embody the consciousness of anti-peace. Nevertheless, the absence of conflict is not peace. What then is peace? It is a vibration, an energy of God, an active ingredient. Peace is not passive, peace is not sitting back, doing nothing.

You may look at the Buddha sitting in meditation. You may look at him as the epitome of peace, but he is not sitting there passively meditating. He is sitting there in oneness with the divine quality of peace or another divine quality. He is radiating that peace as an active vibration to the entire planet, and that is how he is holding the balance for the entire planet. Holding the balance is not a matter of being passive; it is not a matter of being in some equilibrium where you are not radiating conflict but not radiating anything else either. Holding the balance means that you are actively emitting, sending out as a sun, a particular God quality, which then holds the balance for the perversions of that God quality.

When students come to my retreat (the retreat that I share with Jesus and other ascended masters over Saudi Arabia), they

3 | Becoming Peace Is the Highest Level of Service

will first go through some instructions about what I have told you. We will take them up to a place where they can, so to speak, look down over the earth as a whole. They can see the particular areas of anti-peace. Of course, our retreat is located over Saudi Arabia because the Middle East is one of the most active areas of anti-peace on the planet, as you can truly see, going on right now as I give this dictation. There is fighting in Syria, unrest in other countries, and then, of course, the absolutely meaningless protests and demonstrations against a movie that seemingly insults the Prophet Muhammad. As if an insult to a true prophet of God could ever justify the killing of other human beings.

It is very simple. Either Muhammad was not a true prophet of God or the modern followers who want to kill in the name of Muhammad are not true followers of a true prophet of God. It can be no other way. Killing in the name of a true prophet is impossible—it is simply *impossible*. There can never be any justification for killing in the name of God, killing in the name of Muhammad, killing in the name of Jesus, killing in the name of the Buddha, killing in the name of Krishna or any other true representative of the light of God.

We show the students not only where there is unrest, but we show them the psychology, the psychological mechanisms, that cause people to be the open doors for the forces of anti-peace that exist beyond the physical. People in physical embodiment are simply like marionettes, like robots. The dark forces in the astral plane are pulling their strings, stirring them into conflict at the least provocation, for they are always stirred. They are never at peace.

My beloved, out of the seven billion people on this planet, over eighty percent of them are constantly in a state of unpeace. Some call it stress, others call it other names. There is a constant agitation in their chakras, and especially in the solar plexus chakra that is meant to be the sun of peace in your auric field. We show the students that anti-peace is a force, is a vibration. We show them also – which they already know from the previous rays they have been on – that the only way to consume such a vibration is with a higher vibration.

Many of the people who come to our retreat for the first time have been given, or have acquired, a misunderstanding of peace; seeing it as something passive. They think the best way to promote peace on this planet is to be a pacifist, like for example exemplified by Gandhi and others. Was Jesus truly a pacifist? If he had been, would he have been arrested and crucified and condemned by the authorities? Nay, for they are not threatened by those who sit in a cave and meditate upon God. They are threatened by those who go out and play an active role in society by challenging the lies that the elite is using to trap the people and to keep them indefinitely trapped in their schemes of anti-peace.

Anti-peace must be stirred up

Jesus was not a pacifist. He was an example of the active force of peace that goes out and challenges, not only by his words and actions but by his mere Presence, his mere vibration. There were people who, by encountering the auric field of Jesus, were instantly stirred into agitation. There were people who would yell profanities at Jesus whenever they met him. Surely, you could say they were possessed by demons. Nevertheless, when they encountered the intense vibration of peace, the unrest and anti-peace in their beings came out.

You cannot simply judge that a person who is truly at peace within himself will always have peace around him and will always encourage peace in people around him. The first

3 | Becoming Peace Is the Highest Level of Service

thing that must happen before you can attain peace is that the anti-peace in your being must be stirred up so that you can see it, see it for what it is. Then, you can choose to let go of the false beliefs, and then choose to invoke the active Flame of Peace that consumes the vibration, the energy, of anti-peace.

When students come to my retreat, I take them through the process I have described. Then, they are taken into a room – again similar to what other Chohans have described in their retreats – a room where you can sit and there is a screen around you. On that screen we display the images that you yourself find to be the most tranquil and peaceful. Then, you are asked to sit there and look at these images. It may be a forest, green and lush, a mist hanging between the trunks of the trees that stand like pillars in a cathedral. The morning sun is slowly arising, the light is increasing. The entire space is filled with the beautiful, tranquil song of the birds. As you become engrossed in this scene, there is absolutely nothing from outside yourself that stirs up any form of anti-peace. The room that I describe is completely and absolutely sealed from the vibrations on the physical planet, in the astral belt, in the mental and even in the etheric. It is a complete energy vacuum.

What is now displayed is the scene that you find the most peaceful. As you sit there, you become absorbed in the scene. Then, you start noticing that there are certain things, certain impulses from within yourself, that come up and they are not peaceful. As soon as they come up, they are displayed on the screen with the images that are associated with the energies and the beliefs. You can now see how this tranquil, beautiful scene is disturbed in various ways by the images that you hold in your subconscious mind, in the four levels of your being, or at least in one or two or three of those four levels of your being. When you see them, you are, of course, given assistance.

The teachings in the Sixth Ray Retreat

We create a three-dimensional map of your auric field. Then, you are taken into a room where we have another kind of projector where we can display this three-dimensional map so that you can see it. You now learn how you can use your decrees and invocations to invoke the active Flame of Peace to go down and consume these energies, these specific pockets of misqualified energies in your auric field. As you consume them, you then begin to see the beliefs behind them. Then, you can resolve those beliefs. When you let go of them, you have cleared your energy field from that particular accumulation of anti-peace.

Perhaps it would be advantageous for you that after you have given our decrees or invocations, you take a few moments, a few minutes, to sit quietly. Perhaps, you have a notebook next to you where you can either sketch images or write down words that come to you as you meditate on the elements of anti-peace in your being. The more conscious you are of this process, the greater the effect will be and the quicker you can clear your energy field from the elements of anti-peace. When you do clear your own energy field, at least to a sufficient level, you will be able to serve as an active force of peace.

We will, at our retreat, take you to another room where you have something similar to a laser gun that can direct your momentum of invoking the Flame of Peace to specific areas of the planet. Often, this is areas where you have embodied, or at least where you have traveled so that you have first-hand experience of the energies and the mindset of the people there. You can begin to direct these very focused, very precise, laser beams of the active Flame of Peace to consume what stands in the way of people in general seeing the elements of anti-peace, seeing the illusions, thereby being able to let them go.

Our gratitude

I wish to express our gratitude for those of you who have been faithful, many of you for years, in giving decrees and invocations, many of you in invoking positive energies in other ways. We truly say that had it not been for the relatively small number of people who have served as the shock troops for Saint Germain, then long ago there would have been such calamities manifest that the golden age would have been postponed for decades. Yet, as it is, there is still a hope that the golden age can begin to manifest within the next one to two decades so that there is a shift in the bringing forth of new ideas, new inventions, new technology. This can begin to make the golden age vision something that more and more people can grasp and accept as an actual, realistic potential rather than some utopian pipe dream, dreamed up by a mind that is out of touch with reality.

The shift we are looking for is that a great number of people begin to see that their minds, the common collective consciousness, is what is out of touch with reality. Truly, the Mother Light can manifest whatever image is projected upon it through the collective mind. It is just a matter of what the collective mind decides that it wants and decides that it can believe is real—for that is what will be manifest on planet earth. This is the eternal truth.

Become a sun that radiates the Flame of Peace from your solar plexus, from your sun center. I thank you for your attention and I say: Nada I AM! Peace I AM! When *you* become peace, you will begin to be the highest level of service that you can give on the Sixth Ray. Truly, being the sun center for peace is the ultimate service on the Sixth Ray. And *that* sun center, I AM!

4 | HOW TO LIVE WITHOUT MAKING KARMA

I AM the Ascended Master Nada. I AM the Chohan of the Sixth Ray. You are now at the first level of the initiations you will go through in my retreat over Saudi Arabia. As the very first step when students come here, I gather them together in a room, and the first thing I have them do is to vocalize their expectations. What do you expect when you come to the Sixth Ray? What is the initiation that you expect to go through?

Many students, as they vocalize this, talk about service. All students, of course, know that the Sixth Ray is traditionally the ray of peace and service. Many students who come here feel that, because they have been on the path under the other five Chohans for so long and have made so much progress, it must now be time that they start focusing on the service they are here to give, the gift that they want to bring to this planet. What is in their Divine plan that they should do to help raise the consciousness of humankind?

Now, my beloved, this is an understandable expectation. As always, we have no blame, we have no pointing the finger. I must tell you that many students come with an unrealistic expectation of what it means to be initiated on the Sixth Ray. It is not so that the Sixth Ray is *not* focused on service. Naturally, service is part of the initiations on the Sixth Ray, however, how can you give true service? What *is* true service? True service is what raises the planet above the dualistic state of consciousness. How can you make a contribution to raising the planet beyond the dualistic state of consciousness unless you are at peace within yourself?

There are, therefore, many students who feel that, based on what they have gone through under the previous five Chohans, they are ready to *do* something. They are ready to be more active, to be more outgoing. They are ready to play some part, perhaps even to do something important. Therefore, they are a little bit disappointed when they hear that the focus at my retreat will be on attaining inner peace.

I can see very clearly in their auras how they have a certain conflict, a sense of being split by two different impulses. On the one hand, they naturally want to listen to what I am saying because they realize I am the one who is going to initiate them. On the other hand, they still want to *do* something. They feel that, with all they have gone through, all the many initiations on the five rays, they must now be ready to go into some kind of service. Of course, you *are* ready to go into service, but the question is: Do you have a realistic view of what service means and what your highest form of service is?

The non-linear cause of human conflict

In order to get people started on questioning their view of service, it is convenient that my retreat is located over Arabia. Naturally, in an etheric retreat, geographical location is of no real importance, but it is certainly easy to point the students to just take a look at what is happening in the Middle East and what has been happening in this region now for thousands upon thousands of years. It is relatively easy for most of the students to come to see that there has been a conflict in this region, and it is an ongoing conflict.

I now have the students take a look at this, and I have them work in groups so that they begin to look at what are the causes of this conflict. They start with the present situation, and then they look at the various conflicts, and they try to trace: What is the historical background, what is the historical cause, of the present situation. As they trace this back, they see new conflicts, other conflicts, more conflicts. They begin to see that conflict led to conflict that led to conflict that led to conflict. As they trace this chain of "conflict generating conflict" back through the mists of history, they begin to realize that if you want to understand why there is conflict in the Middle East, it is not enough to look at the outer cause of the conflict. You cannot look at the Middle East – or for that matter planet earth – and look at the outer conditions. You cannot look at, for example, that *this* group of people attacked *that* group of people so many years ago, and that is why the second group of people are now seeking to take revenge or seeking to protect themselves. You cannot look at these outer things and thereby find the cause of the conflict.

The students very quickly begin to realize that you can keep going back into history, and you can see how one outer situation generated a conflict that led to an outbreak of violence. This outbreak of violence, however it outplayed itself, created a new conflict, a new level of animosity, which set the stage for a future conflict. You can keep tracing this back for thousands of years. Even if you could find an initial cause, an initial action, that created the first conflict, it would be meaningless to say that this first action (which took place thousands of years ago) is the cause of the present conflict. On the other hand, it would also be meaningless to look at the present situation and say that the previous outbreak of conflict or violence is the cause of the present situation. What the students begin to realize here is that the traditional, linear view of cause and effect simply cannot be applied to the Middle East, and it cannot actually be applied to human conflict, in general.

Surely, our students know about the fallen beings, and they have learned and studied the teachings we have given on the fallen beings. You know that the fallen beings fell in previous spheres, and they have brought their agenda with them into this sphere. You know that it is the fallen beings that brought warfare to this planet and who originally created most of the conflict. What the students begin to see, when they trace the conflict in the Middle East back through time, is that you cannot actually say that the fallen beings are the *only* cause of conflict. Surely, they are the *outer* cause, but they are not the *inner* cause. What the students realize very quickly is that, if you want to understand why there is conflict in the Middle East (or even in the world at large), you cannot look at outer events and outer so-called causes. You need to look within. You need to look at the psychology of the people and why they react the way they do.

This, of course, is not new for most of the students. It *is* new for them to begin to see this in this large historical perspective that they can suddenly see at my retreat where they have access to the Akashic records and they can go back to events that are not even recorded in present history. I give the students some time to work in groups to come up with this, and we discuss it in the larger group. Then, I wait. I let the discussions go on. If the students have not gained the insight that I am seeking to help them gain, then we study history some more. After some time, it begins to dawn on the students – usually one first, then a couple, and then more and more, until the whole group gets it – that the real cause of conflict is a state of mind. This state of mind cannot bring peace. It is important that you truly get this with your conscious mind—that is why I am bringing it up here so that you can integrate with your conscious mind the insights you are getting at my retreat.

Why you cannot stop war through reason

You see, my beloved, there is a consciousness in the world that is aware that warfare is not right, that warfare should not be here, that warfare should be stopped. You can see many, many well-meaning people around the world who have a desire to stop war. Some of them are philosophers, some of them are artists, some of them are intellectuals, some of them are politicians. Some of them can be found in many areas of life, including international organizations, from religious organizations to the United Nations, political organizations or charitable organizations of various kinds. There are millions of people who are aware that war needs to be stopped. However, they think that it is possible to reason with the people who are engaged in warfare and conflict.

You will see, even in the recent decades of history, how from time to time, some country or some organization decides to make an effort to bring, for example, the Israelis and the Palestinians to the negotiating table so that they can negotiate an end to the conflict between them. Now, we have said before, of course, that this cannot happen. The Israelis can never make peace with the Palestinians or with the other Arabs in the region. The reason for this is that the national identity of Israel and the national identity of Arab nations are defined in such a way that they can only be in conflict. What it will take is that the Israelis accelerate to a new national identity and the Palestinians or other Arab groups also accelerate to a new national or group identity. Then, perhaps, these new identities can find some kind of peaceful coexistence. As long as people's group identity is defined based on conflict, peace is not possible. Many, many well-meaning people around the world continue to think that if they can just find the right argument, if they can just find the right incentive, then there can be constructive negotiations and a peaceful settlement can be reached.

This is not difficult for ascended master students to see because you already know what you know about the fallen beings, about the ego, and about perception filters and many other things. What I want to take the students to in my retreat is a deeper understanding of this. In order to illustrate this, let me give you a brief view of karma.

How karma actually works

You, of course, are familiar with the concept of karma but are you really familiar with how it works? Karma in the East is traditionally seen as action. You perform an action, and this creates a consequence. That consequence is then karma. It sets the stage for the next situation. As you take an action in the next situation, you create new karma that sets the stage for the next situation, and so forth on the wheel of rebirth, the Sea of Samsara, the treadmill of human existence.

What the students very quickly can see is that in the Middle East, people have created karma. Groups of people have created karma with each other over thousands of years. I have a screen where I can show, for example, a particular situation where there was a conflict between two groups of people. I can show what happens at the energetic level where you can see that the conflict, especially when it broke into physical violence, created energetic traces, energetic matrices, in the emotional, mental, and identity bodies and realms. These energetic matrices were partly in the individual auras (energy fields) of the people involved. They were also in a group aura, a group consciousness. They are even, to some degree, attached to a geographical location.

What the students come to see is that the people reacted to the original situation in a certain way and this created an energetic matrix. They can then see how this matrix lingers and how, when the people come back into their next embodiment, they are still carrying the matrix in their individual bodies. This causes them to tune in to – or even to be possessed by – the collective matrix. The reaction that people had in the first situation generates a matrix that very much limits the people's options for choosing their reaction to the next situation, whether it be in their next lifetime or later in that lifetime.

Because people have reacted with violence before, their perception is warped, their perception is colored, their perception is limited by this reaction. When the next situation happens where there is conflict, they cannot see a peaceful way to respond to this. They can only see a way that accelerates what they did previously. They are more prone to respond with violence, they more easily respond with violence.

The students can see how these people have created these karmic traces that they carry with them from generation to generation. They can see how the people build these collective matrices that become more and more powerful and therefore more easily overpower the minds of individuals who are born into them. The students can even see that a particular group of people are engaged in a conflict with another group of people, and when people from the first group died, some of them would in their next lifetime incarnate in the other group. You were a Jew in one lifetime; in your next lifetime you might be an Arab, and vice versa. The students can see that even though people change sides, they still carry the matrix with them of responding with violence and hatred. Therefore, it really does not matter what side they are on. They still react the same way.

Now, the students can also very clearly see that there is a fundamental difference between feeling hatred towards another group of people and then acting on this with physical violence. It is clear that when you take a physical action, you are doing something in a physical way, and it is very obvious that you are *doing* something. It also has a more severe consequence. Nevertheless, the students also quickly begin to see that if you have a strong feeling of hatred that you are directing against another group of people, you are actually doing something at the emotional level. If you have very strong thoughts about why this other group of people are bad and what they have done to your people in the past, then you are doing something at the mental level. If you have a very strong sense of identity that you are better than this other group of people because of whatever criteria you have, then this is doing something at the identity level. The students can see that the people are actually projecting energy out with all four of their lower bodies, and this is all *doing,* this is all taking action. It is all creating these karmic matrices that will limit people's perception, limit their freedom to choose their actions.

How to avoid making karma

What the students quickly come to realize here is that if there is to be peace in the Middle East, the people need to stop *doing.* They need to stop taking actions that create karma. Now this, of course, for some students represents somewhat of an enigma. Most of the students who are at this level can very quickly resolve it because it does not mean, naturally, that you do nothing. We are not here saying that in order to avoid making karma, you cannot live an active life. We are not saying you should retreat to a cave in the Himalayas and meditate on God twenty-four hours a day.

What you need to realize, and what is easy for the students to realize, is that you cannot take action through the dualistic state of consciousness, through the fear-based mind. Therefore, it becomes obvious to the students that what Jesus attempted to do was to show people a way to break these karmic patterns, these karmic matrices, by raising themselves above the fear-based response. "Love your enemies. Turn the other cheek. Do unto others what you want them to do unto you." These are all directions to stop people from taking actions at the physical level that create karma for them. It is to help them stop taking action at the emotional level, at the mental level, at the identity level.

Jesus taught people – indirectly – that they are not Jews or Arabs, for example. They are sons and daughters of God. He taught them how to overcome the anger and hatred. He taught them how to overcome the actions that create karma. Even the teachings given through Mohammed (at least the pure, original teachings) contain these elements. If they had been heeded by those who received them, they could have also helped stop the karmic spirals. You, as students of the ascended masters, can quickly see how it is necessary that the people stop taking dualistic, fear-based actions if there is to be peace.

Now, when students have gone through this period (however long it takes) where they have come to see this in the Middle East, I, of course, do what we of the ascended masters always do. I discuss with the students the insights they have gained about how it works in the Middle East, how it works for other people, and then I say: "Now, I have not had you study this so that you can go and create peace in the Middle East. I have had you study it because I wanted you to realize that the same mechanism that you see in the Middle East applies to you."

Overcoming violence in the higher bodies

Now, of course, most students have already stopped taking violent actions, but most students have not entirely stopped *doing* through the dualistic consciousness, through the emotional, mental and identity bodies. What I confront the students with is the absolute necessity that before they can move beyond the first level of my retreat, they absolutely need to stop taking fear-based, dualistic actions at the identity, mental, and emotional levels. You cannot get beyond the first level of my retreat until you have stopped doing this. For some, this is a bit of a shock because they thought they had already overcome this. They thought they had already overcome most of their anger and aggression, most of their fear, and that they were not taking fear-based actions, projecting out a fear-based energy through the three higher bodies.

Naturally, as I spoke about in another dictation, I can take them into a room where they are sealed from the influences of the world and where they go through visualizing the most peaceful scenario they can visualize. Then, they gradually feel how the elements of unpeace come up from inside their beings. This is a very helpful exercise for people because they come to see where they still have certain things that they have not resolved. Of course, we have the entire teachings, the true teachings of Jesus, about forgiveness, turning the other cheek, about unconditional forgiveness, and how you need to forgive unconditionally in order to truly forgive. It is not a matter of the other people being punished, changing or living up to certain conditions. *You* need to forgive because it is the only way *you* are going to be free of the situation. Your concern is not the other people, your concern is that you, yourself, are free of the past and you are free of the pattern of projecting out.

The quicksand of non-peace

When students have taken some time to go through this, then we can take the next step. It is an initiation that may seem somewhat harsh from a normal, waking perspective. You know that on earth there is a substance called quicksand, and you know that many people have walked into a puddle of quicksand and have died because they sank into it and kept sinking. We have in my retreat a similar substance. The difference is, of course, that you are in your identity body. You do not need to breathe oxygen in order to survive so you cannot die from this exercise.

What I do is, I put the students into a puddle of this etheric quicksand and I simply allow them to sink or swim. This, of course, causes the vast majority of the students to sink into this substance. They are still alive but they realize that they are sinking deeper and deeper. The reason they are sinking into it is that they are struggling against the quicksand. They are struggling in order to try to stay afloat.

As long as the students are struggling, I must allow them to struggle. I cannot help them. I *cannot* help them. I cannot offer them any help. They are allowed to continue to struggle. This means that some of them sink quite deeply into the quicksand. They are completely surrounded by this quicksand. They even feel that the deeper they sink, the more their movements are limited, the less they can move. They keep struggling until they come to a point where now they surrender. They give up. They realize that their struggles are getting them nowhere.

Now, some of them get it on their own, but others eventually come to a point where they suddenly remember that they are in the retreat of the Chohan of the Sixth Ray. Suddenly, the thought comes to them: "What if Nada could help me?" So they cry out: "Nada, help me!" I naturally send an impulse to them: "Stop struggling. Stop *doing*. Lie completely still." Then, most of the students have an epiphany. It is a ground-breaking, an earth-shattering, a decisive epiphany.

They realize that it was their struggles that caused them to sink. When they realize this, they immediately become completely still. They experience that the moment they become completely still, they stop sinking. Now, most of the students do not start rising, but they stop sinking. They realize that when they do not struggle, they do not sink. They also realize that if they had not struggled from the very beginning, they would still be floating on the surface of the quicksand. Now, they realize they have sunk deeply into the quicksand, and how do they get back to the surface?

After having contemplated this, some find the answer on their own, others again ask me for help. I say, again (even though this is their identity body): "You have stopped moving at what is the equivalent of the physical level. You have stopped *doing* physically, but you also need to stop *doing* emotionally, mentally and at the identity level. You need to calm your actions, your emotions, your thoughts and your sense of identity. You need to go into neutral where you are just observing. You are in pure awareness, just observing without *doing*." When they go into this state of mind, they experience that they slowly but surely rise back towards the surface. When they come back to the surface, I am there to greet them. Now, I give them a further idea. I say: "This quicksand is a representative of the four levels of the material universe in which you live with your four lower bodies. I want you now to start moving through this quicksand from the state of mind of being neutral. I want you to move without *doing* the move."

This is something that can take a little time for the students to internalize. Before too long, they get it. They realize that it is possible for them to move in their etheric bodies, up and down, back and forth, in the quicksand without doing, without struggling and therefore without sinking. They actually realize that the quicksand is not an enemy, it is not a limitation, it is not something that is out to get them. Therefore, it is possible for them to move through the quicksand in a different way where they are not creating karma by moving. Naturally, when people have experimented with the quicksand, they get out of it again. We meet in the group, and then the students realize that what they could do with the quicksand, they can now start doing with the four levels of the material universe, including the physical.

Doing without making karma

The initiation of the first level of my retreat is that you begin to contemplate and realize that it is actually possible for you to live on planet earth – as dense and as conflict-ridden as it is right now – and you can still be active. You can still live a normal, active life, but you are not making karma by doing so. You are not creating energetic traces that will limit your future actions and choices. There are students who, even though they have been on the spiritual path for some time and studied a variety of spiritual teachings, have never actually contemplated this. Many ascended master students, for example, have been so focused on balancing karma by giving the violet flame that they thought the major requirement for your ascension was that you gave enough violet flame to balance all your karma. They have not been so focused on how *not* to make karma, other than they have thought that, if they do not take any violent, physical actions, then they are not making more karma than they can balance.

The higher goal that I am setting for you at the first level of my retreat is that I am not concerned about having you balance all your karma and get out of here as quickly as possible. I am concerned about having you stay in the world so that you are *in* the world but not *of* the world. You are moving and acting in the world without making karma for yourself. Therefore, we could say that, in a certain sense, whether you are in the world or ascended, it no longer makes such a difference to you.

Consider this: I know very well, my beloved, that all spiritual students have certain feelings about the limitations and the density of the physical realm or even the four realms of earth. For all of you, it is unpleasant to be here. You have various reactions, from being deeply disturbed about being here to feeling it is unpleasant and limiting to be here. My beloved, the vision I give you here is that it is possible for you to rise above these feelings. It is possible for you to come to a point where you can live in the world and be at peace with living in the world because you know you can navigate this world without making karma. This does not mean that you cannot take action. There are certain actions you naturally would not take, but there are actions you *can* take, and it does not make karma for yourself because you are taking them from a higher state of consciousness.

This is, for the vast majority of students who come to this level, a major shift in consciousness. In fact, it is such a major shift that it usually takes some time for people to begin to even contemplate and integrate this idea. I am not asking you, as a result of the first level, to come to the point where you can navigate the world without making karma. This is one of the goals of the entire sojourn you have in my retreat. I am asking you to contemplate the *possibility* of navigating the world without making karma.

Because I know that this is a radical idea that will take some time to integrate, I am asking you to take more time on this first lesson. We have said that you can give a particular lesson for nine days. You study the dictation and you give the invocation associated with it once a day for nine days. For this first lesson, I am asking you to extend that to thirty-three days because it will be a more radical shift for most of you. Therefore, it is very good for you to take the time to integrate this. I know that for some it will seem like a very long time. Some of you will think that you have gotten the lesson already now and why do you need to repeat it? I assure you that there are reasons for doing this, and it is that, as you give the invocation for these thirty-three days, you will integrate the lesson, you will purify your three higher bodies of these traces of always thinking you have to *do*.

The trap of doing

My beloved, it is important for you to realize that the fallen beings do not give up just because you find the spiritual path and an ascended master teaching. The fallen beings did not give up when you found this course and decided to commit yourself to going through it. They will seek to derail you at any level. One of the more subtle ways in which they seek to derail you is to play on the fact that you know you have a Divine plan and you are here to affect some positive change on earth. They will then seek to color this, to color your mind, with this very old consciousness that is on this planet that you have to *do* something on earth. In other words, over the course of history, many, many spiritual students have come to a certain level of understanding the spiritual reality. They have then attained the vision of how many things are not right on earth and how many things need to change. They have then been seduced by the fallen beings into thinking it was their role to do something to change certain manifestations that they see as being not right. Therefore, many of them have gone on a crusade – we might call it a campaign – to eradicate a certain problem.

Now, in some cases, of course, it is part of your Divine plan to take action and to engage in some aspect of life. It is not part of your Divine plan to do this from this state of mind of *doing,* of acting from a dualistic, fear-based perspective. If you are to fulfill your Divine plan, you cannot do it from that level of consciousness. You need to recognize here that the fallen beings have been very clever at setting up this idea that you need to *do*.

If you look at the world today, you will see that many of the people who are engaged, for example, in some effort to bring peace, are actually at a level of consciousness where they *could* move on to the path of Christhood. They are prevented from moving to the path of Christhood (at least at the conscious level) because they are so focused on doing something in the outer world. They are focused on doing something with the level of vision, the level of perception, that they have at the moment. They are not open to the possibility that they could receive a higher vision whereby they would still be doing something, but they would be doing it from a completely different framework and basis. What they are doing would be so different that they cannot even see it right now.

We have before talked about the fact that many spiritual students have a correct sense of *what* needs to be done, but they do not have a clear vision of *how*. This is, of course, because many students have a sense that they are here to do something that is part of your Divine plan, but you think you can do this with your present level of consciousness, your present perception.

Seeking a higher perception before doing

What I am telling you here is that you need to step back from your present way of looking at life, looking at the planet, looking at yourself. I know you have already gone through this under Hilarion of purifying your vision. The fact is that I am taking this to a higher level by having you step back and realize that it is possible to *do* something on earth, it is possible to navigate the four levels of matter, without making karma. You are not going to fulfill your Divine plan by making more karma for yourself, my beloved.

I know that, for some people, this will be a radical statement because some of you have been seduced by another clever plot of the fallen beings, namely that the end can justify the means. In other words, there is a cause that is so important that even if you make a little bit of karma, it is necessary (it is worth it) in order to attain this so epically important goal. You see, my beloved, the entire epic consciousness is a creation of the fallen beings and has nothing whatsoever to do with the cause of the ascended masters.

The ascended masters have not created the epic struggle. Although you can go back to previous ascended master organizations and see that, in a sense, they did not challenge the epic struggle, I am telling you that it is now time – both in your personal development and in the planetary development – to step beyond this. It is time to rise above the dualistic struggle, to put this behind you. It is time to recognize that you can be in physical embodiment, you can take actions and live an active life, without doing it through the epic mindset, without doing it with a dualistic impulse that creates karma for yourself.

We have said before that we are not focused on achieving a particular outer result on this planet. Our real focus is to raise the collective consciousness, but for you individually, our real focus is to raise *your* consciousness. It is not my concern at this level of your path whether you accomplish some outer goal in this world. My concern right now is that you pass the initiation at the first level of my retreat so you can move on to the second level. I have now given you all the keys for how you can pass that initiation, and I can assure you that, at the etheric level, you will not move on to the second initiation until you have passed the first.

I realize that we have given you a book that is in the physical level. Therefore, you can decide with the outer mind: "Oh, I have passed the first initiation, I am going to move on to the second chapter." My beloved, this will not mean that you move on at the etheric level. You can go through the rest of this book, but until you get and pass the initiation at the first level, you will not move on at the etheric level.

Have I made myself clear?

5 | INVOKING THE SKILL TO LIVE WITHOUT MAKING KARMA

In the name I AM THAT I AM, Jesus Christ, I call to my I AM Presence to flow through the I Will Be Presence that I AM and give this invocation with full power. I call to beloved Elohim Peace and Aloha and Hercules and Amazonia, Archangel Uriel and Aurora and Michael and Faith, Nada and Master MORE to help me know how to live on earth without making karma. Help me see and surrender all patterns that block my oneness with Nada and with my I AM Presence, including …

[Make personal calls]

Part 1

1. True service is what raises the planet above the dualistic state of consciousness. To give this kind of service, I must be at peace within myself.

> O Elohim Peace, in Unity's Flame,
> there is no more room for duality's game,
> we know that all form is from the same source,
> empowering us to plot a new course.
>
> **O Elohim Peace, through your tranquility,**
> **we are free from the chaos of duality,**
> **in oneness with God a new identity,**
> **we are raising the earth into Infinity.**

2. The real cause of conflict is a state of mind. This state of mind cannot bring peace.

> O Elohim Peace, the bell now you ring,
> causing all atoms to vibrate and sing,
> we give up the sense of a separate "me,"
> we're crossing Samsara's turbulent sea.
>
> **O Elohim Peace, through your tranquility,**
> **we are free from the chaos of duality,**
> **in oneness with God a new identity,**
> **we are raising the earth into Infinity.**

3. People are projecting energy out with all four of their lower bodies, and this is all *doing,* this is all taking action. It is all creating karmic matrices.

5 | Invoking the Skill to Live Without Making Karma

O Elohim Peace, you help us to know,
that Jesus has come your Flame to bestow,
upon all who are ready to give up the strife,
by following Christ into infinite life.

**O Elohim Peace, through your tranquility,
we are free from the chaos of duality,
in oneness with God a new identity,
we are raising the earth into Infinity.**

4. If there is to be peace in the world, people need to stop *doing*. They need to stop taking actions that create karma.

O Elohim Peace, through your eyes we see,
that only in oneness will we ever be free,
we now see that there is no separate thing,
to the ego-based self we no longer cling.

**O Elohim Peace, through your tranquility,
we are free from the chaos of duality,
in oneness with God a new identity,
we are raising the earth into Infinity.**

5. Not doing does not mean that I do nothing. I can still live an active life and avoid making karma.

O Elohim Peace, you show us the way,
for clearing the mind from duality's fray,
you pierce the illusions of both time and space,
separation consumed by your Infinite Grace.

**O Elohim Peace, through your tranquility,
we are free from the chaos of duality,
in oneness with God a new identity,
we are raising the earth into Infinity.**

6. To avoid making karma, I cannot take action through the dualistic state of consciousness, through the fear-based mind.

O Elohim Peace, what beauty your name,
consuming within us duality's shame,
the earth is set free from burden of fear,
accepting your peace is now manifest here.

**O Elohim Peace, through your tranquility,
we are free from the chaos of duality,
in oneness with God a new identity,
we are raising the earth into Infinity.**

7. Jesus attempted to show me a way to break these karmic patterns, these karmic matrices, by raising myself above the fear-based response.

O Elohim Peace, with Christ at our side,
no force of duality can evermore hide,
It was through the vibration of your Golden Flame,
that Christ the illusion of death overcame.

**O Elohim Peace, through your tranquility,
we are free from the chaos of duality,
in oneness with God a new identity,
we are raising the earth into Infinity.**

8. "Love your enemies. Turn the other cheek" are directions to stop me from taking karma-making actions at the physical, emotional, mental and identity level.

> O Elohim Peace, you bring now to earth,
> the unstoppable flame of Cosmic Rebirth,
> we give up the sense that something is "mine,"
> allowing your Light through our beings to shine.
>
> **O Elohim Peace, through your tranquility,**
> **we are free from the chaos of duality,**
> **in oneness with God a new identity,**
> **we are raising the earth into Infinity.**

9. Although I have already stopped taking violent actions, I have not entirely stopped *doing* through the dualistic consciousness, through the emotional, mental and identity bodies.

> O Elohim Peace, as peace now we feel,
> all records of war you totally heal,
> the earth is now free from forces of war,
> restoring her purity known from before.
>
> **O Elohim Peace, through your tranquility,**
> **we are free from the chaos of duality,**
> **in oneness with God a new identity,**
> **we are raising the earth into Infinity.**

Part 2

1. I see the absolute necessity that before I can move beyond the first level of Nada's retreat, I need to stop taking fear-based, dualistic actions at the identity, mental, and emotional levels.

> O Hercules Blue, we're one with your will,
> all space in our beings with Blue Flame you fill,
> a beacon that radiates light to the earth,
> bringing about our planet's rebirth.
>
> **O Hercules Blue, all life you defend,**
> **giving us power to always transcend,**
> **in you the expansion of self has no end,**
> **as we in God's infinite spirals ascend.**

2. Nada, help me see my anger, aggression and fear. I am willing to see how I am taking fear-based actions, projecting out a fear-based energy through the three higher bodies.

> O Hercules Blue, your wisdom so great,
> within us a sense of knowing create,
> a new frame of reference we suddenly gain,
> for going beyond duality's pain.
>
> **O Hercules Blue, all life you defend,**
> **giving us power to always transcend,**
> **in you the expansion of self has no end,**
> **as we in God's infinite spirals ascend.**

3. I need to forgive unconditionally in order to truly forgive. I need to forgive because it is the only way *I* am going to be free of the situation.

> O Hercules Blue, we lovingly raise,
> our voices in giving God infinite praise,
> in feeling your flame, so clearly we see,
> transcending the self is the true alchemy.
>
> **O Hercules Blue, all life you defend,
> giving us power to always transcend,
> in you the expansion of self has no end,
> as we in God's infinite spirals ascend.**

4. I am not concerned about other people, my concern is that *I* am free of the past, and I am free of the pattern of projecting out.

> O Hercules Blue, all life now you heal,
> enveloping all in your Blue-flame Seal,
> we're grateful for playing a personal part,
> In God's infinitely intricate work of art.
>
> **O Hercules Blue, all life you defend,
> giving us power to always transcend,
> in you the expansion of self has no end,
> as we in God's infinite spirals ascend.**

5. Nada, help me see how I am struggling against something on earth and how this causes me to sink deeper and deeper into karmic quicksand.

> O Hercules Blue, your Temple of Light,
> revealed to us all through our inner sight,
> your power allows us to forge on until,
> we pierce every veil and climb every hill.
>
> **O Hercules Blue, all life you defend,**
> **giving us power to always transcend,**
> **in you the expansion of self has no end,**
> **as we in God's infinite spirals ascend.**

6. I see that it was my struggles that caused me to sink. Nada, help me to stop doing emotionally, mentally and at the identity level.

> O Hercules Blue, I pledge now my life,
> in helping this planet transcend human strife,
> duality's lies are pierced by your light,
> restoring the fullness of our inner sight.
>
> **O Hercules Blue, all life you defend,**
> **giving us power to always transcend,**
> **in you the expansion of self has no end,**
> **as we in God's infinite spirals ascend.**

7. Nada, help me calm my actions, my emotions, my thoughts and my sense of identity.

> O Hercules Blue, we set all life free,
> from the subtlest lies of duality,
> the prince of this world no more has a bond,
> for with you we go completely beyond.

5 | Invoking the Skill to Live Without Making Karma

**O Hercules Blue, all life you defend,
giving us power to always transcend,
in you the expansion of self has no end,
as we in God's infinite spirals ascend.**

8. Nada, help me go into neutral where I am just observing. I am in pure awareness, just observing without *doing*.

O Hercules Blue, in oneness with thee,
we open our hearts to your reality,
your electric-blue fire within us reveal,
our innermost longing for all that is real.

**O Hercules Blue, all life you defend,
giving us power to always transcend,
in you the expansion of self has no end,
as we in God's infinite spirals ascend.**

9. Nada, help me see how to move through the four levels of the material universe from the state of mind of being neutral. Help me to move without *doing* the move.

O Hercules Blue, you fill every space,
with infinite Power and infinite Grace,
you embody the key to creativity,
the will to transcend into Infinity.

**O Hercules Blue, all life you defend,
giving us power to always transcend,
in you the expansion of self has no end,
as we in God's infinite spirals ascend.**

Part 3

1. It is possible for me to move in my four bodies without *doing*, without struggling, and therefore without sinking.

> Uriel Archangel, immense is the power,
> of angels of peace, all war to devour.
> The demons of war, no match for your light,
> consuming them all, with radiance so bright.
>
> **Uriel Archangel, use your great sword,**
> **Uriel Archangel, consume all discord,**
> **Uriel Archangel, we're of one accord,**
> **Uriel Archangel, we walk with the Lord.**

2. The matter world is not an enemy, it is not a limitation, it is not something that is out to get me.

> Uriel Archangel, intense is the sound,
> when millions of angels, their voices compound.
> They build a crescendo, piercing the night,
> life's glorious oneness revealed to our sight.
>
> **Uriel Archangel, use your great sword,**
> **Uriel Archangel, consume all discord,**
> **Uriel Archangel, we're of one accord,**
> **Uriel Archangel, we walk with the Lord.**

3. It is possible for me to live on planet earth and I can still live a normal, active life, but I am not making karma by doing so.

5 | Invoking the Skill to Live Without Making Karma

Uriel Archangel, from out the Great Throne,
your millions of trumpets, sound the One Tone.
Consuming all discord with your harmony,
the sound of all sounds will set all life free.

**Uriel Archangel, use your great sword,
Uriel Archangel, consume all discord,
Uriel Archangel, we're of one accord,
Uriel Archangel, we walk with the Lord.**

4. I can live without creating energetic traces that will limit my future actions and choices.

Uriel Archangel, all war is now done,
for you bring a message, from heart of the One.
The hearts of all men, now singing in peace,
the spirals of love, forever increase.

**Uriel Archangel, use your great sword,
Uriel Archangel, consume all discord,
Uriel Archangel, we're of one accord,
Uriel Archangel, we walk with the Lord.**

5. I see the need to focus on how *not* to make karma with all four of my energy bodies.

Uriel Archangel, your infinite peace,
from all warring beings our planet release,
war is a prison from which we are free,
embracing the peace of true unity.

**Uriel Archangel, use your great sword,
Uriel Archangel, consume all discord,
Uriel Archangel, we're of one accord,
Uriel Archangel, we walk with the Lord.**

6. The higher goal is to stay in the world so that I am *in* the world but not *of* the world. I am moving and acting in the world without making karma for myself.

Uriel Archangel, we send forth the call,
reveal now the oneness that unifies all,
help us the vision of peace now to see,
so we from all conflicts and struggles are free.

**Uriel Archangel, use your great sword,
Uriel Archangel, consume all discord,
Uriel Archangel, we're of one accord,
Uriel Archangel, we walk with the Lord.**

7. When I can do this, whether I am in the world or ascended, it no longer makes such a difference to me.

Uriel Archangel, in service to life,
you give us release from struggle and strife,
forgetting the self is truly the key,
to living a life in true harmony.

**Uriel Archangel, use your great sword,
Uriel Archangel, consume all discord,
Uriel Archangel, we're of one accord,
Uriel Archangel, we walk with the Lord.**

5 | Invoking the Skill to Live Without Making Karma

8. Nada, help me see my feelings about the limitations and the density of the physical realm or even the four realms of earth. Help me see my reactions to being here.

> Uriel Archangel, the earth now you raise,
> out of duality's death-bringing haze,
> we call now upon your great Flame of Peace,
> commanding that all petty squabbles do cease.
>
> **Uriel Archangel, use your great sword,**
> **Uriel Archangel, consume all discord,**
> **Uriel Archangel, we're of one accord,**
> **Uriel Archangel, we walk with the Lord.**

9. Nada, help me see that it is possible for me to rise above these feelings. It is possible for me to live in the world and be at peace with living in the world because I can navigate this world without making karma.

> Uriel Archangel, as peace is the norm,
> to your higher vision the earth does conform,
> as people have found your peace from within,
> a Golden Age is the prize that we win.
>
> **Uriel Archangel, use your great sword,**
> **Uriel Archangel, consume all discord,**
> **Uriel Archangel, we're of one accord,**
> **Uriel Archangel, we walk with the Lord.**

Part 4

1. This does not mean that I cannot take action. There are actions I *can* take, and it does not make karma for myself because I am taking them from a higher state of consciousness.

> Michael Archangel, in your flame so blue,
> there is no more night, there is only you.
> In oneness with you, we're filled with your light,
> what glorious wonder, revealed to our sight.

> **Michael Archangel, your Knowing so strong,**
> **Michael Archangel, oh sweep us along.**
> **Michael Archangel, we're singing your song,**
> **Michael Archangel, with you we belong.**

2. I am willing to go through this shift in consciousness and contemplate the possibility of navigating the world without making karma.

> Michael Archangel, protection you give,
> within your blue shield, we ever shall live.
> Sealed from all creatures, roaming the night,
> we remain in your sphere, of electric blue light.

> **Michael Archangel, your Knowing so strong,**
> **Michael Archangel, oh sweep us along.**
> **Michael Archangel, we're singing your song,**
> **Michael Archangel, with you we belong.**

3. The fallen beings do not give up just because I find the spiritual path and an ascended master teaching.

Michael Archangel, what power you bring,
as millions of angels, praises will sing.
Consuming the demons, of doubt and of fear,
we know that your Presence, will always be near.

**Michael Archangel, your Knowing so strong,
Michael Archangel, oh sweep us along.
Michael Archangel, we're singing your song,
Michael Archangel, with you we belong.**

4. The fallen beings did not give up when I found this course and decided to commit myself to going through it.

Michael Archangel, God's will is your love,
you bring to us all, God's light from Above.
God's will is to see, all life taking flight,
transcendence of self, our most sacred right.

**Michael Archangel, your Knowing so strong,
Michael Archangel, oh sweep us along.
Michael Archangel, we're singing your song,
Michael Archangel, with you we belong.**

5. The fallen beings will seek to derail me at any level of the path.

Michael Archangel, you are the best friend,
from all worldly dangers you do us defend,
the devil no match for your power of light,
and therefore our souls can freely take flight.

**Michael Archangel, your Knowing so strong,
Michael Archangel, oh sweep us along.
Michael Archangel, we're singing your song,
Michael Archangel, with you we belong.**

6. One of the more subtle ways in which they seek to derail me is to play on the fact that I have a Divine plan, and I am here to affect some positive change on earth.

Michael Archangel, as children we play,
we're bringing the earth into a new day,
we raise it from all of the patterns so old,
our planet's life story is by us retold.

**Michael Archangel, your Knowing so strong,
Michael Archangel, oh sweep us along.
Michael Archangel, we're singing your song,
Michael Archangel, with you we belong.**

7. The fallen beings will seek to color my mind with this very old consciousness that I have to *do* something on earth.

Michael Archangel, God's power you show,
that you are invincible, this we do know,
you are undivided and thus can withstand,
anything coming from serpentine band.

**Michael Archangel, your Knowing so strong,
Michael Archangel, oh sweep us along.
Michael Archangel, we're singing your song,
Michael Archangel, with you we belong.**

8. Many spiritual students have come to see that many things are not right on earth and need to change. They have then been seduced by the fallen beings into thinking it was their role to do something, to change something.

> Michael Archangel, come raise now the earth,
> giving her thus a complete rebirth,
> collective the mind that we do now raise,
> for this we do give our infinite praise.

> **Michael Archangel, your Knowing so strong,**
> **Michael Archangel, oh sweep us along.**
> **Michael Archangel, we're singing your song,**
> **Michael Archangel, with you we belong.**

9. Many students have gone on a crusade or campaign to eradicate a certain problem.

> Michael Archangel, the earth is now new,
> covered in Blue-flame as the morning dew,
> our planet now sparkles throughout all of space,
> as we are receiving your infinite Grace.

> **Michael Archangel, your Knowing so strong,**
> **Michael Archangel, oh sweep us along.**
> **Michael Archangel, we're singing your song,**
> **Michael Archangel, with you we belong.**

Part 5

1. Nada, help me see how it is part of my Divine plan to take action and to engage in some aspect of life.

> Master Nada, beauty's power,
> unfolding like a sacred flower.
> Master Nada, so sublime,
> a will that conquers even time.
>
> **Master Nada, peace you give,**
> **forevermore in peace we live,**
> **our planet has a peaceful morn,**
> **the Golden Age is hereby born.**

2. Nada, help me see how to avoid doing this from the state of mind of *doing,* of acting from a dualistic, fear-based perspective.

> Master Nada, you bestow,
> upon us wisdom's rushing flow.
> Master Nada, mind so strong
> rising on your wings of song.
>
> **Master Nada, peace you give,**
> **forevermore in peace we live,**
> **our planet has a peaceful morn,**
> **the Golden Age is hereby born.**

3. If I am to fulfill my Divine plan, I cannot do it from the dualistic level of consciousness.

5 | Invoking the Skill to Live Without Making Karma

Master Nada, precious scent,
your love is truly heaven-sent.
Master Nada, kind and soft
on wings of love we rise aloft.

**Master Nada, peace you give,
forevermore in peace we live,
our planet has a peaceful morn,
the Golden Age is hereby born.**

4. I recognize that the fallen beings have been very clever at setting up this idea that I need to *do*.

Master Nada, mother light,
our hearts are rising like a kite.
Master Nada, from your view,
all life is pure as morning dew.

**Master Nada, peace you give,
forevermore in peace we live,
our planet has a peaceful morn,
the Golden Age is hereby born.**

5. I am willing to see if I am so focused on *doing* something in the outer world that it prevents me from moving onto the path of Christhood.

Master Nada, truth you bring,
as morning birds in love do sing.
Master Nada, we now feel,
your love that all four bodies heal.

**Master Nada, peace you give,
forevermore in peace we live,
our planet has a peaceful morn,
the Golden Age is hereby born.**

6. Nada, help me see where I am focused on doing something with the level of vision, the level of perception, that I have at the moment.

Master Nada, serve in peace,
as all emotions we release.
Master Nada, life is fun,
the solar plexus is a sun.

**Master Nada, peace you give,
forevermore in peace we live,
our planet has a peaceful morn,
the Golden Age is hereby born.**

7. I am open to the possibility that I could receive a higher vision whereby I would still be doing something, but I would be doing it from a completely different framework and basis.

Master Nada, love is free,
conditions we no longer see.
Master Nada, rise above,
all human forms of lesser love.

**Master Nada, peace you give,
forevermore in peace we live,
our planet has a peaceful morn,
the Golden Age is hereby born.**

8. Many spiritual students have a correct sense of *what* needs to be done, but we do not have a clear vision of *how*.

> Master Nada, balance all,
> the seven rays upon our call.
> Master Nada, rise and shine,
> your radiant beauty most divine.
>
> **Master Nada, peace you give,**
> **forevermore in peace we live,**
> **our planet has a peaceful morn,**
> **the Golden Age is hereby born.**

9. I realize that I cannot fulfill my Divine plan with my present level of consciousness, my present perception.

> Nada Dear, your Presence here,
> filling up the inner sphere.
> Life is now a sacred flow,
> God Peace we do on all bestow.
>
> **Master Nada, peace you give,**
> **forevermore in peace we live,**
> **our planet has a peaceful morn,**
> **the Golden Age is hereby born.**

Part 6

1. Nada, help me step back from my present way of looking at life, looking at the planet, looking at myself.

> Master MORE, come to the fore,
> we will absorb your flame of MORE.
> Master MORE, our will so strong,
> our power centers cleared by song.
>
> **Master MORE, your Sacred Heart,**
> **from this we will no more depart,**
> **we are forever in your flow,**
> **of Diamond Will that you bestow.**

2. Nada, help me realize that it is possible to do something on earth, it is possible to navigate the four levels of matter, without making karma.

> Master MORE, your wisdom flows,
> as our attunement ever grows.
> Master MORE, we have a tie,
> that helps us see through Serpent's lie.
>
> **Master MORE, your Sacred Heart,**
> **from this we will no more depart,**
> **we are forever in your flow,**
> **of Diamond Will that you bestow.**

3. I am not going to fulfill my Divine plan by making more karma for myself.

> Master MORE, your love so pink,
> there is no purer love, we think.
> Master MORE, you set us free,
> from all conditionality.
>
> **Master MORE, your Sacred Heart,**
> **from this we will no more depart,**
> **we are forever in your flow,**

4. I see through the plot of the fallen beings, namely that the end can justify the means. I see that it is *not* worth it to make karma in order to fulfill an epic goal.

> Master MORE, we will endure,
> your discipline that makes us pure.
> Master MORE, intentions true,
> as we are always one with you.
>
> **Master MORE, your Sacred Heart,**
> **from this we will no more depart,**
> **we are forever in your flow,**
> **of Diamond Will that you bestow.**

5. I see that the entire epic consciousness is a creation of the fallen beings and has nothing whatsoever to do with the cause of the ascended masters.

> Master MORE, our vision raised,
> the will of God is always praised.
> Master MORE, creative will,
> raising all life higher still.

> Master MORE, your Sacred Heart,
> from this we will no more depart,
> we are forever in your flow,
> of Diamond Will that you bestow.

6. I see that it is now time – both in my personal development and in the planetary development – to rise above the dualistic struggle, to put this behind me.

> Master MORE, your peace is power,
> the demons of war it will devour.
> Master MORE, we serve all life,
> our flames consuming war and strife.

> Master MORE, your Sacred Heart,
> from this we will no more depart,
> we are forever in your flow,
> of Diamond Will that you bestow.

7. Nada, help me recognize that I can be in physical embodiment, I can take actions and live an active life, without *doing* it through the epic mindset, without *doing* it with a dualistic impulse that creates karma for myself.

> Master MORE, we are so free,
> eternal bond from you we see.
> Master MORE, we find rebirth,
> in flow of your eternal mirth.

> Master MORE, your Sacred Heart,
> from this we will no more depart,
> we are forever in your flow,
> of Diamond Will that you bestow.

8. Nada, help me integrate the realization that the ascended masters are not focused on achieving a particular outer result on this planet.

> Master MORE, you balance all,
> the seven rays upon our call.
> Master MORE, forever MORE,
> we are the Spirit's open door.

> **Master MORE, your Sacred Heart,**
> **from this we will no more depart,**
> **we are forever in your flow,**
> **of Diamond Will that you bestow.**

9. Your real focus is to raise the collective consciousness, but for me individually, my real focus is to raise *my* consciousness. It is not my concern at this level of my path whether I accomplish some outer goal in this world.

> Master MORE, your Presence here,
> filling up the inner sphere.
> Life is now a sacred flow,
> God Power we on all bestow.

> **Master MORE, your Sacred Heart,**
> **from this we will no more depart,**
> **we are forever in your flow,**
> **of Diamond Will that you bestow.**

Sealing:

In the name of the Divine Mother, I fully accept that the power of these calls is used to set free the River of Life, so it can outpicture the perfect vision of Christ for my own life, for all people and for the planet. In the name I AM THAT I AM, it is done! Amen.

6 | ALL CONDITIONS ON EARTH ARE OPPORTUNITIES

I AM the Ascended Master Nada, and I welcome you to the second level of initiation at my retreat. Now, you may think that my first message was quite sobering, especially for a lady master. Some people still have an expectation that the lady masters are more gentle than the male masters. My beloved, I *was,* indeed, much more gentle than a male master because if Archangel Michael had delivered the same message, it would have been much more sobering and much more serious.

My beloved, what you realize is that, as the other masters have told you, you are now at a level where we are not playing any games with you. We are not sort of giving you the gentle version. We are speaking freely and directly to you because you are at the level where you are ready for this. Therefore, there is no reason to play any sort of games, the sort of games that people often play on earth. It is not really a matter of catering to your egos and not offending your egos because, at this point, you need to start looking beyond the ego, looking through the ego. You need to start identifying that when certain reactions come up in you, you know that this comes from the ego. Therefore, you can distance yourself from it, avoid being wrapped up in it. You can avoid reacting the way the ego reacts.

What not to expect from yourself

This does not mean that you do not have a reaction. Now my beloved, there is, of course, the concept of the Buddha who, in his final initiation before going into Nirvana, was sitting under the Bo tree, being approached by the demons of Mara. These demons attempted to get him to react to them in some way. Because he did not react, he passed the initiation and was able to go into Nirvana. We are not at that level. You are not at the point of being ready to go into Nirvana. You are at the second level of my retreat and you are below the 96th level of consciousness. We are not in any way asking you not to have a reaction. It is not so, my beloved, that we want you to go around feeling bad about yourselves if you react to conditions in the world. It is natural for you to react to the world at your level of consciousness.

What we are asking you to do is to come to the point where you begin to consciously realize that the reaction is not coming from *you,* meaning your true inner being. The reaction is coming from what we have called your ego, what we have called an internal spirit or a separate self. In other words, it is a reaction that is in your four lower bodies, but it is not *your* reaction. I have put the goal before you that I want you to come to the point where you can navigate the four realms of the material universe – you can be *in* the world – but you are not *doing* with the separate state of consciousness. You are acting, you are living an active life. You are doing, but you are not *doing*. You are doing from a state of being, a state of inner peace.

Now, the initiation you needed to get at the first level was that you realize that you cannot create peace by *doing*, by doing more, by doing something different. It is not a matter of discovering this secret that nobody else has discovered before, and then you can create peace. There is no secret to discover—other than what we have given you about the duality consciousness and rising above it. This, of course, happens gradually. It happens in increments. We are not asking you at this point to be completely above the dualistic consciousness and to have no reaction to conditions on earth.

We are asking you to begin to separate yourself from your reactions so you know that, even though the reactions are there in your four lower bodies, they are not truly *your* reactions. Of course, this does not mean you need to ignore the reactions because you realize that when you have a reaction, this is a sign that you have an internal spirit, a separate self, a part of your ego that is reacting. Therefore, it is an opportunity for you to look at this, to distance yourself from it, and thereby transcend it, rise above it.

You understand that when I talked about how you can be in this quicksand and how the entire physical world with its four levels is a form of quicksand, then what I am truly saying is that as long as you are in the world and you are constantly reacting and allowing yourself to be pulled into reactionary patterns by some condition in the world, then you are making karma, then you are *doing*, then you are sinking into the quicksand. It is only by coming to the point where you are free of a certain reaction that this quicksand no longer has any pull on you, and you can avoid sinking. What I said in my last lesson was that I desire you to begin to contemplate what it is that takes away your inner peace and causes you to *do,* to go into these reactionary patterns where you are *doing.*

How you created your Divine plan

In this lesson, I want to point out a certain element of this, a certain mechanism. Now, I said before that most spiritual students have a certain reaction to the world. In fact, we could say that all human beings in embodiment have a reaction to the world. Even those who are not particularly spiritual have a certain reaction, a certain way of looking at the world. Naturally, the fallen beings have a certain reaction to the world of not wanting to be here, not feeling it is just that they are here, and so on. You who are the spiritual people (most of you probably being avatars, if you have started this course, but certainly, this course is also for the original inhabitants of the earth) you have a reaction, a feeling, that things are not the way they should be on earth. Here is one of these enigmas that you need to resolve in order to avoid being pulled into a reactionary pattern.

Naturally, you have a Divine plan. When you created that Divine plan, you were looking at earth, you were seeing that there were certain conditions that were not what we might call natural on this planet. You saw that it was the goal of the ascended masters to help the planet rise above these conditions, and you decided that you wanted to play a part in fulfilling this goal. What you need to recognize here is that when you are creating your Divine plan, you are in a higher state of consciousness. Now, this does not mean that you create your Divine plan for this lifetime from some ultimate state of consciousness where you are completely free of ego. What it does mean is that you create your Divine plan from the highest state of consciousness to which you have the potential to rise in this lifetime. Now, your Divine plan has two levels. One is what you want to do in the world, what you want to accomplish. The other is how you want to grow, how much you want to raise your consciousness. You recognize here that your Divine plan operates with the present level of consciousness that you had when you left your last embodiment, and then, the goal that you and your teachers evaluate as realistic for you to attain at the end of this lifetime. Your Divine plan is made from the highest state of consciousness you have the potential to rise to in this embodiment.

Of course, when you then come down into embodiment, you start at the same level that you were at in your last embodiment—meaning the lowest level of consciousness that is the potential for this embodiment. This means that you forget the state of consciousness from which you made your Divine plan. You often have a tendency to look at your Divine plan through a very linear mindset and think that if the ascended masters have the goal, for example, to remove war, and if you are here to help do this, then you need to take active measures, you need to do something actively, in order to accomplish this.

My beloved, in order to truly accomplish the goal of doing what you are here to do in your Divine plan, you first need to rise to the state of consciousness – not necessarily the absolute highest state but at least to a close proximity to it – that you can attain in this lifetime. In other words, if you are to fulfill your Divine plan, you need to rise to a higher level of consciousness than when you started this embodiment. This, of course, you have already done. Nevertheless, what I am pointing out to you is that it is easy to keep a certain sense with you that you have to do something actively. Many ascended master students, when they found our teachings, decided with their outer minds, based on the level of consciousness they had when they found the teachings, what they were going to do. They were going to give decrees and invocations and so forth and so on.

What do you feel about earth?

What I am asking you to do at this level is to put this aside, to realize that the goal here is to rise to a higher level of consciousness where you can gain a different view of your Divine plan, a different view of what you are here to do. In order to do this, I need you at this level to again look at the earth with your present, waking consciousness. In fact, what I have the students do in groups at my retreat is that I have them verbalize what they think, what they feel, about the earth in its present state. You can even do this as an exercise yourself. You can go into a quiet room, and you verbalize what you feel about the earth, life on earth, human beings, fallen beings and this and that. Most students at this level clearly feel that something is wrong on earth, something has gone wrong.

Naturally, as an avatar, you would have a remembrance of what it means to be on a natural planet. You would know that the earth is far below the state of a natural planet. If you are one of the original inhabitants of the earth, you will have (in your inner memory) a sense that there was a time in the past when the earth was at a higher level, and it has now fallen below it. For example, in the past, there was no warfare on earth, and now there is. All spiritual students have this sense that something is wrong, something is not right, something needs to be corrected, something needs to change. This is where the enigma comes in.

6 | All Conditions on Earth Are Opportunities

The enigma of changing things on earth

You see, my beloved, in a sense, this is all correct. We of the ascended masters do want to take the earth through a process where we raise it so that certain manifestations are not found here, including war. This is, in a certain sense, a linear process. We start at a certain level, we gradually go to the next level up, and then the next level and so forth and so on. We are raising the collective consciousness increment by increment until we come to one of these turning points where a certain manifestation has been overcome. This has not yet happened with war. It has to a large degree happened with slavery and certain other conditions that you do not see anymore, at least not so much more in the developed world.

In a sense, there *is* a goal. In a sense, there *is* a linear process towards that goal. What I need you to recognize is that there is an element of your ego, there is an internal spirit, there is a separate self, which has adopted (or rather, is created from) the belief that you cannot be a fully spiritual person, you cannot be a Christed being, you cannot be fully at peace with yourself until a certain condition on earth has changed.

You see, my beloved, most spiritual people have a sense that something needs to change, but they often do not realize that underneath that sense is a personal reaction where you feel that because of this condition being the way it is, you cannot fully be who you are. For example, you cannot fully be at peace, you cannot fully accept being here, you cannot fully enjoy life, you cannot fully engage in life or in the spiritual path. There is something you cannot *do,* something you cannot *be,* because outer conditions are not the way they are meant to be.

This, my beloved, is an absolute illusion that you absolutely need to overcome. I am not asking you to fully overcome it at this level, but I am asking you to become conscious of it. There are many reasons for this. First of all, you will not feel good about yourself as long as you are trapped in this pattern. It is actually a reactionary pattern. You are looking at conditions on earth and you are reacting to them by feeling limited. You are feeling that you cannot fully be the open door for your I AM Presence because of this outer condition, and this is a reactionary pattern that limits you. You cannot fully feel good about yourself as long as you have this pattern. You cannot be fully at peace within yourself because you cannot be at peace with being in embodiment on earth.

My beloved, many people have heard me say that it is the goal of your course at my retreat to be at peace within yourself. They have not actually realized that in order to be at peace within yourself, you need to be at peace with being on earth, being in embodiment on earth. Therefore, they have not realized that they have a reactionary pattern in their subconscious minds that says: "Oh, I cannot be at peace as long as this condition is the way it is." Do you see here that there is a mechanism, a reactionary pattern, in you that actually prevents you from being at peace because certain outer conditions are the way they are?

Now, with the linear mind, with the outer mind, with the ego, with the internal spirit, with the separate self there is only one solution to this condition and it is that the outer condition must change. There are ascended master students who have been in ascended master teachings for decades, and they are still trapped in this pattern of focusing their attention on the outer conditions that must change, feeling that they cannot be at peace within themselves until this or that condition has changed. They are focusing their attention outside themselves, always directing their attention at how they can make a contribution to changing the outer condition.

The subtle inner frustration

Since they obviously feel somewhat powerless to change many outer conditions, such as war, then there is a certain frustration in their beings. This causes them to, in many cases, go into having a subtle sense of blame against other people, against the fallen beings, against the Mother Light—whatever it may be. In many cases, they blame all three. You have many students here who actually feel: "I can't be at peace because the outer condition hasn't changed and the outer condition hasn't changed because other people don't want to change, the fallen beings are here and the Mother Light is just the way it is and has manifested these conditions and will not change." There is a frustration here. Hence, my beloved, how can I help you to be at peace with yourself as long as you have this frustration?

I need you to recognize the frustration, verbalize it if you like. Go into a quiet room, verbalize the frustration you feel about it. Then, I need you to come to a simple realization, and it is this: "If I cannot change the outer condition, does that mean it is impossible for me to be at peace?" Some students believe this. I do everything *I* can at the etheric level of my retreat here to help them get that this is not correct. I am asking you to do everything *you* can to get it at the conscious level. We have, of course, said this before, but I still find many students who come to this level of initiation at my retreat and have not gotten it with the conscious mind.

The obvious flaw in the reasoning that you cannot change until the outer conditions have changed is that the entire idea of our teachings is that you are on the path of becoming psychologically, spiritually, psycho-spiritually independent of conditions on earth. This is why the Buddha passed that initiation under the Bo tree. He was psycho-spiritually independent of any condition on earth. There was no condition that had any hold on him because he did not think that there was any condition on earth that could take away his inner peace. The obvious resolution to the enigma is that if you cannot change the outer condition, you can still come to feel inner peace by working on yourself, by changing yourself.

It is true that it could be part of your Divine plan to help bring about certain outer changes on earth, but it is also part of your Divine plan to attain inner peace. You need to recognize here that there are *outer* goals and there are *inner* goals. The inner goal is your own growth in consciousness, and there is no condition on earth that can stop or limit your growth in consciousness. On the contrary, my beloved, conditions on earth are actually the *facilitators* of your growth in consciousness. They are not the enemy of your growth in consciousness; they are the opportunity for growing. How do you grow in consciousness? By overcoming a particular internal spirit that causes you to react to a certain condition on earth. When you no longer react to the condition, then you have grown in consciousness, and then, you have taken one step closer to being at peace within yourself.

Do you not see, my beloved, that this is what the spiritual path is all about? It always has been. The other Chohans have said the same thing but there are levels of internalizing this truth. You may think you had gotten it at the First Ray initiations or the Second Ray or another ray, but there are deeper levels of it. At this level I need you to recognize here that your inner peace has nothing whatsoever to do with conditions on earth. It is an *inner* condition. There is no *outer* condition that can stop your *inner* peace. If you think, or have been thinking until now, that a certain condition can stop your inner peace, then that particular condition is your opportunity to rise to a higher level.

What disturbs you the most on earth

Do you see, my beloved, that what I am asking you to do at this level is to step back, look at your life, look at your spiritual path, look at your psychology. Then, look at the earth and say: "What is the condition that most disturbs my peace on earth? What is the condition that most often causes me to feel resentment, resistance towards being here, feeling that something is wrong, something shouldn't be the way it is?" Identify that condition, and then realize that this is the particular condition that you need to rise above at this level of initiation at my retreat. This condition is not the enemy of your spiritual growth; it is your opportunity to grow. Therefore, the condition is the facilitator of your growth.

How can you make peace with being in embodiment? Why are you not at peace? Because you have a certain spiritual goal in front of you, but you have a mechanism somewhere in your four lower bodies that prevents you from reaching that goal. It prevents you from reaching the goal because you think that you cannot reach the *inner* goal until an *outer* condition has changed. The entire opportunity for spiritual growth is to recognize that all of the conditions on earth are opportunities for overcoming some attachment, some reactionary pattern.

If you can make that shift, my beloved, then you can actually be at peace with being in embodiment on a planet as dense and as low as the earth is right now. What I am seeking to help you rise above is this constant inner struggle where you know you are in embodiment, you know you cannot just snap your fingers and leave embodiment, but yet you feel frustrated, you feel limited by being here. I am hoping to help you make the shift where you look at life and say: "But this is not a limitation—it's an opportunity."

Now, I know that your mind will conjure up this idea: "But what about the outer conditions? Am I not supposed to do something?" My beloved, all I am asking you here is that you temporarily, while you are undergoing these initiations at my retreat, put aside your desire to do something in the world. You may, indeed, do something later, but it will be done when you have a higher vision. You will not get that vision as long as you are so focused *outside* of yourself instead of being focused *inside*. I need you, while you are going through these initiations at my retreat, to pull your conscious attention away from what you change in the world to look at what you change in yourself. I need you to look at what takes away your peace and look at this condition as an opportunity.

My beloved, the spiritual path, the path towards the ascension, is an *inner* path, and it is inner precisely because there are no *outer* conditions you need to overcome. There are only *inner* conditions you need to overcome. Most of these inner conditions are the reactionary patterns you have to outer conditions where you – or rather your ego, your separate self, your internal spirit – believes that the outer condition can limit your spiritual growth.

The belief behind internal spirits

Now, my beloved, we have talked about the internal spirits, the separate selves and aspects of the ego. What I am asking you to do here is to realize that when you first heard these concepts, you were at a certain level of consciousness. Therefore, in your outer mind, you formed a view of these concepts based on that level of consciousness. Now that you have followed this course until this point on the Sixth Ray, you have risen higher in consciousness. This means that it is time to step up to a higher view of these concepts.

How is an internal spirit, a separate self, created? It is created out of a certain belief. Now, in most cases, these beliefs are not something that have been created inside your mind because they have been floating around in the collective consciousness for a long time. The fallen beings have created many of them, and therefore, there are certain collective spirits. What the fallen beings are very good at doing is exposing you to a condition here on earth that is very difficult on the outer, that leads to some traumatic situation. In order to deal with this, you create, then, a separate self, an internal spirit. This internal spirit is created based on a certain belief.

This could be the belief, for example, that as long as there is war on earth (and therefore there is a risk that you could be exposed to war again), you cannot be fully at peace. You always need to be on guard. You always need to be aware that something could happen, a war could break out that would affect you. This is why you see so many spiritual people, so many people in the New Age arena, who go into these negative prophesies. They are always waiting for 2012 or whatever year is prophesied that there would be this major, dramatic change, or there would be some breakdown or a major war. They are always looking at the dire prophecies, being wrapped up in this. They cannot let go of it, and it is simply because they have an internal spirit.

My beloved, again, there is no blame from our side. All of us, who have been in physical embodiment on earth, have been exposed to severe trauma generated by the fallen beings. It may not have been directed at you personally, but it may be that you were exposed to a war. For example, you saw your family killed, you were killed, you suffered greatly, you were wounded, whatever it may be. All of us who have been in embodiment have been exposed to these traumas. There is no blame here for you having created this spirit. I am not asking you to feel bad about having these internal spirits. We have all had them while we were in embodiment. We also ascended and are no longer in embodiment because we overcame them one by one. That is why: "What one has done, all can do." *We* have done it. We know *you* can do it, and we are simply taking you through that process—one spirit at a time.

How to overcome spirits of anti-peace

The spirit I am asking you to deal with now is the spirit that says you cannot be at peace because there is this or that condition on earth that should not be here. I am asking you to begin to separate yourself and see that this is a reactionary pattern and it is not *your* reaction. It is not *your* belief. It is programmed into the internal spirit. The next thing you need to recognize is that the internal spirit will never overcome it.

There are spiritual students (and, of course, we are now at the second level of my retreat, which is the combination of the Sixth Ray and the Second Ray of wisdom) who think that they can reason with their egos, they can reason with their internal spirits, their separate selves. They think that you can look at a certain spirit, you can see that it is based on a certain belief, and then you can come up with an argument. The spirit will suddenly see that it has been wrong and, therefore, it will be dissolved.

This is not the way it happens. The spirit will *never* see anything wrong about its programming. The illusion based on which the spirit was created is an absolute, infallible truth to the spirit—and it always will be. What you can do is that you can come to a point where *you* fully see the illusion for what it is. Therefore, you let the spirit, you let the separate self, die. You let it fall away because you realize: "This is not me. This has been part of me, but I do not want to drag it around with me any longer. I want to let it go."

This is the entire process of the spiritual path. I know that for some students this will be a sense of disappointment. Some students have gotten this earlier because the other Chohans have said this in more or less direct ways. Some come to this level of my retreat and they have not fully internalized this. When they are confronted with this truth at the etheric level, then they feel a certain disappointment. Now, you recognize that what we have been saying all along here is that when you are engaging in this course, you are in your identity body going to the retreat of the Chohan at night. What you need to recognize here is that when you are at the retreat in your identity body, it is much easier for you to get the lesson, to see the next insight, than it is with your conscious mind.

What often happens is that a student gets it at the identity level, but there is a resistance in, for example, the emotional body or the mental body that prevents them from getting it at the conscious level. You could say that the outer books, the outer dictations and the invocations, only have one purpose, and that is to help you get at the physical, conscious level what you have already gotten at the identity level so that it filters down to the conscious mind. Therefore, you integrate it, you fully accept it. You can therefore at the conscious level see through the illusion, let the spirit go, let the separate self go, and therefore, you can adopt that higher attitude to life.

What I am hoping with this second lesson is to get you to a point where you fully realize that you have had this mechanism of resisting being in embodiment because you saw the earth or some condition on earth as being a limitation to your spiritual growth. I am hoping to help you make the shift where you now come to see that any condition on earth is your opportunity to overcome that internal spirit, that internal mechanism, that reactionary pattern.

Being at peace with being on earth

When you can do this at the conscious level, then you can really make peace with being here on earth. I, of course, know very well how difficult it is to be on earth. Again, there is no blame, my beloved. I know that there are so many conditions on earth that are pulling on you to get you to react to them. I know how difficult it is to stop reacting. I also know that I do not want you to live the rest of your time in embodiment with your current frustration, with your current sense of not wanting to be here, not wanting to engage fully in life or in the spiritual path. I desire to help you come to the point where you have risen above the internal spirit that is resisting being on earth so that you can feel at peace with being here.

My beloved, if you step back with your conscious mind, as you can easily do with your identity mind, and look at earth from a bigger perspective, from a cosmic perspective, then you might realize that although the earth is a dark, dense and difficult planet, it is also a tremendous growth opportunity. Those of you who are here and who have found the teachings of the ascended masters, you have a tremendous potential to grow for the rest of this lifetime. In order to realize that potential, you need to overcome the internal spirit that causes you to resist being here. You have chosen to come here, or if you are one of the original inhabitants, you have chosen to be here, to remain here, in many cases, because you wanted to raise the earth. Do you not see that if this is a choice you made, then it is not some punishment that you are here. It is not unfair that you are here. It is actually the opportunity you chose because you saw that this was your personal opportunity to grow—the best possible opportunity that you could have at your present level of spiritual, cosmic growth.

If you could look at your lifestream consciously the way you can do at the identity level (and you *can,* of course, if you are willing to step outside your normal sense of identity), then you could be completely at peace by recognizing that you have chosen to be in this embodiment in your specific conditions because they represent the maximum opportunity for growth for you personally.

Personal growth versus service

Now, I know that there are students who at this level will say: "But isn't the spiritual path about overcoming selfishness? Isn't it so that the lower you go in consciousness towards the lowest level on earth, the more self-centered and selfish people become? So, isn't it so that there comes a point on the path where we need to focus on serving a greater cause than just ourselves?" There are students who will feel that what I am telling them is that they need to focus so much on themselves (there are even students who feel this way about the whole course and the ascended master teachings in general) that it actually prevents you from giving your service. You are supposed to focus so much on your spiritual growth, your personal growth and not on giving service to life.

What did I say in my previous lesson? You cannot, truly, give service to earth by *doing.* This is what people in the Middle

East have been doing for thousands of years. They have been thinking that: "The cause of warfare is those other people, and if we can just destroy those other people, there will be peace on earth." They are trying to do, *do, do* and all they do is create more and more karma, more and more conflict. The only way to raise the planet above a certain manifestation, such as war, is to raise the collective consciousness until a critical mass of people see the lie behind war and transcend it.

How do you raise the collective consciousness, my beloved? You can help this along by enlightening other people, by telling them about the path, or certain lies and initiations and truths. My beloved, the primary way that you personally help raise the collective is to raise your own consciousness. When you are in physical embodiment, you are a part of the collective consciousness on earth. The more you raise your personal consciousness, the more you raise the collective. It is inevitable, my beloved. If you were to look at this in very strict terms, you could say that even if you lived an entire lifetime where you focused one-hundred percent on raising your own consciousness and never, ever attempted to change the mind of any other person, you would still make the maximum possible contribution to raising the collective consciousness.

However, most of you are not meant to sit in a cave in the Himalayas. You are meant to live active lives in society. This means, for you, that the maximum opportunity is some interaction where you are raising your own consciousness and you are interacting with other people. Whether you are directly telling them about ascended master teachings or higher truth or not, you are still giving them an example of how to live a more spiritual life. For you, it is an interaction but you understand that this interaction is a figure-eight flow. How can you help other people see a certain truth unless you have seen it yourself? There is an exchange here where you raise your own consciousness, then you can help others, then you raise your own consciousness some more and then you can help others overcome another illusion.

Raising consciousness versus spreading truth

If you look at spiritual movements, if you look at religious movements, if you look at political movements, charitable movements, you can see that many of them are based on a particular idea: "We have the truth, and if only all other people could see the same truth that we see, then the planet would be changed." This is based on a view of truth with the outer, linear mind where you think that if you go out and convert other people to *your* belief system, if you convince them of *your* truth, then you will have changed the collective consciousness. My beloved, changing the collective consciousness is not a matter of giving people an intellectual understanding. An intellectual understanding is part of changing the collective consciousness, but it is not the main part of it because you also need to change people's emotional bodies and their identity bodies.

How can you do this? There are plenty of examples of people in the world who have become missionaries, who are going on a crusade trying to convert others (whether it is to a religion or scientific materialism or whatever) and they are trying to do this with the linear, intellectual, analytical mind. They think that if they can convince other people of a certain truth, the world will have moved forward.

Unless you have integrated that truth with all four of your lower bodies, you cannot really help other people rise higher, and you are not truly helping to raise the collective consciousness. I need you to recognize here that as part of your service, you need to raise your own consciousness at all four levels.

You need to overcome these spirits, and therefore, you need to overcome the illusion that your service is dependent on changing other people. Your service is *not* dependent on changing other people; your service is dependent on raising your own consciousness—changing yourself.

Changing the world without changing yourself

There is a subtle illusion in the world among spiritual people that you can change the world without changing yourself by simply changing other people or giving decrees or invocations or whatever spiritual practice you have. In reality, it is, first of all, about changing your own consciousness, raising that consciousness up.

There is another illusion that says that you cannot give real service by focusing too much on yourself. What I am asking you to do here is to step up to recognize that focusing on your personal growth of overcoming your attachments and your internal spirits is fundamentally different from the narcissistic self-focus you see with people who are below the 48th level of consciousness. You have risen far beyond the 48th level. Therefore, you are not selfish the way they are. You are not focused on yourself in a narcissistic way. Now, it is possible (until you pass the initiation at the 96th level and go into the higher levels of Christhood) that you can revert back to a narcissistic self-focus of wanting to elevate yourself. That is precisely why I am giving you these insights now because one of the ways that people are often pulled into this is through the illusion that they need to change something outside themselves. Doing so is so important that they actually need to set aside their own growth, they do not need to look at themselves, and they can focus on changing other people. There are people who can be pulled into that even up to the 96th level and therefore they can start going down the hill again.

You need to begin to contemplate these ideas. I know I have given you a large mouthful in this dictation, but I hope you recognize that the initiations are not becoming easier as you are going higher on the spiritual path. There is more for you to contemplate, more for you to wrap your mind around, as they say, but it is not really a matter of wrapping your mind around it. It is matter of *un*wrapping your mind because what the internal spirits do is that they cause your mind to be wrapped around a certain belief so that you cannot step back from it and see it for the illusion that it is. You think it is some absolute truth or some condition that could not be changed.

My beloved, there is ultimately no condition on earth that cannot be changed. There are, of course, for you certain conditions that you cannot change right now. There is no condition on earth that can prevent you from changing yourself, and that is the truth and the insight that you need to get with the conscious mind at this level.

Then, you need to make the determination that you are willing to change yourself, you are willing to look at any condition that is causing you to feel resentment towards being in physical embodiment. You will look for the illusion, and you will separate yourself from the illusion and allow yourself to feel: "Yes, I am here right now because I want to be here. I want to rise higher in consciousness and I rise higher by transcending the specific condition that I am facing right now."

Once you see that condition from the outside, once you separate yourself from it and see that it is not *your* condition (it is only the condition of an internal spirit), then, my beloved, you can be free. You can feel at peace about being yourself and about being in embodiment. *That* peace I truly desire you to have, for I am the Chohan of the Sixth Ray of Peace.

7 | INVOKING THE VISION THAT ALL CONDITIONS ARE OPPORTUNITIES

In the name I AM THAT I AM, Jesus Christ, I call to my I AM Presence to flow through the I Will Be Presence that I AM and give this invocation with full power. I call to beloved Elohim Peace and Aloha and Apollo and Lumina, Archangel Uriel and Aurora and Jophiel and Christine, Nada and Lord Lanto to help me accept that all conditions on earth are opportunities for growth. Help me see and surrender all patterns that block my oneness with Nada and with my I AM Presence, including …

    [Make personal calls]

Part 1

1. Nada, help me look beyond the ego, look through the ego and identify when my reactions come from the ego. Help me distance myself from the ego's reactions, avoid being wrapped up in them. Help me avoid reacting the way the ego reacts.

> O Elohim Peace, in Unity's Flame,
> there is no more room for duality's game,
> we know that all form is from the same source,
> empowering us to plot a new course.
>
> **O Elohim Peace, through your tranquility,**
> **we are free from the chaos of duality,**
> **in oneness with God a new identity,**
> **we are raising the earth into Infinity.**

2. Nada, help me consciously realize that the reaction is not coming from me, meaning my true inner being. The reaction is coming from my ego, an internal spirit, a separate self. It is a reaction that is in my four lower bodies, but it is not *my* reaction.

> O Elohim Peace, the bell now you ring,
> causing all atoms to vibrate and sing,
> we give up the sense of a separate "me,"
> we're crossing Samsara's turbulent sea.
>
> **O Elohim Peace, through your tranquility,**
> **we are free from the chaos of duality,**
> **in oneness with God a new identity,**
> **we are raising the earth into Infinity.**

7 | Invoking the Vision that all Conditions Are Opportunities

3. I realize that the reaction is a sign that I have an internal spirit, a separate self, a part of my ego that is reacting. This is an opportunity for me to look at this, to distance myself from it, and thereby transcend it.

> O Elohim Peace, you help us to know,
> that Jesus has come your Flame to bestow,
> upon all who are ready to give up the strife,
> by following Christ into infinite life.
>
> **O Elohim Peace, through your tranquility,**
> **we are free from the chaos of duality,**
> **in oneness with God a new identity,**
> **we are raising the earth into Infinity.**

4. As long as I am constantly reacting and allowing myself to be pulled into reactionary patterns by some condition in the world, then I am making karma, then I am *doing,* then I am sinking into the quicksand.

> O Elohim Peace, through your eyes we see,
> that only in oneness will we ever be free,
> we now see that there is no separate thing,
> to the ego-based self we no longer cling.
>
> **O Elohim Peace, through your tranquility,**
> **we are free from the chaos of duality,**
> **in oneness with God a new identity,**
> **we are raising the earth into Infinity.**

5. It is only by coming to the point where I am free of a certain reaction that this world no longer has any pull on me, and I can avoid sinking.

O Elohim Peace, you show us the way,
for clearing the mind from duality's fray,
you pierce the illusions of both time and space,
separation consumed by your Infinite Grace.

**O Elohim Peace, through your tranquility,
we are free from the chaos of duality,
in oneness with God a new identity,
we are raising the earth into Infinity.**

6. I recognize that when I created my Divine plan, I was in a higher state of consciousness, but not an ultimate state of consciousness.

O Elohim Peace, what beauty your name,
consuming within us duality's shame,
the earth is set free from burden of fear,
accepting your peace is now manifest here.

**O Elohim Peace, through your tranquility,
we are free from the chaos of duality,
in oneness with God a new identity,
we are raising the earth into Infinity.**

7. I created my Divine plan from the highest state of consciousness to which I have the potential to rise in this lifetime.

O Elohim Peace, with Christ at our side,
no force of duality can evermore hide,
It was through the vibration of your Golden Flame,
that Christ the illusion of death overcame.

**O Elohim Peace, through your tranquility,
we are free from the chaos of duality,
in oneness with God a new identity,
we are raising the earth into Infinity.**

8. When I come down into embodiment, I start at the same level that I was at in my last embodiment.

O Elohim Peace, you bring now to earth,
the unstoppable flame of Cosmic Rebirth,
we give up the sense that something is "mine,"
allowing your Light through our beings to shine.

**O Elohim Peace, through your tranquility,
we are free from the chaos of duality,
in oneness with God a new identity,
we are raising the earth into Infinity.**

9. This means that I forget the state of consciousness from which I made my Divine plan.

O Elohim Peace, as peace now we feel,
all records of war you totally heal,
the earth is now free from forces of war,
restoring her purity known from before.

**O Elohim Peace, through your tranquility,
we are free from the chaos of duality,
in oneness with God a new identity,
we are raising the earth into Infinity.**

Part 2

1. Nada, help me see my tendency to look at my Divine plan through a very linear mindset and think that if the ascended masters have a goal and if I am here to help, then I need to take active measures in order to accomplish this.

> Beloved Apollo, with your second ray,
> you open our eyes to see a new day,
> We see through duality's lies and deceit,
> transcending the mindset producing defeat.
>
> **Beloved Apollo, thou Elohim Gold,**
> **your radiant light our eyes now behold,**
> **as pages of wisdom you gently unfold,**
> **our planet is free from all that is old.**

2. Nada, help me see that in order to truly accomplish the goal of doing what I am here to do in my Divine plan, I first need to rise to the highest state of consciousness I can attain in this lifetime.

> Beloved Apollo, in your flame we know,
> that your living wisdom is always a flow,
> in your light we see our own highest will,
> immersed in the stream that never stands still.
>
> **Beloved Apollo, thou Elohim Gold,**
> **your radiant light our eyes now behold,**
> **as pages of wisdom you gently unfold,**
> **our planet is free from all that is old.**

7 | Invoking the Vision that all Conditions Are Opportunities

3. I see that when I found the teachings, I decided with my outer mind, based on the level of consciousness I had, what I was going to do in terms of giving decrees and invocations.

> Beloved Apollo, your light makes it clear,
> why we have taken embodiment here,
> exposing all lies causing the fall,
> you help us reclaim the oneness of all.

> **Beloved Apollo, thou Elohim Gold,**
> **your radiant light our eyes now behold,**
> **as pages of wisdom you gently unfold,**
> **our planet is free from all that is old.**

4. I am going to put this aside and realize that the goal is to rise to a higher level of consciousness where I can gain a different view of my Divine plan and what I am here to do.

> Beloved Apollo, exposing all lies,
> we hereby surrender all ego-based ties,
> we know our perception is truly the key,
> to transcending the serpentine duality.

> **Beloved Apollo, thou Elohim Gold,**
> **your radiant light our eyes now behold,**
> **as pages of wisdom you gently unfold,**
> **our planet is free from all that is old.**

5. Nada, help me see that there is an element of my ego, there is an internal spirit, there is a separate self, which is created from the belief that I cannot be a fully spiritual person, I cannot be a Christed being, I cannot be fully at peace with myself until a certain condition on earth has changed.

Beloved Apollo, we heed now your call,
drawing us into Wisdom's Great Hall,
working to raise our own cosmic sphere,
together we form the tip of the spear.

**Beloved Apollo, thou Elohim Gold,
your radiant light our eyes now behold,
as pages of wisdom you gently unfold,
our planet is free from all that is old.**

6. Nada, help me see my personal reaction where I feel that because of this condition being the way it is, I cannot fully be who I am.

Beloved Apollo, your wisdom so clear,
in oneness with you, no serpent we fear,
the beam in our eye we willingly see,
we're free from the serpent's own duality.

**Beloved Apollo, thou Elohim Gold,
your radiant light our eyes now behold,
as pages of wisdom you gently unfold,
our planet is free from all that is old.**

7. Nada, help me see the belief that there is something I cannot do, something I cannot be, because outer conditions are not the way they are meant to be.

Beloved Apollo, you help us to see
through your knowing eyes we truly are free,
we willingly stand in your piercing gaze,
empowered, we exit duality's maze.

> Beloved Apollo, thou Elohim Gold,
> your radiant light our eyes now behold,
> as pages of wisdom you gently unfold,
> our planet is free from all that is old.

8. Nada, help me see that this is a reactionary pattern. I am looking at conditions on earth and I am reacting to them by feeling limited. I am feeling that I cannot fully be the open door for my I AM Presence because of this outer condition, and this is a reactionary pattern that limits me.

> Beloved Apollo, our vision we raise,
> we see that the earth is in a new phase,
> for nothing can stop the knowledge you bring,
> exposing that there's no separate thing.

> Beloved Apollo, thou Elohim Gold,
> your radiant light our eyes now behold,
> as pages of wisdom you gently unfold,
> our planet is free from all that is old.

9. I cannot fully feel good about myself as long as I have this pattern. I cannot be fully at peace within myself because I cannot be at peace with being in embodiment on earth.

> Beloved Apollo, in wisdom's great mirth,
> we all are together uplifting the earth,
> as you now the true Flame of Wisdom reveal,
> all of earth's people can see what is real.

**Beloved Apollo, thou Elohim Gold,
your radiant light our eyes now behold,
as pages of wisdom you gently unfold,
our planet is free from all that is old.**

Part 3

1. I realize that, in order to be at peace within myself, I need to be at peace with being on earth, being in embodiment on earth.

> Uriel Archangel, immense is the power,
> of angels of peace, all war to devour.
> The demons of war, no match for your light,
> consuming them all, with radiance so bright.

> **Uriel Archangel, use your great sword,
> Uriel Archangel, consume all discord,
> Uriel Archangel, we're of one accord,
> Uriel Archangel, we walk with the Lord.**

2. Nada, help me see the reactionary pattern in my subconscious mind that says: "Oh, I cannot be at peace as long as this condition is the way it is."

> Uriel Archangel, intense is the sound,
> when millions of angels, their voices compound.
> They build a crescendo, piercing the night,
> life's glorious oneness revealed to our sight.

**Uriel Archangel, use your great sword,
Uriel Archangel, consume all discord,
Uriel Archangel, we're of one accord,
Uriel Archangel, we walk with the Lord.**

3. Nada, help me see if there is a frustration in my being that is caused by me feeling powerless to change outer conditions.

Uriel Archangel, from out the Great Throne,
your millions of trumpets, sound the One Tone.
Consuming all discord with your harmony,
the sound of all sounds will set all life free.

**Uriel Archangel, use your great sword,
Uriel Archangel, consume all discord,
Uriel Archangel, we're of one accord,
Uriel Archangel, we walk with the Lord.**

4. Nada, help me see any subtle sense of blame against other people, against the fallen beings, against the Mother Light.

Uriel Archangel, all war is now done,
for you bring a message, from heart of the One.
The hearts of all men, now singing in peace,
the spirals of love, forever increase.

**Uriel Archangel, use your great sword,
Uriel Archangel, consume all discord,
Uriel Archangel, we're of one accord,
Uriel Archangel, we walk with the Lord.**

5. I will do everything I can to see that this is based on an illusion. No outer condition can prevent me from being the open

door for my I AM Presence. I can still be at peace even if I cannot change outer conditions.

> Uriel Archangel, your infinite peace,
> from all warring beings our planet release,
> war is a prison from which we are free,
> embracing the peace of true unity.

Uriel Archangel, use your great sword,
Uriel Archangel, consume all discord,
Uriel Archangel, we're of one accord,
Uriel Archangel, we walk with the Lord.

6. The idea of ascended master teachings is that I am on the path of becoming psychologically, spiritually, psycho-spiritually independent of conditions on earth. There is no condition on earth that can take away my inner peace.

> Uriel Archangel, we send forth the call,
> reveal now the oneness that unifies all,
> help us the vision of peace now to see,
> so we from all conflicts and struggles are free.

Uriel Archangel, use your great sword,
Uriel Archangel, consume all discord,
Uriel Archangel, we're of one accord,
Uriel Archangel, we walk with the Lord.

7. The obvious resolution to the enigma is that if I cannot change the outer condition, I can still come to feel inner peace by working on myself, by changing myself.

> Uriel Archangel, in service to life,
> you give us release from struggle and strife,
> forgetting the self is truly the key,
> to living a life in true harmony.
>
> **Uriel Archangel, use your great sword,**
> **Uriel Archangel, consume all discord,**
> **Uriel Archangel, we're of one accord,**
> **Uriel Archangel, we walk with the Lord.**

8. My Divine plan has *outer* goals and *inner* goals. The inner goal is my own growth in consciousness, and there is no condition on earth that can stop or limit my growth in consciousness.

> Uriel Archangel, the earth now you raise,
> out of duality's death-bringing haze,
> we call now upon your great Flame of Peace,
> commanding that all petty squabbles do cease.
>
> **Uriel Archangel, use your great sword,**
> **Uriel Archangel, consume all discord,**
> **Uriel Archangel, we're of one accord,**
> **Uriel Archangel, we walk with the Lord.**

9. Conditions on earth are actually the facilitators of my growth in consciousness. They are not the enemy of my growth in consciousness; they are the opportunity for growing.

> Uriel Archangel, as peace is the norm,
> to your higher vision the earth does conform,
> as people have found your peace from within,
> a Golden Age is the prize that we win.

**Uriel Archangel, use your great sword,
Uriel Archangel, consume all discord,
Uriel Archangel, we're of one accord,
Uriel Archangel, we walk with the Lord.**

Part 4

1. I grow in consciousness by overcoming a particular internal spirit that causes me to react to a certain condition on earth. When I no longer react to the condition, then I have grown in consciousness, and I have taken one step closer to being at peace within myself.

> Jophiel Archangel, in wisdom's great light,
> all serpentine lies exposed to our sight.
> So subtle the lies that creep through the mind,
> yet you are the greatest teacher we find.

> **Jophiel Archangel, exposing all lies,
> Jophiel Archangel, cutting all ties.
> Jophiel Archangel, clearing the skies,
> Jophiel Archangel, the mind truly flies.**

2. I recognize that my inner peace has nothing whatsoever to do with conditions on earth. It is an *inner* condition. There is no *outer* condition that can stop my *inner* peace.

> Jophiel Archangel, your wisdom we hail,
> your sword cutting through duality's veil.
> As you show the way, we know what is real,
> from serpentine doubt, we instantly heal.

7 | Invoking the Vision that all Conditions Are Opportunities

**Jophiel Archangel, exposing all lies,
Jophiel Archangel, cutting all ties.
Jophiel Archangel, clearing the skies,
Jophiel Archangel, the mind truly flies.**

3. Nada, help me see the condition that most disturbs my peace on earth. Help me realize that this condition is not the enemy of my spiritual growth; it is my opportunity to grow. The condition is the facilitator of my growth.

Jophiel Archangel, your reality,
the best antidote to duality.
No lie can remain in your Presence so clear,
with you on our side, no serpent we fear.

**Jophiel Archangel, exposing all lies,
Jophiel Archangel, cutting all ties.
Jophiel Archangel, clearing the skies,
Jophiel Archangel, the mind truly flies.**

4. Nada, help me see that I cannot make peace with being in embodiment if I have a certain spiritual goal and a mechanism in my four lower bodies that prevents me from reaching that goal.

Jophiel Archangel, God's mind is in me,
and through your clear light, its wisdom we see.
Divisions all vanish, as we see the One,
and truly, the wholeness of mind we have won.

**Jophiel Archangel, exposing all lies,
Jophiel Archangel, cutting all ties.
Jophiel Archangel, clearing the skies,
Jophiel Archangel, the mind truly flies.**

5. The mechanism prevents me from reaching the goal because I think I cannot reach the *inner* goal until an *outer* condition has changed.

Jophiel Archangel, now show us the way,
that leads us beyond duality's fray,
we long to discern the truth and the lie,
so we the serpentine knots can untie.

**Jophiel Archangel, exposing all lies,
Jophiel Archangel, cutting all ties.
Jophiel Archangel, clearing the skies,
Jophiel Archangel, the mind truly flies.**

6. I realize that the entire opportunity for spiritual growth is to see that all of the conditions on earth are opportunities for overcoming some attachment, some reactionary pattern.

Jophiel Archangel, your Presence is here,
and therefore our minds are perfectly clear,
in wisdom's great fount we do take a bath,
and now we withstand the devil's own wrath.

**Jophiel Archangel, exposing all lies,
Jophiel Archangel, cutting all ties.
Jophiel Archangel, clearing the skies,
Jophiel Archangel, the mind truly flies.**

7 | Invoking the Vision that all Conditions Are Opportunities

7. I am making that shift and I am at peace with being in embodiment on a planet as dense and as low as the earth is right now. I am rising above this constant inner struggle where I am in embodiment and I feel frustrated and limited by being here. I say: "But this is not a limitation—it's an opportunity."

> Jophiel Archangel, it is your great task,
> to raise all mankind, if only we ask,
> so now on behalf of those who are blind,
> we ask for your help in wisdom to find.

> **Jophiel Archangel, exposing all lies,**
> **Jophiel Archangel, cutting all ties.**
> **Jophiel Archangel, clearing the skies,**
> **Jophiel Archangel, the mind truly flies.**

8. I am temporarily putting aside my desire to *do* something in the world. I want a higher vision, but I will not get that vision as long as I am so focused outside myself, instead of being focused inside.

> Jophiel Archangel, your Presence we hail,
> your Light cutting through the serpentine veil,
> the serpents can no longer people deceive,
> for all now your Flame of Wisdom receive.

> **Jophiel Archangel, exposing all lies,**
> **Jophiel Archangel, cutting all ties.**
> **Jophiel Archangel, clearing the skies,**
> **Jophiel Archangel, the mind truly flies.**

9. The path towards the ascension is an *inner* path precisely because there are no *outer* conditions I need to overcome.

There are only inner conditions I need to overcome. Most of these inner conditions are the reactionary patterns I have to outer conditions where I – or rather an internal spirit – believes that the outer condition can limit my spiritual growth.

> Jophiel Archangel, where else can we go,
> when we long the highest wisdom to know?
> You share with us gladly all that you are,
> and now our vision goes ever so far.
>
> **Jophiel Archangel, exposing all lies,**
> **Jophiel Archangel, cutting all ties.**
> **Jophiel Archangel, clearing the skies,**
> **Jophiel Archangel, the mind truly flies.**

Part 5

1. When I first heard about internal spirits, I was at a certain level of consciousness. In my outer mind, I formed a view of these concepts based on that level of consciousness. Nada, help me step up to a higher view of these concepts.

> Master Nada, beauty's power,
> unfolding like a sacred flower.
> Master Nada, so sublime,
> a will that conquers even time.
>
> **Master Nada, peace you give,**
> **forevermore in peace we live,**
> **our planet has a peaceful morn,**
> **the Golden Age is hereby born.**

2. An internal spirit is created out of a certain belief. The fallen beings are very good at exposing me to a condition on earth that is very difficult. In order to deal with this, I create an internal spirit, and it is created based on a certain belief.

> Master Nada, you bestow,
> upon us wisdom's rushing flow.
> Master Nada, mind so strong
> rising on your wings of song.
>
> **Master Nada, peace you give,**
> **forevermore in peace we live,**
> **our planet has a peaceful morn,**
> **the Golden Age is hereby born.**

3. I am rising above the spirit that says I cannot be at peace because there is this or that condition on earth that should not be here. I am separating myself and I see that this is a reactionary pattern and it is not *my* reaction. It is not my belief.

> Master Nada, precious scent,
> your love is truly heaven-sent.
> Master Nada, kind and soft
> on wings of love we rise aloft.
>
> **Master Nada, peace you give,**
> **forevermore in peace we live,**
> **our planet has a peaceful morn,**
> **the Golden Age is hereby born.**

4. I recognize that the internal spirit will never overcome the belief out of which it was created.

Master Nada, mother light,
our hearts are rising like a kite.
Master Nada, from your view,
all life is pure as morning dew.

**Master Nada, peace you give,
forevermore in peace we live,
our planet has a peaceful morn,
the Golden Age is hereby born.**

5. I realize that I cannot reason with my ego, with my internal spirits, my separate selves. I give up the desire to come up with an argument that will make a spirit see that it has been wrong.

Master Nada, truth you bring,
as morning birds in love do sing.
Master Nada, we now feel,
your love that all four bodies heal.

**Master Nada, peace you give,
forevermore in peace we live,
our planet has a peaceful morn,
the Golden Age is hereby born.**

6. The spirit will never see anything wrong about its programming. The illusion based on which the spirit was created is an absolute, infallible truth to the spirit—and it always will be.

Master Nada, serve in peace,
as all emotions we release.
Master Nada, life is fun,
the solar plexus is a sun.

7 | Invoking the Vision that all Conditions Are Opportunities

**Master Nada, peace you give,
forevermore in peace we live,
our planet has a peaceful morn,
the Golden Age is hereby born.**

7. I fully see the illusion for what it is, and therefore, I let the spirit die. I let it fall away because I realize: "This is not me. This has been part of me, but I do not want to drag it around with me any longer. I am letting it go."

Master Nada, love is free,
conditions we no longer see.
Master Nada, rise above,
all human forms of lesser love.

**Master Nada, peace you give,
forevermore in peace we live,
our planet has a peaceful morn,
the Golden Age is hereby born.**

8. Nada, help me get at the conscious level what I have already gotten at the identity level so that it filters down to my conscious mind and I can integrate it and fully accept it.

Master Nada, balance all,
the seven rays upon our call.
Master Nada, rise and shine,
your radiant beauty most divine.

**Master Nada, peace you give,
forevermore in peace we live,
our planet has a peaceful morn,
the Golden Age is hereby born.**

9. Nada, help me, at the conscious level, see through the illusion, let the spirit go, let the separate self go. I am adopting a higher attitude to life.

> Nada Dear, your Presence here,
> filling up the inner sphere.
> Life is now a sacred flow,
> God Peace we do on all bestow.
>
> **Master Nada, peace you give,**
> **forevermore in peace we live,**
> **our planet has a peaceful morn,**
> **the Golden Age is hereby born.**

Part 6

1. I realize that I have had this mechanism of resisting being in embodiment because I saw the earth or some condition as being a limitation to my spiritual growth. I am making the shift and I now see that any condition on earth is my opportunity to overcome an internal spirit, an internal mechanism, a reactionary pattern.

> Master Lanto, golden wise,
> expose in us the ego's lies.
> Master Lanto, will to be,
> we will to win our mastery.

7 | Invoking the Vision that all Conditions Are Opportunities

**Master Lanto, Wisdom's Fount,
with blessings we can hardly count,
you are for earth a shining light,
your Golden Wisdom oh so bright.**

2. I am doing this at the conscious level, and I am really making peace with being here on earth.

Master Lanto, balance all,
for wisdom's balance we do call.
Master Lanto, help us see,
that balance is the Golden Key.

**Master Lanto, Wisdom's Fount,
with blessings we can hardly count,
you are for earth a shining light,
your Golden Wisdom oh so bright.**

3. I do not want to live the rest of my time in embodiment with this frustration, with the sense of not wanting to be here, not wanting to engage fully in life or in the spiritual path. I am rising above the internal spirit that is resisting being on earth and I feel at peace with being here.

Master Lanto, from Above,
we call forth discerning love.
Master Lanto, love's not blind,
through love, God vision we do find.

**Master Lanto, Wisdom's Fount,
with blessings we can hardly count,
you are for earth a shining light,
your Golden Wisdom oh so bright.**

4. Although the earth is a dark, dense and difficult planet, it is also a tremendous growth opportunity. I have a tremendous potential to grow for the rest of this lifetime. In order to realize that potential, I need to overcome the internal spirit that causes me to resist being here.

> Master Lanto, we are sure
> as Christic lamb intentions pure.
> Master Lanto, we'll transcend,
> acceleration is our truest friend.
>
> **Master Lanto, Wisdom's Fount,**
> **with blessings we can hardly count,**
> **you are for earth a shining light,**
> **your Golden Wisdom oh so bright.**

5. I have chosen to come here, I have chosen to be here. Since this is a choice I made, then it is not some punishment that I am here. It is not unfair that I am here. It is actually the opportunity I chose because I saw that this was my personal opportunity to grow—the best possible opportunity that I could have at my present level of spiritual growth.

> Master Lanto, we are whole,
> no more division in the soul.
> Master Lanto, healing flame,
> all balance in your sacred name.
>
> **Master Lanto, Wisdom's Fount,**
> **with blessings we can hardly count,**
> **you are for earth a shining light,**
> **your Golden Wisdom oh so bright.**

7 | Invoking the Vision that all Conditions Are Opportunities

6. I am willing to step outside my normal sense of identity and look at my lifestream consciously the way I do at the identity level. Therefore, I am completely at peace by recognizing that I have chosen to be in this embodiment in my specific conditions because they represent the maximum opportunity for growth for me personally.

> Master Lanto, serve all life,
> as we transcend all inner strife.
> Master Lanto, peace you give,
> to all who want to truly live.

> **Master Lanto, Wisdom's Fount,**
> **with blessings we can hardly count,**
> **you are for earth a shining light,**
> **your Golden Wisdom oh so bright.**

7. There is ultimately no condition on earth that cannot be changed. There are certain conditions that I cannot change right now, but there is no condition on earth that can prevent me from changing myself.

> Master Lanto, free to be,
> in balanced creativity.
> Master Lanto, we employ,
> your balance as the key to joy.

> **Master Lanto, Wisdom's Fount,**
> **with blessings we can hardly count,**
> **you are for earth a shining light,**
> **your Golden Wisdom oh so bright.**

8. I am willing to change myself, I am willing to look at any condition that is causing me to feel resentment towards being in physical embodiment. I will look for the illusion, and I will separate myself from the illusion and allow myself to feel: "Yes, I am here right now because I want to be here. I want to rise higher in consciousness and I rise higher by transcending the specific condition that I am facing right now."

> Master Lanto, balance all,
> the seven rays upon our call.
> Master Lanto, we take flight,
> the threefold flame a blazing light.
>
> **Master Lanto, Wisdom's Fount,**
> **with blessings we can hardly count,**
> **you are for earth a shining light,**
> **your Golden Wisdom oh so bright.**

9. I see the condition from the outside, I separate myself from it, and see that it is not *my* condition (it is only the condition of an internal spirit). Therefore, I am free, I am at peace about being myself and about being in embodiment.

> Lanto dear, your Presence here,
> filling up the inner sphere.
> Life is now a sacred flow,
> God Wisdom we on all bestow.
>
> **Master Lanto, Wisdom's Fount,**
> **with blessings we can hardly count,**
> **you are for earth a shining light,**
> **your Golden Wisdom oh so bright.**

Sealing:

In the name of the Divine Mother, I fully accept that the power of these calls is used to set free the River of Life, so it can outpicture the perfect vision of Christ for my own life, for all people and for the planet. In the name I AM THAT I AM, it is done! Amen.

8 | HOW TO STOP BLAMING YOURSELF

I AM the Ascended Master Nada. At this third level of the initiations of my retreat, I want to start out by referring to something I said in a previous lesson. I pointed out to you that there is a mechanism in your consciousness where you are feeling that because certain conditions in the world, specifically here on planet earth, are not the way they should be, you cannot be a certain way. You cannot be at peace, you cannot be yourself, you cannot fully express yourself on earth.

Now my beloved, what is really behind this psychological condition? Why is it that you have come to accept that because of certain conditions on earth, you cannot express your creativity, you cannot express your Christhood, you cannot give the gift that you came to this planet to give? Here, it is necessary, my beloved, to recognize that the fallen beings are very, very subtle and very, very clever and they are very, very determined to prevent anyone from expressing Christhood.

Naturally, we have given teachings about the concept that many spiritual people are avatars who came to earth specifically to assist in the process of raising the collective consciousness. I can assure you that the fallen beings are also very, very determined to prevent any of the original inhabitants of the earth from rising to the level of Christhood and beginning to express that Christhood because, truly, that is the greater threat to them.

As we have pointed out before, the real progress of this planet depends on the original inhabitants of the earth. The avatars can help raise the collective consciousness but they cannot really cause the planet to make a decisive leap forward. It takes a critical mass of the original inhabitants to rise above a certain level of consciousness before there is a decisive shift. Of course, for such a shift too happen among the original inhabitants, it is necessary that some of them reach the level of Christhood and begin to express that Christhood so the fallen beings are very anxious to prevent this.

Being hammered down for expressing yourself

What has happened to you in the past is that you have dared to express something that is beyond the ordinary. You have dared to not follow the crowd, and the fallen beings have been there to hammer you down, to create some kind of trauma so that you have associated pain and fear (or a sense of hopelessness and despair, a sense that nothing really matters) with expressing yourself, expressing your creativity, taking a stand for a higher truth or in other ways acting beyond the norm. Many of you have this mechanism where you actually fear that the moment you begin to express yourself, you will be exposed to ridicule, criticism or even physical consequences, such as being killed, tortured, imprisoned or whatever. What you have built in your own mind is a mechanism that says: "I don't want to express my Christhood, but I know I am here to express my Christhood so I need to have a justification for why I cannot express my Christhood." Of course, this then is what causes you to think that until a certain outer condition has changed, you cannot express your Christhood.

This makes your ego and certain internal spirits feel very secure because, naturally, it could take a very long time (or least so it has seemed in the past) before the earth is ready to overcome war. You know that for several future embodiments you will not have to worry about expressing your Christhood because you have the perfect excuse. The expression of your Christhood is tied to the change of a certain outer condition that is difficult and will take a long time to change so your ego can feel safe for a while.

Watch your internal reaction

Now, when exposing something like this to you, I am asking you to look at your internal reaction to what I am telling you. In a sense, you could say that I am being very direct, very merciless, here in exposing this mechanism. Some people might feel I should not be so direct. Some people might feel I should not expose this at all. There may be a reaction in you and it could take one of two forms. One is that you feel I should not have been so direct in bringing this to your attention. The other is that you accept what I am saying and that you immediately feel bad about yourself for having this mechanism.

What I am pointing out to you here is that in my last lesson, I said that you cannot really be at peace within yourself as long as you do not accept conditions on earth and accept being in embodiment. If you are constantly struggling against being in embodiment, resisting being here, naturally you cannot feel at peace. What I need you to recognize in this lesson is that if you are not accepting *yourself,* then likewise you cannot be at peace. Why am I bringing this up by pointing out this mechanism where you are postponing your Christhood? Well, it is because when I am pointing out to you that there is a mechanism in you, it will often create a reaction. The reaction can help you see what it is in you that is preventing you from accepting yourself, from feeling at peace with being who you are.

Now, there are some of you (not most of you, but some of you) who will react by feeling almost offended that I would bring this to your attention. This is because you are still at the point where you are seeking to avoid looking at yourself by always projecting out that this or that should not have happened. I need you to become aware of this reaction and I need you to see that it is simply an internal spirit – a part of your ego – that is resisting this way. It is a defense mechanism where the ego does not want you to see the mechanism that is giving the ego power over you. It is causing you to always project your attention out and saying that this or that should not have happened.

I need you to start separating yourself from this, and I know very well that when you do this, then you will realize that you need to look at yourself, you need to look at the mechanism. Instead of saying that I should not have said this, you need to look at the fact that you have this mechanism, this tendency to postpone your Christhood. This, then, allows you to do what many other students have already been doing for a while, namely looking at yourself, looking at whatever you have in you that needs to be resolved.

I know that for many of you, in fact *most* of you, it will be painful to look at this condition. Many of you have felt on a number of occasions, as you have been taking this course or even as you have been following the spiritual path before this course, that when something has been exposed inside of you, it is painful. It causes a reaction in you.

Ascended masters are not sadists

Now my beloved, ascended masters are not sadists; we are not deliberately, consciously torturing you. We are not enjoying pointing out a mechanism in your psychology that makes you feel pain, that makes you feel bad about yourself. On the contrary, I have no greater desire at this level of my retreat than to help you come to the point where you can look at yourself without feeling pain, without feeling bad about yourself.

The entire purpose of this third lesson at my retreat is to get you to a point where you can overcome this very, very subtle tendency to feel bad whenever you come to see something in yourself that you need to overcome. Many of you will feel that you come to see something that should not be there, that should not have been there in the first place. Now my beloved, you need to recognize here that this very reaction is created by the fallen beings. I should perhaps rephrase this by saying that the reaction, of course, is not created by the fallen beings, but that the outer conditions that cause you to react this way were created by the fallen beings.

Sometime in a past lifetime you did dare to express an aspect of your Christhood and the fallen beings did everything they could to hammer you down so that you could not continue in that lifetime to express that Christhood. You need to recognize that the fallen beings are not satisfied with just stopping you in that embodiment. The fallen beings are looking at anyone who dares to express an element of Christhood. There are fallen beings in the identity, mental, and emotional realms who are using the fallen beings in physical embodiment to deliberately try to make sure that you will never again dare to express your Christhood. They do this by trying to in some way insert a reaction in your being that makes you feel that you were wrong for expressing your Christhood. You were wrong for challenging them, you were wrong for speaking out. You were wrong because you were too different from the norm, from the other people or any number of such mechanisms.

Christhood means challenging status quo

What I need you to recognize is that one of the major triumphs of the fallen beings is when they can take a lifestream, who has come to the point where it is ready to express its Christhood, and then it can insert a mechanism in the four lower bodies of that being. The mechanism makes you feel that it is wrong to express your Christhood, that *you* are wrong for expressing your Christhood, so you never dare to do it again.

This is why you have the other mechanism that causes you to tie the expression of your Christhood to certain conditions on earth. In other words, you know that you are here to express your Christhood. There is deep within you a certain memory that this is why you are here. What you experienced back then in time was that you got a very negative reaction for expressing your Christhood. Somehow, you tied this to the outer conditions on earth, thinking that they were not favorable. You are waiting for certain outer conditions to change so that it is then safe to express your Christhood.

You understand, my beloved, that Christhood has one purpose only and that is to challenge status quo so that people can see that there is an alternative to the status quo. There will never *ever* come conditions on earth where it is safe to express your Christhood. Even if you took the manifestation of Saint Germain's Golden Age in its fullest expression, you would still have a society where it would not be safe to express Christhood.

Now of course, if you look at today's society and say: "Where will you be criticized for expressing your Christhood," then you can project forward to the golden age and see that in the golden age what is today condemned will be perfectly normal and acceptable. There will still be some people in the golden age who have a certain sense of status quo. This means that in order to express Christhood, you need to challenge that sense of status quo. It is a much higher sense of status quo than what you have now, but it is still a sense that things are the way they should be and should not be changed because there will still be people who have that need for security. The role of a Christed being, no matter what society he or she is in, no matter what time he or she is in, is always to challenge the norm. It will never be safe, it will never be popular, it will never be accepted to express your Christhood. This I need you to understand consciously because you have already understood it at the level of your identity body.

I need you to pull this down in your conscious awareness and recognize that the role of a Christed being is always to challenge status quo. Therefore, my beloved, expressing your Christhood will never be approved by the fallen beings. Neither will it be popular among many, if not most, of the general population. Recognize one thing: Expressing your Christhood is not a popularity contest. It never *has* been, it never *will* be, it cannot be by the very nature of what it means to express Christhood. You need to come to the recognition here that sometime in your past you reasoned, you accepted the belief, that you were wrong for challenging status quo, that you should not have challenged the fallen beings, that you should not have challenged the people around you. You should have just stayed within the norm of what was acceptable behavior and speech in your society.

I need you to recognize that they reacted negatively to you and you took this negative reaction into your own being and you accepted the belief that you were wrong for standing out from the crowd. Then, I need you to look at this belief and recognize that this belief created an internal spirit, a separate self, and you still have this in you. My beloved, you need to start recognizing consciously that it is just *that:* It is just an internal spirit, it is just a separate self—it is *not* you. This is not who you are. *You* actually do not feel that you are wrong when you express your Christhood, when you stand above the crowd, when you challenge the status quo.

This internal spirit does feel this way and therefore it is constantly trying to prevent you from expressing your Christhood. One of the ways it does so is to make you think it is tied to some outer condition on earth. Another way that this internal spirit seeks to prevent you is to make you feel that whenever you do something that is not acceptable in society, you should feel bad about yourself, you should feel guilty. In order to avoid this emotional pain of feeling bad about yourself, you tend to adjust your outer behavior, even the way you look at life on earth—what you *can* do, what you *cannot* do and even the way you look at yourself. There are many aspects of your relationship to life on earth that are affected by this mechanism.

Seeking to compensate for what has gone wrong

Now, we have talked about reactionary patterns where you go into a certain outer situation, which causes an inner reaction in you. As a result of that inner reaction, you go into a certain pattern of outer behavior, of feelings, of thoughts. I want to give this a little bit of a twist here to make you recognize that many of these reactionary patterns put you in a certain state of mind and they create a compensatory pattern. In other words, you go into a state of mind where you feel that something has gone wrong and now you are seeking to compensate for it. This has been expressed in a very obvious and very primitive way in, for example, the Christian religion where you have the concept of sin.

The idea is that you were created as a sinner, you have done something wrong in this life and you need to compensate for it. You need to somehow either do something that makes up for it or you need to at least suffer for it for a time and then you will have paid back your sin. You have the concept in eastern religions of karma where people feel they have made a certain karma and now you need to balance this karma. Even many ascended master students have the idea that you have made karma in past lives and you compensate for this by giving enough violate flame to balance the karma. Do you see that this is a compensatory pattern?

What has happened is that many of you have come to believe that there is something wrong with you, at least there is something wrong with you here on earth, and you need to compensate for this. One of the primary ways that I want to bring to your attention here is that these compensatory patterns have often affected how you approach the spiritual path, including our teachings, including this course.

You have the sense that there is something wrong with you or that you have done something wrong in the past. When you find the spiritual path, when you find the ascended master's teachings, and learn about karma, reincarnation and the possibility to balance your karma, then you throw yourself at this with an eagerness that on the one hand is commendable but on the other hand is born of a reactionary pattern. You are seeking to compensate for the supposed mistakes you have made in the past. You see many students who find our teachings and they get to the point where they recognize the opportunity to balance karma. They become very, very eager at giving our decrees and invocations, for example the violet flame. They give hours and hours of invocations and decrees every day. Many students have continued this for years and decades.

Overcoming OCD

Now, if you will be completely, brutally honest about this, you could see that the way many students approach the path, especially how they approach giving decrees and invocations, is actually what psychologists would call OCD, obsessive compulsive disorder. My beloved, this is not psychologically healthy. In the long run, this is not healthy for you and it is not what we want to see for you.

Do you see that this kind of behavior comes from the compensatory pattern where you feel there is something you have to compensate for? Now, many of you are going to say: "But have we not sinned in the past, have we not made karma and do we not have to balance the karma? Are you now saying we don't have to balance karma?" My beloved, this is your linear mind talking and I am asking you to set aside this reaction so that you can actually hear and absorb the explanation I will give you.

I am in no way saying that it has been wrong of you to give invocations and decrees. It has, in fact, been necessary for you. You did have karma that you needed to balance. What I am saying is that you are now at a point where you can step back, look at this and say: "Obviously, at this level of consciousness,

8 | How to Stop Blaming Yourself

I have not qualified for my ascension, I have not balanced all of my karma. It is not that I need to stop giving decrees and invocations, but perhaps I could step back and come to approach the path, including decrees and invocations, from a different perspective where I am not doing it because I am driven by a compensatory pattern that was actually set up in reaction to the fallen beings."

I am asking you to come to the point where you are not approaching the spiritual path based on a reaction to the *fallen beings* but on a reaction to the *ascended masters*. Now, many of you will think that you *are* reacting to the ascended masters by following our teachings. You *are* to some degree but you are not completely approaching the path as a result of reacting to us. You have with you, in your four lower bodies, this compensatory mechanism where the fallen ones have made you believe that you were wrong and that you could only be wrong on earth. Therefore, you are seeking to compensate for this and you are using the teachings of the ascended masters as a way to compensate. This has been acceptable up until this point, but it is no longer necessary for you to drag this with you. In fact, you cannot be at peace with yourself as long as you are dragging this mechanism along with you.

The irony of blaming yourself for blaming yourself

I need you to step back here and see the irony of this. There is a deep irony here because you will notice in yourself, if you are honest, that when I am telling you this, there is a reaction in you. It is most likely that you feel that you were wrong for having this compensatory mechanism and that here is another thing that was wrong with you and it needs to be changed and it needs to be corrected. You may react with certain feelings but do you not see the irony? I am pointing out to you that you have a tendency to think that you are wrong for being here. When I point this out to you, how do you react to what I am saying? You react with the very same mechanism of feeling you were wrong for having the tendency to feel that you were wrong. Do you not see that this is what scientists call an *infinite regress?* It is a closed circle, a treadmill. You can *never* get out of it.

I point out that you have a tendency to blame yourself and then you blame yourself for blaming yourself. When will this stop? When will this reaction stop? Well, it will stop, my beloved, when you see that this is one of these treadmills that you can never get out of by running on it.

If you do not have this picture in your mind, then go and find some video on the Internet of a mouse or a hamster running on one of these treadmills. Then, ask yourself a simple question: "Will the mouse ever get off the treadmill by running faster on the treadmill?" The obvious answer is "No." No matter how fast the mouse runs, it will not get off the treadmill. Well, it may in a sense in that it might actually wear itself out, have a heart attack and die but that is the only way it is going to get off the treadmill.

You realize here that the treadmill I am pointing out to you is in your psychology. This compensatory treadmill may cause you to run faster and faster in your outer life, give more and more decrees, do more and more things—compensate, compensate, *compensate*. Your whole life becomes this total compensation mechanism where you are running faster and faster until you have a heart attack and die. The mechanism is in your three higher bodies so you take that with you to your next lifetime. Then, in your next lifetime, you can also wear out your physical body until you die and you can continue doing this lifetime after lifetime.

There are, in fact, people who have done this. There are ascended master students who have done this and who are doing the same thing in this lifetime that you have done in the last three or four embodiments. My only question here is: "Will you ever get off the emotional, mental and identity level treadmill by running faster in the physical or for that matter in your three higher bodies?" Obviously, you will never get off it that way. There is no linear goal that can be fulfilled in the treadmill because it can only go around in a circle. What do you need to do? *You need to stop struggling.* Then, the treadmill will come to a halt and then you can jump out of the thing.

Using the teachings to blame yourself

I need you to recognize this pattern where you are blaming yourself and where you are even using our teachings to blame yourself, to feel that now you have done another thing wrong. Here is another thing to compensate for and now you need to feel bad so you can run even faster. I need you to simply step back and say: "Why is it necessary to feel bad about myself when I'm on the path of the ascended masters?"

You recognize, my beloved, that most of you have in past lifetimes, perhaps even in this lifetime, encountered false teachers. The Catholic church is an institution that wants its members to feel bad about themselves. It wants its members to feel like sinners because that is the only way they will submit themselves to what the church tells them to do and will not question the illogical doctrines of the church.

You recognize there are many false teachers in the world who want you to feel bad about yourself. They are actually taking advantage of your compensatory mechanism in order to keep you engaged in what they are wanting you to engage in so that you give them your energy. We are the ascended masters, my beloved. We do not need your energy and we certainly do not need or want you to feel bad about yourself. We do not need you to approach the path that we are offering you based on this compensatory mechanism where you feel you have to do more and more on the outer in order to avoid feeling bad about yourself on the inner. My beloved, I do not need you to be on any treadmill in order to follow the initiations at my retreat. I do not *want* you to be on any treadmill. My primary desire at this level is to help you get off the treadmill in your emotional, mental and identity bodies so that you can feel how (as you stop running, as you stop trying to compensate) it just slows down, it stands still. You jump out of it, you look at this self, you look at this internal spirit, and you say: "Get thee behind me Satan, I just don't need you in my life anymore."

Now again, my beloved, I have been in physical embodiment on earth. So have most of the ascended masters, certainly all of the Chohans. We have created these compensatory mechanisms, we have been on a treadmill ourselves. We know what it is like. We know it can be tricky to step out of it but we also know that it is *possible* to step out of it. We know how much more free, how much more at peace you feel when you step off the treadmill of trying to use a spiritual teaching and spiritual tools to compensate for what you think you have done wrong in the past.

Forgiving yourself for reacting

My beloved, Hilarion gave a very, very important teaching that some of you may not have fully locked in to. He said that as you descend into embodiment, you are not just suddenly popping down to the 48th level and take embodiment for the first time at the 48th level. In order to get down to that level, you have to go through all of the levels above it, starting at the 144th level. He also said that for each level you go down, you take on a certain illusion that is associated with that level.

My beloved, do you understand what I am saying here? It does not matter how you came to earth, whether you are an avatar or one of the original inhabitants. Even an avatar, no matter what level of consciousness you had before coming to earth, you still descend to the 48th level for your first embodiment and that means you take on all of these illusions that are above the 48th level. Now my beloved, what does this mean? It means that you may have been an avatar who came from a natural planet and at the level of consciousness you had when you descended to earth, you would have been able to avoid reacting to the fallen beings.

You may feel today that you *should* have been able to avoid reacting to the fallen beings, but you realize that the purpose of you descending into embodiment was to demonstrate to the people on earth that you can start at the 48th level and rise above that level in consciousness. You *had* to descend to the 48th level. *When* you descend to the 48th level on earth, you will react to what the fallen beings expose you to based on the 48th level of consciousness. There is no other way for you to react because you are seeing life on earth through the perception filter of these many illusions you have taken on in order for you to reach the 48th level.

There is no other way to react on earth, my beloved. That means very simply that nobody in the ascended realm blames you for reacting the way you did to the fallen beings. We all did the same thing and that is why nobody in the ascended realm wants you to blame yourself for reacting to the fallen beings the way you did. You understand, my beloved, that at the 48th level of consciousness there is a high and a low reaction but the high reaction at the 48th level is not Buddhic attainment where you can be completely non-attached. *That* only comes at the 144th level.

It was inevitable that you reacted with a lower reaction. You were meant to do this in order to demonstrate that you can rise above the reaction. You understand, my beloved, there is a consciousness projected by the fallen beings that if you are a spiritual person (whether you are one of the original inhabitants who have risen to a certain level or whether you are an avatar) you should never have reacted in any negative way, in any imperfect way. Therefore, the fallen beings (when you dared to express your Christhood in the past) hammered you down. They caused you to have a negative reaction and now they are causing you to blame yourself for having that negative reaction. You are feeling that because you had this, Humpty Dumpty has fallen from the wall and all the king's horses and all the king's men cannot put Humpty Dumpty together again. You feel there is nothing you could do to undo what happened in the past. Therefore, you are caught in this never-ending treadmill of seeking to compensate for it.

The only way to overcome your past

My beloved, there *is* actually something you could do to undo what you did in the past. Many of you have not quite understood this at the conscious level. What can you do to undo what you did in the past? Well, we have actually said it before but I will say it again. You cannot change the physical action that took place in the past but the physical action no longer matters because time has moved on. What matters is what you are carrying with you in your four lower bodies as an internal spirit. My beloved, you can separate yourself from an internal spirit, dismiss it and let it die. When you undo the spirit, so to speak, you have undone what you did in the past.

This is the ultimate compensation and it is the *only* compensation that can work. You understand there is a spirit that causes you to be on a treadmill, feeling that you have to constantly run faster, you have to do something in order to compensate for what you did wrong in the past, right? You have the old saying in popular vernacular: "Two wrongs don't make a right." Do you see, my beloved: "Two rights don't compensate for one wrong." It does not matter how many right things you do, it will not compensate for the wrong thing you did as long as that internal spirit you created is still in your higher bodies.

There are people, and you can find them in most religious and spiritual teachings, who for lifetimes have been seeking to compensate for something they did wrong in the past by doing something right according to their religion or spiritual teaching. There are people, for example, in Tibet who spend most of their time rotating a prayer wheel, thinking this will compensate for something they did wrong in the past. There are people everywhere who give prayers, go to mass, light candles, do yoga, do decrees, do this, do that.

My beloved, there is a mechanical aspect in the sense that you did something, you made karma. You can balance the karma by, for example, giving a certain amount of decrees. When you come to this level of the path of self-mastery, you need to recognize that the primary problem you are having right now is not a matter of balancing karma. By rising to this level, by giving the decrees and invocations you have given, most of you are already well on the way to balancing your karma, at least a great part of it. It is not so that you will have balanced all the karma when you complete this course. You are on the path of balancing it at the end of this lifetime because you recognize that for each of the levels up to the 144th level, there is a certain portion of karma that needs to be balanced at that level.

It is not a matter of balancing *all* of your karma at this level of your path, but it is a matter of balancing the karma up to your present level. Do you see? You can be behind balancing karma but you can also come to a point where you catch up with the level you are at on the path, meaning you do not have any karma lingering from the lower levels. You have balanced all the karma up to whether you are on the 48th, or the 56th or the 63rd or the 85th level. You have balanced this karma and that means you are caught up and you do not need to worry about balancing karma. As you keep giving invocations and decrees at higher levels, you will continue to balance the karma for each level.

There is nothing wrong with you

What I am concerned about here is to get you to the point where you realize that it is a matter of dissolving these internal spirits. My beloved, this is the internal spirit that you need to overcome right now: this entire feeling that there is something wrong with you.

Do you understand, my beloved, that what the fallen ones want you to feel is that rising to your present level of consciousness makes you wrong? It is wrong for you to be in embodiment on earth and rise to this level. They want you to feel this way because you are a threat to them, and you can surely see that this is not something you want to accept. You do not want to accept their reasoning, and naturally you *are* not wrong for rising to your present level of consciousness. You need to let go of this mechanism. You need to get to the point where you can consciously accept a very simple fact: "There is *nothing* wrong with me." It may be necessary (as this messenger did many years ago) to go through a period where you make this your mantra. You monitor yourself and you see how (sometimes in an outer situation, sometimes just out of the blue) there comes an impulse to you that you were wrong, that you did something wrong, that you should not have done this, you should not have done that. You may need to go through a period where you monitor yourself and then, whenever this impulse comes to you, you counteract it by consciously saying, perhaps aloud, perhaps silently: "There is nothing wrong with me. I fully accept that there is nothing wrong with me."

My beloved, when you go through this and when you keep going through this, then you can come to that point where you have separated yourself enough from this spirit, this separate self. You can look at it and you just feel that it has no more pull on you. At that moment, it will collapse because what is holding it up is the energy you give it by still believing in the illusion that there is something wrong with you.

You are not wrong for being on earth

You see my beloved, what we are taking you through in this course is helping you rise above the illusions at each level between the 48th and 96th level of consciousness. One of these illusions is the entire idea that there is something wrong with you here on earth.

If you are an avatar, you have never experienced any accusation on a natural planet that there was something wrong with you. In the distant past, before the earth descended into duality, you had never experienced this either if you are one of the original inhabitants. There is within you some sense that there is really nothing wrong with you. Because you have experienced so many times from the outer (both from the fallen beings and from other people and society at large) that they have accused you of being wrong, then you have come to think that perhaps there *is* something wrong with you here on earth. Perhaps it is the earth that makes you wrong, that makes you feel wrong? This is, of course, one reason you find it difficult to accept being here.

If you look at yourself, you will perhaps recognize that many spiritual people have felt like outcasts. As children you have felt like you did not fit in, there was nobody you could talk to about your spiritual beliefs. Many of you have been ridiculed for your spiritual beliefs. Many of you have perhaps even found a spiritual movement, followed it for a while and then (when you started expressing some questions that challenged the status quo of that movement) you were perhaps even persecuted by that movement.

You have maybe come to feel: "Where do I actually belong, where do I actually fit in?" This, of course, has fed this compensatory mechanism that I have exposed to you. Once you can let go of that mechanism, you can come to a new level of the spiritual path where it is truly based on love. You are not following the spiritual path in order to compensate for anything. You are following it because there is something you love, whatever it is individually. For you it is a love-based motivation, not a compensation-based motivation.

Overcoming fear of being creative

This is where you can overcome your obsessive-compulsive disorder and start approaching the path from a non-obsessive, non-compulsive way. This is not a disorder, it is simply your natural love-based, built-in drive for rising higher, for experiencing something that is more and for expressing that something that is more.

Truly, my beloved, as long as you are compensating, you cannot feel free to express yourself, you cannot feel free to be creative. You will be afraid of being creative because what is creativity? Well, it is going beyond status quo. You are only creative when you go beyond status quo. When you are compensating, you are actually basing your desire to compensate on status quo because you are saying: "Status quo is that I did something wrong in the past and I need to compensate for this."

Compensation and creativity are incompatible and you will never be a fully creative being as long as you are trying to compensate for anything. There are, of course, people who are considered artists and who are driven by a compensatory pattern in their psychology and seeking to compensate for this through their art. You can even see people who have been obsessed with painting as many paintings as possible or doing sculptures or whatever it is. You see many artists, for example, who are really driven by an OCD to express art that challenges the status quo. Even though they are challenging the status quo, they are *not* actually doing so in a creative way. That is why so much of modern art is not balanced and it is not aesthetically pleasing. It is jagged, it is inharmonious. It is meant to be provocative but not in a sense that uplifts you but simply in a way that jars people out of their sense of what is aesthetically pleasing.

Many people have the sense of what is aesthetic but many modern artists have attempted to compensate for this because they have thought that this is actually status quo and they need to challenge this. You see, my beloved, aesthetics is not a matter of status quo even though, of course, in the past there have been many examples of how a certain style of painting has been considered the only right one and therefore it became status quo. Nevertheless, there is a difference here because there are certain aesthetics, a certain sense of beauty, that you have with you and most modern art simply falls outside of the sense of beauty that most people have. These artists may think they are challenging status quo but they are coming from this obsessive-compulsive, compensatory mechanism that causes them to actually think they have to challenge society's sense of status quo instead of challenging their own sense of the compensatory mechanism. They are focusing on changing society instead of changing themselves, transcending their own state of consciousness.

We, of course, want our students to be creative but we want you to be creative from a love-based foundation, not from this compensatory mechanism that drives you to do something unusual just to get attention. My beloved, I have taken up enough of your attention for this particular lesson, and I thank you for being willing to walk the path that I put before you.

9 | INVOKING FREEDOM FROM BLAME

In the name I AM THAT I AM, Jesus Christ, I call to my I AM Presence to flow through the I Will Be Presence that I AM and give this invocation with full power. I call to beloved Elohim Peace and Aloha and Heros and Amora, Archangel Uriel and Aurora and Chamuel and Charity, Nada and Paul the Venetian to help me overcome all tendency to blame myself. Help me see and surrender all patterns that block my oneness with Nada and with my I AM Presence, including ...

[Make personal calls]

Part 1

1. In the past, I did not follow the crowd, and the fallen beings tried to create a trauma so that I have associated pain and fear with expressing myself.

O Elohim Peace, in Unity's Flame,
there is no more room for duality's game,
we know that all form is from the same source,
empowering us to plot a new course.

**O Elohim Peace, through your tranquility,
we are free from the chaos of duality,
in oneness with God a new identity,
we are raising the earth into Infinity.**

2. This is a mechanism where I fear that the moment I begin to express myself, I will be exposed to ridicule, criticism or even physical consequences, such as being killed, tortured or imprisoned.

O Elohim Peace, the bell now you ring,
causing all atoms to vibrate and sing,
we give up the sense of a separate "me,"
we're crossing Samsara's turbulent sea.

**O Elohim Peace, through your tranquility,
we are free from the chaos of duality,
in oneness with God a new identity,
we are raising the earth into Infinity.**

3. What I have built in my mind is a mechanism that says: "I don't want to express my Christhood, but I know I am here to express my Christhood so I need to have a justification for why I cannot express my Christhood."

O Elohim Peace, you help us to know,
that Jesus has come your Flame to bestow,
upon all who are ready to give up the strife,
by following Christ into infinite life.

O Elohim Peace, through your tranquility,
we are free from the chaos of duality,
in oneness with God a new identity,
we are raising the earth into Infinity.

4. This is what causes me to think that until a certain outer condition has changed, I cannot express my Christhood. This makes my ego and internal spirits feel secure.

O Elohim Peace, through your eyes we see,
that only in oneness will we ever be free,
we now see that there is no separate thing,
to the ego-based self we no longer cling.

O Elohim Peace, through your tranquility,
we are free from the chaos of duality,
in oneness with God a new identity,
we are raising the earth into Infinity.

5. I am willing to look at my internal reaction to this revelation. The reaction can help me see what it is in me that is preventing me from accepting myself and feeling at peace with being who I am.

O Elohim Peace, you show us the way,
for clearing the mind from duality's fray,
you pierce the illusions of both time and space,
separation consumed by your Infinite Grace.

> **O Elohim Peace, through your tranquility,
> we are free from the chaos of duality,
> in oneness with God a new identity,
> we are raising the earth into Infinity.**

6. I am letting go of the internal spirit that wants to avoid looking at myself by always projecting out that this or that should not have happened.

> O Elohim Peace, what beauty your name,
> consuming within us duality's shame,
> the earth is set free from burden of fear,
> accepting your peace is now manifest here.

> **O Elohim Peace, through your tranquility,
> we are free from the chaos of duality,
> in oneness with God a new identity,
> we are raising the earth into Infinity.**

7. This is a defense mechanism where the ego does not want me to see the mechanism that is giving the ego power over me. It is causing me to project my attention out and not looking at myself.

> O Elohim Peace, with Christ at our side,
> no force of duality can evermore hide,
> It was through the vibration of your Golden Flame,
> that Christ the illusion of death overcame.

> **O Elohim Peace, through your tranquility,
> we are free from the chaos of duality,
> in oneness with God a new identity,
> we are raising the earth into Infinity.**

8. I am willing to look at the fact that I have this mechanism, this tendency to postpone my Christhood. I am willing to look at myself, look at whatever I have in me that needs to be resolved, even if it is painful.

> O Elohim Peace, you bring now to earth,
> the unstoppable flame of Cosmic Rebirth,
> we give up the sense that something is "mine,"
> allowing your Light through our beings to shine.
>
> **O Elohim Peace, through your tranquility,**
> **we are free from the chaos of duality,**
> **in oneness with God a new identity,**
> **we are raising the earth into Infinity.**

9. Nada, help me come to the point where I can look at myself without feeling pain, without feeling bad about myself.

> O Elohim Peace, as peace now we feel,
> all records of war you totally heal,
> the earth is now free from forces of war,
> restoring her purity known from before.
>
> **O Elohim Peace, through your tranquility,**
> **we are free from the chaos of duality,**
> **in oneness with God a new identity,**
> **we are raising the earth into Infinity.**

Part 2

1. Nada, help me overcome the subtle tendency to feel bad whenever I come to see something in myself that I need to overcome.

> O Heros-Amora, in your love so pink,
> we care not what others about us may think,
> in oneness with you, we claim a new day,
> as innocent children, we frolic and play.
>
> **O Heros-Amora, we reap what we sow,**
> **yet this is Plan B for helping us grow,**
> **for truly, Plan A is that we join the flow,**
> **immersed in the Infinite Love you bestow.**

2. This reaction is created by the fallen beings. Sometime in a past lifetime I did dare to express an aspect of my Christhood and the fallen beings did everything they could to hammer me down.

> O Heros-Amora, a new life begun,
> we laugh at the devil, the serious one,
> the serpent is stuck in his duality,
> but we are set free by Love's reality.
>
> **O Heros-Amora, we reap what we sow,**
> **yet this is Plan B for helping us grow,**
> **for truly, Plan A is that we join the flow,**
> **immersed in the Infinite Love you bestow.**

9 | Invoking Freedom from Blame

3. I recognize that the fallen beings are not satisfied with just stopping me in one embodiment. They want to make sure that I will never again dare to express my Christhood.

> O Heros-Amora, awakened we see,
> in true love is no conditionality,
> we bathe in your glorious Ruby-Pink Sun,
> knowing our God allows life to be fun.
>
> **O Heros-Amora, we reap what we sow,**
> **yet this is Plan B for helping us grow,**
> **for truly, Plan A is that we join the flow,**
> **immersed in the Infinite Love you bestow.**

4. They do this by trying to insert a reaction in my being that makes me feel that I was wrong for expressing my Christhood. I was wrong for challenging them, I was wrong for speaking out. I was wrong because I was too different from the norm.

> O Heros-Amora, life is such a joy,
> we see that the world is like a great toy,
> whatever the mind into it projects,
> the mirror of life exactly reflects.
>
> **O Heros-Amora, we reap what we sow,**
> **yet this is Plan B for helping us grow,**
> **for truly, Plan A is that we join the flow,**
> **immersed in the Infinite Love you bestow.**

5. One of the major triumphs of the fallen beings is when they can insert a mechanism in my four lower bodies that makes me feel that it is wrong to express my Christhood, that I am wrong for expressing my Christhood, so I never dare to do it again.

O Heros-Amora, conditions you burn,
we know we are free to take a new turn,
Immersed in the stream of infinite Love,
we know that the Spirit came from Above.

**O Heros-Amora, we reap what we sow,
yet this is Plan B for helping us grow,
for truly, Plan A is that we join the flow,
immersed in the Infinite Love you bestow.**

6. This is why I have the other mechanism that caused me to tie the expression of my Christhood to certain conditions on earth. I tied the negative reaction for expressing my Christhood to the outer conditions on earth, thinking that they were not favorable.

O Heros-Amora, we feel that at last,
we've risen above the trap of the past,
in true love we claim our freedom to grow,
forever we're one with Love's Infinite Flow.

**O Heros-Amora, we reap what we sow,
yet this is Plan B for helping us grow,
for truly, Plan A is that we join the flow,
immersed in the Infinite Love you bestow.**

7. Christhood has one purpose only, and that is to challenge status quo so that people can see that there is an alternative to the status quo. There will never come conditions on earth where it is safe to express my Christhood.

9 | Invoking Freedom from Blame

O Heros-Amora, conditions are ties,
forming a net of serpentine lies,
but you have the antidote setting us free,
you take us beyond conditionality.

**O Heros-Amora, we reap what we sow,
yet this is Plan B for helping us grow,
for truly, Plan A is that we join the flow,
immersed in the Infinite Love you bestow.**

8. The role of a Christed being, no matter what society I am in, no matter what time I am in, is always to challenge the norm. It will never be safe, it will never be popular, it will never be accepted to express my Christhood.

O Heros-Amora, your love is no bond,
for love only wants to take us beyond,
your love has no bounds, forever it flies,
raising all life into Ruby-Pink skies.

**O Heros-Amora, we reap what we sow,
yet this is Plan B for helping us grow,
for truly, Plan A is that we join the flow,
immersed in the Infinite Love you bestow.**

9. Expressing my Christhood is not a popularity contest. It never has been, it never will be. It cannot be by the very nature of what it means to express Christhood.

O Heros-Amora, love bathing the earth,
filling all people with infinite mirth,
for fear and despair there is no more room,
as all are awakened by love's sonic boom.

**O Heros-Amora, we reap what we sow,
yet this is Plan B for helping us grow,
for truly, Plan A is that we join the flow,
immersed in the Infinite Love you bestow.**

Part 3

1. Sometime in my past I accepted the belief that I was wrong for challenging status quo, that I should not have challenged the fallen beings, that I should not have challenged the people around me.

> Uriel Archangel, immense is the power,
> of angels of peace, all war to devour.
> The demons of war, no match for your light,
> consuming them all, with radiance so bright.
>
> **Uriel Archangel, use your great sword,
> Uriel Archangel, consume all discord,
> Uriel Archangel, we're of one accord,
> Uriel Archangel, we walk with the Lord.**

2. I came to think that I should have just stayed within the norm of what was acceptable behavior and speech in my society.

> Uriel Archangel, intense is the sound,
> when millions of angels, their voices compound.
> They build a crescendo, piercing the night,
> life's glorious oneness revealed to our sight.

9 | Invoking Freedom from Blame

> **Uriel Archangel, use your great sword,**
> **Uriel Archangel, consume all discord,**
> **Uriel Archangel, we're of one accord,**
> **Uriel Archangel, we walk with the Lord.**

3. People reacted negatively to me and I took this negative reaction into my own being and I accepted the belief that I was wrong for standing out from the crowd.

> Uriel Archangel, from out the Great Throne,
> your millions of trumpets, sound the One Tone.
> Consuming all discord with your harmony,
> the sound of all sounds will set all life free.

> **Uriel Archangel, use your great sword,**
> **Uriel Archangel, consume all discord,**
> **Uriel Archangel, we're of one accord,**
> **Uriel Archangel, we walk with the Lord.**

4. I recognize that this belief created an internal spirit, a separate self, and I still have this in me.

> Uriel Archangel, all war is now done,
> for you bring a message, from heart of the One.
> The hearts of all men, now singing in peace,
> the spirals of love, forever increase.

> **Uriel Archangel, use your great sword,**
> **Uriel Archangel, consume all discord,**
> **Uriel Archangel, we're of one accord,**
> **Uriel Archangel, we walk with the Lord.**

5. I recognize that it is just that: It is just an internal spirit, it is just a separate self—it is not *me*. This is not who I am. I actually do not feel that I am wrong when I express my Christhood.

> Uriel Archangel, your infinite peace,
> from all warring beings our planet release,
> war is a prison from which we are free,
> embracing the peace of true unity.
>
> **Uriel Archangel, use your great sword,**
> **Uriel Archangel, consume all discord,**
> **Uriel Archangel, we're of one accord,**
> **Uriel Archangel, we walk with the Lord.**

6. This internal spirit does feel this way and therefore it is constantly trying to prevent me from expressing my Christhood. One of the ways it does so is to make me think I should feel bad about myself, I should feel guilty.

> Uriel Archangel, we send forth the call,
> reveal now the oneness that unifies all,
> help us the vision of peace now to see,
> so we from all conflicts and struggles are free.
>
> **Uriel Archangel, use your great sword,**
> **Uriel Archangel, consume all discord,**
> **Uriel Archangel, we're of one accord,**
> **Uriel Archangel, we walk with the Lord.**

7. In order to avoid this emotional pain of feeling bad about myself, I adjust my outer behavior, even the way I look at life. Many aspects of my relationship to life on earth are affected by this mechanism.

9 | Invoking Freedom from Blame

> Uriel Archangel, in service to life,
> you give us release from struggle and strife,
> forgetting the self is truly the key,
> to living a life in true harmony.
>
> **Uriel Archangel, use your great sword,**
> **Uriel Archangel, consume all discord,**
> **Uriel Archangel, we're of one accord,**
> **Uriel Archangel, we walk with the Lord.**

8. This reactionary tendency creates a compensatory pattern in me. I feel that something has gone wrong and now I am seeking to compensate for it.

> Uriel Archangel, the earth now you raise,
> out of duality's death-bringing haze,
> we call now upon your great Flame of Peace,
> commanding that all petty squabbles do cease.
>
> **Uriel Archangel, use your great sword,**
> **Uriel Archangel, consume all discord,**
> **Uriel Archangel, we're of one accord,**
> **Uriel Archangel, we walk with the Lord.**

9. I believe there is something wrong with me here on earth and I need to compensate for this.

> Uriel Archangel, as peace is the norm,
> to your higher vision the earth does conform,
> as people have found your peace from within,
> a Golden Age is the prize that we win.

Uriel Archangel, use your great sword,
Uriel Archangel, consume all discord,
Uriel Archangel, we're of one accord,
Uriel Archangel, we walk with the Lord.

Part 4

1. These compensatory patterns give me an unbalanced approach to the spiritual path, bordering on an obsessive-compulsive disorder.

> Chamuel Archangel, in ruby ray power,
> we know we are taking a life-giving shower.
> Love burning away all perversions of will,
> we suddenly feel our desires falling still.

> **Chamuel Archangel, descend from Above,**
> **Chamuel Archangel, with ruby-pink love,**
> **Chamuel Archangel, so often thought-of,**
> **Chamuel Archangel, o come Holy Dove.**

2. I am willing to step back and come to approach the path, including decrees and invocations, from a different perspective where I am not doing it because I am driven by a compensatory pattern that was actually set up in reaction to the fallen beings.

> Chamuel Archangel, a spiral of light,
> as ruby ray fire now pierces the night.
> All forces of darkness consumed by your fire,
> consuming all those who will not rise higher.

9 | Invoking Freedom from Blame

**Chamuel Archangel, descend from Above,
Chamuel Archangel, with ruby-pink love,
Chamuel Archangel, so often thought-of,
Chamuel Archangel, o come Holy Dove.**

3. Nada, help me come to the point where I am not approaching the spiritual path based on a reaction to the fallen beings but on a reaction to the ascended masters.

Chamuel Archangel, your love so immense,
with clarified vision, our lives now make sense.
The purpose of life you so clearly reveal,
immersed in your love, God's oneness we feel.

**Chamuel Archangel, descend from Above,
Chamuel Archangel, with ruby-pink love,
Chamuel Archangel, so often thought-of,
Chamuel Archangel, o come Holy Dove.**

4. Nada, help me see that when you are pointing out that I have a tendency to think that I was wrong for being here, I react with the same mechanism of feeling I was wrong for having the tendency to feel that I was wrong.

Chamuel Archangel, what calmness you bring,
we see now that even death has no sting.
For truly, in love there can be no decay,
as love is transcendence into a new day.

**Chamuel Archangel, descend from Above,
Chamuel Archangel, with ruby-pink love,
Chamuel Archangel, so often thought-of,
Chamuel Archangel, o come Holy Dove.**

5. I see that when you point out that I have a tendency to blame myself, I blame myself for blaming myself. I see that this is one of these treadmills that I can never get out of by running on it.

> Chamuel Archangel, God's Love Flame bestow,
> on all those longing God's true love to know,
> conditions we know can never be real,
> and this is the love you always reveal.

> **Chamuel Archangel, descend from Above,**
> **Chamuel Archangel, with ruby-pink love,**
> **Chamuel Archangel, so often thought-of,**
> **Chamuel Archangel, o come Holy Dove.**

6. This compensatory treadmill causes me to run faster and faster, seeking to do more and more things—compensate, compensate, compensate.

> Chamuel Archangel, love's seed you have sown,
> in hearts of all those who don't seek to own,
> for love that possesses is nothing but fear,
> that pierces the heart with duality's spear.

> **Chamuel Archangel, descend from Above,**
> **Chamuel Archangel, with ruby-pink love,**
> **Chamuel Archangel, so often thought-of,**
> **Chamuel Archangel, o come Holy Dove.**

7. There is no linear goal that can be fulfilled in the treadmill because it can only go around in a circle. Therefore, I need to stop struggling.

9 | Invoking Freedom from Blame

> Chamuel Archangel, we don't want control,
> for this is the devil's hold on the soul,
> your love will now break the serpentine chain,
> so we are set free God's love to reclaim.

> **Chamuel Archangel, descend from Above,**
> **Chamuel Archangel, with ruby-pink love,**
> **Chamuel Archangel, so often thought-of,**
> **Chamuel Archangel, o come Holy Dove.**

8. I recognize the pattern where I am blaming myself and I am using spiritual teachings to blame myself.

> Chamuel Archangel, you are so adept,
> at helping us God's true love to accept,
> we know that the love for which we so yearn,
> is not something we on earth have to earn.

> **Chamuel Archangel, descend from Above,**
> **Chamuel Archangel, with ruby-pink love,**
> **Chamuel Archangel, so often thought-of,**
> **Chamuel Archangel, o come Holy Dove.**

9. I now see that it is not necessary to feel bad about myself when I am on the path of the ascended masters.

> Chamuel Archangel, for love to accept,
> we do not need to be so perfect,
> for love is not static but always a flow,
> demanding only we're willing to grow.

Chamuel Archangel, descend from Above,
Chamuel Archangel, with ruby-pink love,
Chamuel Archangel, so often thought-of,
Chamuel Archangel, o come Holy Dove.

Part 5

1. Nada, help me get off the treadmill in my emotional, mental and identity bodies so that I can jump out of it. I see the internal spirit and say: "Get thee behind me Satan, I just don't need you in my life anymore."

> Master Nada, beauty's power,
> unfolding like a sacred flower.
> Master Nada, so sublime,
> a will that conquers even time.

> **Master Nada, peace you give,**
> **forevermore in peace we live,**
> **our planet has a peaceful morn,**
> **the Golden Age is hereby born.**

2. Nada, help me see any tendency to feel that I should not have reacted to the fallen beings from a lower state of consciousness.

> Master Nada, you bestow,
> upon us wisdom's rushing flow.
> Master Nada, mind so strong
> rising on your wings of song.

9 | Invoking Freedom from Blame

Master Nada, peace you give,
forevermore in peace we live,
our planet has a peaceful morn,
the Golden Age is hereby born.

3. I reacted the way I did because in order to take embodiment on earth, I had to take on the illusions that brought me to a lower level of consciousness. It is natural that I react with that level of consciousness.

Master Nada, precious scent,
your love is truly heaven-sent.
Master Nada, kind and soft
on wings of love we rise aloft.

Master Nada, peace you give,
forevermore in peace we live,
our planet has a peaceful morn,
the Golden Age is hereby born.

4. Nobody in the ascended realm blames me for reacting the way I did to the fallen beings. Nobody in the ascended realm wants me to blame myself for reacting to the fallen beings the way I did.

Master Nada, mother light,
our hearts are rising like a kite.
Master Nada, from your view,
all life is pure as morning dew.

**Master Nada, peace you give,
forevermore in peace we live,
our planet has a peaceful morn,
the Golden Age is hereby born.**

5. It was inevitable that I reacted with a lower reaction. I was meant to do this in order to demonstrate that I can rise above the reaction.

Master Nada, truth you bring,
as morning birds in love do sing.
Master Nada, we now feel,
your love that all four bodies heal.

**Master Nada, peace you give,
forevermore in peace we live,
our planet has a peaceful morn,
the Golden Age is hereby born.**

6. The fallen beings have projected that if I am a spiritual person, I should never have reacted in any imperfect way. The fallen beings hammered me down. They caused me to have a negative reaction and now they are causing me to blame myself for having that negative reaction.

Master Nada, serve in peace,
as all emotions we release.
Master Nada, life is fun,
the solar plexus is a sun.

9 | Invoking Freedom from Blame

**Master Nada, peace you give,
forevermore in peace we live,
our planet has a peaceful morn,
the Golden Age is hereby born.**

7. I am feeling that this could never be undone, and therefore I am caught in this never-ending treadmill of seeking to compensate for it.

Master Nada, love is free,
conditions we no longer see.
Master Nada, rise above,
all human forms of lesser love.

**Master Nada, peace you give,
forevermore in peace we live,
our planet has a peaceful morn,
the Golden Age is hereby born.**

8. I cannot change the physical action that took place in the past but the physical action no longer matters because time has moved on. I am carrying with me an internal spirit, but I can separate myself from that spirit, dismiss it and let it die. When I undo the spirit, I have undone what I did in the past.

Master Nada, balance all,
the seven rays upon our call.
Master Nada, rise and shine,
your radiant beauty most divine.

> **Master Nada, peace you give,**
> **forevermore in peace we live,**
> **our planet has a peaceful morn,**
> **the Golden Age is hereby born.**

9. Nada, help me overcome the spirit behind the feeling that there is something wrong with me. The fallen beings want me to feel that rising to my present level of consciousness makes me wrong. It is wrong for me to be in embodiment.

> Nada Dear, your Presence here,
> filling up the inner sphere.
> Life is now a sacred flow,
> God Peace we do on all bestow.

> **Master Nada, peace you give,**
> **forevermore in peace we live,**
> **our planet has a peaceful morn,**
> **the Golden Age is hereby born.**

Part 6

1. They want me to feel this way because I am a threat to them. This is not something I want to accept. I do not want to accept their reasoning, and I am not wrong for rising to my present level of consciousness. I now consciously accept this fact: "There is nothing wrong with me."

9 | Invoking Freedom from Blame

Master Paul, venetian dream,
your love for beauty's flowing stream.
Master Paul, in love's own womb,
your power shatters ego's tomb.

**Master Paul, your love so true,
and therefore we apply to you,
to set all free in the great love,
that you are shining from Above.**

2. I will monitor myself and whenever I feel this projection that there is something wrong with me, I say: "There is nothing wrong with me. I fully accept that there is nothing wrong with me."

Master Paul, your counsel wise,
our minds are raised to lofty skies.
Master Paul, in wisdom's love,
such beauty flowing from Above.

**Master Paul, your love so true,
and therefore we apply to you,
to set all free in the great love,
that you are shining from Above.**

3. I am separating myself from this spirit. I look at it and I feel that it has no more pull on me. It is collapsing because what is holding it up is the energy I give it by still believing in the illusion that there is something wrong with me.

Master Paul, love is an art,
it opens up the secret heart.
Master Paul, love's rushing flow,
our hearts awash in sacred glow.

Master Paul, your love so true,
and therefore we apply to you,
to set all free in the great love,
that you are shining from Above.

4. Nada, help me overcome my obsessive compulsive disorder and start approaching the path from a non-obsessive, non-compulsive way that is not a disorder. It is my natural drive for experiencing something that is more and for expressing that something more.

Master Paul, accelerate,
upon pure love we meditate.
Master Paul, intentions pure,
our self-transcendence will ensure.

Master Paul, your love so true,
and therefore we apply to you,
to set all free in the great love,
that you are shining from Above.

5. As long as I am compensating, I cannot feel free to express myself, I cannot feel free to be creative.

Master Paul, your love will heal,
our inner light you do reveal.
Master Paul, all life console,
with you we're being truly whole.

**Master Paul, your love so true,
and therefore we apply to you,
to set all free in the great love,
that you are shining from Above.**

6. Creativity is going beyond status quo. I am only creative when I go beyond status quo.

Master Paul, you serve the All,
by helping us transcend the fall.
Master Paul, in peace we rise,
as ego meets its sure demise.

**Master Paul, your love so true,
and therefore we apply to you,
to set all free in the great love,
that you are shining from Above.**

7. When I am compensating, I am actually basing my desire to compensate on status quo because I am saying: "Status quo is that I did something wrong in the past and I need to compensate for this."

Master Paul, love all life free,
your love is for eternity.
Master Paul, you are the One,
to help us make the journey fun.

**Master Paul, your love so true,
and therefore we apply to you,
to set all free in the great love,
that you are shining from Above.**

8. Compensation and creativity are incompatible and I will never be a fully creative being as long as I am trying to compensate for anything.

> Master Paul, you balance all,
> the seven rays upon our call.
> Master Paul, you paint the sky,
> with colors that delight the I.
>
> **Master Paul, your love so true,**
> **and therefore we apply to you,**
> **to set all free in the great love,**
> **that you are shining from Above.**

9. I am creative from a love-based foundation, not from this compensatory mechanism that drives me to do something unusual to get attention. I am free to express the creativity of my I AM Presence.

> Master Paul, your Presence here,
> filling up the inner sphere.
> Life is now a sacred flow,
> God Love we do on all bestow.
>
> **Master Paul, your love so true,**
> **and therefore we apply to you,**
> **to set all free in the great love,**
> **that you are shining from Above.**

Sealing:

In the name of the Divine Mother, I fully accept that the power of these calls is used to set free the River of Life, so it can outpicture the perfect vision of Christ for my own life, for all people and for the planet. In the name I AM THAT I AM, it is done! Amen.

10 | THE ILLUSION OF PERFECTIONISM

I AM the Ascended Master Nada, and I would like for this fourth lesson to begin with what I talked about in my last lesson about the compensatory mechanism. Now, I said in my last lesson that in the past you have had a sense that you did something wrong and you are trying to compensate for it. I said, of course, that you need to become conscious of this mechanism so that you can look at it, separate yourself from it and let it go. You stop basing your path on this obsessive-compulsive desire to compensate. I want to take this one step further by looking at this concept of doing something wrong. What does it actually mean to do something wrong?

We have given many teachings over the years through this messenger about the dualistic state of mind, about the epic consciousness. We have given many teachings on the fallen beings and how they have tried to manipulate every aspect of life on earth. Of course, one of the more subtle ways that they have attempted to manipulate life and manipulate human beings is by them defining the standard for what is right and wrong. The most subtle aspect of this is that in many cultures they have managed to make most people believe that it is not *they* who have defined a standard for right and wrong, it is *God*. There is some higher authority beyond the material realm who has defined a standard for what is right and wrong. There is an angry God in the sky who is observing your every action and judging you based on this standard of right and wrong. If you do what is wrong, you will be punished by this God, perhaps by burning forever in some fiery hell.

As the ascended master students you are, you can see that in most cultures (wherever you could have grown up on this planet) there is in the collective consciousness this mechanism, defined by the fallen beings. People believe that God has actually defined a standard for right and wrong. It is almost impossible for you to grow up on this planet without being affected by this. Again, there is no reason to feel bad about it but it is time to become conscious of how this has affected you. You will be able to see very quickly that if you in the past had a sense that you did something wrong but that sense was based on the standard defined by the fallen beings, then you may not have done somethings wrong at all. Therefore, it is not very constructive for you to continue the pattern of seeking to compensate for what you did wrong—if in fact you did not do anything wrong.

Now, you can see that all of you have taken a certain sense of responsibility for yourself. You have a sense that: "I have made karma in the past and I do need to balance that karma." In a sense, you could say that balancing your karma is a compensatory effort. You are compensating for something you did in the past. As I said in my last lesson, you need to balance whatever karma you have but there is a difference between balancing karma from a neutral state of mind and balancing karma from this obsessive-compulsive desire to compensate. I trust you can begin to see this after having integrated my last lesson.

Looking at your spiritual practice

Naturally, we need to be neutral and observant here. We need to simply observe that you have made a certain karma in the past, you need to balance it and you need to do what you need to do in order to balance it—whether it is taking certain actions or giving decrees and invocations. First of all, balancing your karma is a matter of raising your consciousness, letting go of the internal spirits you had that caused you to do the act that created the karma in the first place. The step we need to take here is that if you are in this compensatory pattern, you will have a sense that if you stop doing what you have been doing in an attempt to compensate, this will be bad. I need you to look at yourself honestly and ask yourself this: "What have I been doing for the last years? Have I been giving invocations and decrees?" Then you need to contemplate: "How would I feel if I stopped giving invocations and decrees today?" If you can feel that there is some reaction in you to this, there is perhaps some fear-based sense that something bad will happen or that this would be wrong for you, then this is a compensatory pattern, this is obsessive-compulsive.

I am not telling you to stop giving decrees and invocations. I am telling you to monitor your reaction to it. You can see that if you are driven by an obsessive-compulsive desire to compensate for what you have done wrong in the past, you are not fully in control of your reactions. You are reacting, as I said in my last lesson, to the fallen beings rather than the ascended masters. We want you to balance your karma and when you have balanced your karma, we need you to move on to something else instead of continuing to do the same thing.

Again, you find the teachings of the ascended masters, you learn about the spiritual path and karma, you learn that you can balance karma by giving violet flame, for example, and you decide with your outer mind that you have to give an hour of violet flame a day. You think that this is what you have to do for the rest of your life in order to make sure that you have balanced your karma. As I said in my last lesson, there comes a point where you have caught up with your present level of consciousness, you have balanced the karma up until that level and now you no longer need to do the exact same thing that you decided you had to do, perhaps several years ago.

Now you need to tune in to what is the challenge you face at your present level of consciousness and how do you move on from there? All I am asking you here is to go into a deeper sense of attunement with where you are at on your path. Then, you look at: "Did I make a decision two, five, ten, thirty years ago that I have to do a certain outer practice every day for the rest of my life?" If you did, is it constructive to carry on that decision? Would it not be more constructive to tune in to what is your present level of consciousness and what you need to do at this level to rise to the next level up.

You can see the irony, of course, that if the fallen beings in the past made you believe that you have done something wrong and this set up a compensatory pattern but in reality you did not do something wrong, then it is pointless to try to compensate for something that was not wrong. You can see that you were trying to balance karma but the karma is not there.

There are levels of Christhood

I now need you to step back here and take a look at your concept of right and wrong. I need you, actually, to be willing to open your mind to a new way of looking at this. This is not to in any way imply that what you have done so far was wrong. It is simply that you have now come to the level of the spiritual path where you are approaching the 90th level of consciousness. You are approaching the initiations of the Seventh Ray under Saint Germain and therefore you are ready to take a look at this.

My beloved, let us approach this by looking at the concept of Christhood. We have given many teachings on Christhood and we have given them for different levels of consciousness. As we have said before, it is natural that when you first hear about the concept of Christhood, you will look at it with your present level of consciousness. In reality, there are many levels of Christhood and therefore you should be aware that you cannot take your first conception of Christhood and carry that with you as you raise your consciousness.

Why is this so? Well, if you take the most common concept of Christhood found on earth, it is the one promoted by the official Christian churches. According to their view, only Jesus could attain Christhood and Christhood was a state of perfection. Many ascended master students have an aspect of the view that Christhood means that – all of a sudden – you reach a certain level of consciousness, and from then you have a clear vision of everything and everything you do is right. They think, for example, that Jesus one day attained Christhood or perhaps even that he had it from birth and therefore nothing he did was ever wrong.

Now, the reality here is much more subtle and it can be understood by tying in to what I said in my last discourse. I said: "Christhood is challenging status quo." What is status quo based on? It is based on an illusion. You now see that for each of the 144 levels of consciousness on earth, there is a certain illusion tied to that level of consciousness. It is this illusion that defines a particular level of consciousness. Therefore, this illusion also defines what people who are still blinded by that level of consciousness see as status quo.

For each of the 144 levels there is a certain sense of status quo based on a certain sense of illusion. What is Christhood? It is challenging the illusion at each of the 144 levels of consciousness. You now see that there are 144 levels of Christhood. My beloved, if you are to challenge the illusion at the lowest possible level of Christhood on earth, in other words, the level where people are the most self-centered, narcissistic, egotistical, then obviously that is very different from challenging the illusion at a much higher level.

Therefore, you now see that there can be different expressions of Christhood. If you are to apply the fallen standard, then many of the acts of Christhood that challenge the illusions at lower levels of consciousness will seem wrong according to that standard. What I need you to realize here is that it is good for you to accept responsibility for what you have done in the past. But the obsessive-compulsive disorder causes you to accept responsibility for what you have *not* done. It causes you to accept responsibility for something that is not your responsibility. I have said that Christhood is never going to be a popularity contest because the fallen beings will never approve of any expression of Christhood. Let me now take you through a different look at your own past.

10 | The Illusion of Perfectionism

Christhood does mean you have to be perfect

In the past, you were at a lower level of consciousness. It does not matter whether you were above or below the 48th level of consciousness. How did you rise to a higher level of consciousness? You rose because you came to see through the illusion of that particular level of consciousness. When you saw through that illusion, this in a sense became a challenge, not only to the fallen beings but to other people around you who were still trapped by the illusion. You realize that, in your past, you may have had certain lifetimes where you came to see through a certain illusion. It may have been an illusion at one of the lower levels and you openly and directly challenged people who were still holding on to that illusion.

You may have challenged certain fallen beings who were leaders of your society and who were keeping your society trapped at that level of illusion, for example, by being in a violent conflict with another nation or another group of people. You may have therefore challenged a certain illusion, a certain sense of status quo, and then the fallen beings did everything they could to make you feel that you were wrong for doing so.

Now, my beloved, this is not just that they in general try to make you feel wrong. What the fallen beings will often do is that they will look at the actions, the words and they will try to find some aspect of it that was not perfect. Ponder very carefully what I am saying here. You are expressing a challenge to the status quo, you are challenging a particular illusion. That illusion may be at a very low level of consciousness, way below the 48th level. This does not necessarily mean that you were at that level of consciousness but you could see the illusion in your society and you challenged it.

This was a low illusion. What does it mean to challenge an illusion, say at the 25th level of consciousness? It does not mean that when you challenge the illusion of that low level, you are doing so by expressing the highest possible truth. Nobody at that level could grasp the highest possible truth, if even there was such a thing as the highest possible truth on earth. When you challenge an illusion at the 25th level of consciousness, your challenge is not going to be "perfect," if there was such a thing as perfection. It is only the fallen beings who have created the concept that there should be something that is perfect.

Do you see what I am saying? You are challenging an illusion at the 25th level of consciousness, you are doing so by expressing a truth that is a little bit higher than the 25th level but certainly not the highest truth that is possible on earth. The fallen beings now look at what you did, look at what you said, and they try to find some little aspect of it that they can then say was not perfect according to their standard. My beloved, how do you react to this? Well, you do not react based on your present level of consciousness, you react based on the level of consciousness you had at the time. Let us say you were at the 48th level of consciousness. You challenged an illusion at the 25th level. You were accused by the fallen ones for not being perfect and naturally you reacted to that based on the 48th level of consciousness.

At that level of consciousness, you did feel that you had to be perfect, you were still very much caught up in the entire concept of perfectionism that has been perpetrated on people by the fallen beings. You, then, used the accusations of the fallen beings to decide: "I was wrong. I was not perfect." This is one of the most insidious, most subtle and also one of the most common reasons why ascended master students dare not express their Christhood. You think that in order to express Christhood, you have to be perfect. You think that there is a standard of perfection that has some validity. You do not think it is the fallen beings who have put this standard upon you because you do not realize that yet. You think it is God or the ascended masters who have defined the standard. You think you were wrong according to this standard in the past when you tried to express your Christhood. Therefore, you have decided that you are not going to try and express your Christhood again until you are sure you are perfect.

Daring to be imperfect

You see, this makes the fallen beings laugh all the way to the bank. You are at the level of consciousness now where you can look at this and say: "I am going to have the last laugh. The fallen beings are *not* going to have the last laugh. They may have had it for several embodiments but they're not going to have it anymore because I'm going to rise above this. I am going to realize that Christhood can and must be expressed at each of the 144 levels of consciousness. And at the lower levels, the expression of Christhood cannot in any way be said to be perfect, to be the highest possible."

"Naturally, the expression of Christhood that challenges the illusion at the 25th level will be a lower expression of Christhood than what you can express at a higher level. That is just the way it is so I am not going to blame myself for having expressed Christhood in the past that was not perhaps the highest expression of Christhood possible on earth. I am going to accept that I expressed that Christhood at the level of consciousness I was at. I expressed it to challenge a particular level of consciousness and therefore my expression of Christhood was good enough, was perfectly acceptable and it did exactly what it did in challenging that particular illusion at that particular level of consciousness. I don't have to be perfect in order to express Christhood today, I simply have to recognize what level of consciousness I am at and then I have to dare to express my Christhood at this level of consciousness based on the vision I have with this level of consciousness."

My beloved, take now what Hilarion said. At each of the levels you descend in consciousness from the 144th level to the 48th, you are taking on a certain illusion. If you are at the 56th or the 85th or the 93rd level of consciousness right now, there is a number of illusions you have that are still in your four lower bodies. There is nothing wrong with this, how else could you walk the path? How could you be in embodiment without taking on these illusions? When you are contemplating expressing your Christhood at this particular level, you cannot and you *should* not expect yourself to be perfect. Naturally, your expression of Christhood will be colored by the illusions you have not yet shed, the illusions that are above your present level of consciousness. It cannot be any other way, my beloved.

Jesus, when he started his embodiment, when he started his public mission, was not at the 144th level of consciousness. Therefore, he reacted the way he did when he threw-out the moneychangers from the temple. It was not the highest possible expression of Christhood but it was the appropriate level of Christhood for the level of consciousness Jesus had at the time. You understand what I am saying here, my beloved?

So many of you have this sense that, for example, if you are being the Christ in action, you should never be angry. My beloved, at certain levels of consciousness where you are dealing with an illusion on a very low level, it can be extremely difficult to handle a situation without feeling some kind of anger or at least a very intense emotional reaction. I know that we have set certain ideals before you, for example Buddhahood where you are completely non-attached. As I said in my last discourse, full Buddhahood is not attained until the 144th level.

10 | *The Illusion of Perfectionism*

Overcoming perfectionism

Do you see that what the fallen beings have tried to create is an unbreachable gap, a gap that you can never cross, between where you are at now and Christhood? It seems like there is such a distance, such a chasm, between you and Christhood that you could not possibly cross it. Or at least, maybe you can do it just before you are ready to ascend. In reality, the distance is much smaller. The distance is not the distance between the 48th and the 144th level of consciousness, which of course you cannot cross in one leap. The distance is the distance between your present level of consciousness and the next. *That* distance you can cross at any moment by shifting your consciousness.

I am not asking you at this level of consciousness to be the Christ the way Jesus was the Christ in the time just before his crucifixion. I am asking you to dare to be the Christ that challenges the illusion of your present level of consciousness even if you are not perfect in doing so. I am actually asking you to shift your mind, to get rid of this internal spirit, this separate self of perfectionism so you say: "But I *am* actually perfect in expressing my Christhood at my current level of consciousness." This is, if you want to use that word, perfection. Perfection is reaching one step higher than your present level. Perfection is not some ultimate level that does not exist, except in the minds of the fallen beings where it, of course, has no reality to it.

One of the challenges you face at this level is to overcome this sense of perfectionism, the sense that you have to be perfect in everything you do. Many ascended master students have used our teachings to build this elaborate sense of how you dress, how you act, how you talk, what you eat, what you do not eat, what you have to do as your spiritual practice, what you have to think and feel—and you never feel angry and you never express any emotions, this and that, all of these things. You are using your outer mind to create almost like a straitjacket and you force yourself into it and now you can only do certain things. Many ascended master students over the past many decades have done this and have used our teachings to do it.

I am asking you to realize here that we are not the ones who want you to do this. We are not the ones who are driving you to do it. It is an internal spirit who is driving you to do it. I am asking you to begin to consciously separate yourself from it so that you can come to see it, see that it is based on a completely impossible goal defined by the fallen beings, that there is no state of perfection that is possible on earth or that is required by the ascended masters.

The masters accept you as you are

My beloved, as other Chohans have expressed before me, I completely and fully and absolutely accept you as you are right now. I do not have a standard in my mind or at my retreat that requires you to be at the 144th level before I will teach you. My role is to work with you at your present level of consciousness and help you take the next step up so you reach the next level—and to keep doing this for these seven steps until I have fulfilled my mission and can now hand you off to Saint Germain who will take you higher. I am not judging you as being imperfect at your present level. I am completely accepting you for who you are at your present level and I am only focused on helping you see that illusion and to take the next step up.

My beloved, I have talked about the need for you to feel at peace with yourself and at peace with being on earth. Well, how

10 | The Illusion of Perfectionism

will you ever feel at peace with yourself if you are judging yourself based on a standard of perfectionism that you can never, *ever* reach? If you always judge yourself as being imperfect, how will you feel at peace with yourself? If you have always judged that you have done something wrong on earth and that you can only do something wrong on earth, how will you ever feel at peace with being here? How will you even feel at peace on the spiritual path if you think that expressing Christhood requires you to be perfect?

Do you not understand, my beloved, that deep within you, you have a certain drive. It is this drive that caused you to find the spiritual path, that caused you to find this course and it has caused you to follow it until this level. You have a certain drive that is driving you in a certain direction. Then, you have certain mechanisms in your identity, mental and emotional body that are working against this drive and this is what makes you feel not at peace with yourself.

What have we been doing throughout this course? What am I specifically doing in this segment? It is to take you through the initiations that help you resolve all the mechanisms that are working against your natural drive so that you can come to a point where you are free to recognize that drive. You are expressing that inbuilt drive, which is the drive from your I AM Presence, the drive to be more, the drive to transcend yourself, the drive to be the open door for the I AM Presence to express itself in this world.

In a sense, you could say that this is a clean-up of your four lower bodies. We are taking you through these mechanisms and pointing out that here is something that is standing in the way of your transcendence to the next level. I know that with the linear mind you can very quickly step back and look at this entire course and say: "But I started at the 48th level and Master MORE told me I had *this* problem and I had *that* tendency and I had *that* hang-up and I needed to overcome *this* and I needed to overcome *that*. Now, I am at the 6th level of the course and Nada is still telling me things to overcome—when will it ever end?" Well, my beloved, it will end at the 144th level when you overcome the last illusion that you have taken on in order to take embodiment on earth—and what is wrong about that? What is so bad about that?

Accept yourself at this level of the path

You see that part of perfectionism is the sense that you did something wrong by coming into embodiment. Something should not have happened and therefore you will never feel at peace until you overcome it. What I am trying to tell you here is that there was nothing wrong that you did by coming into embodiment. You just did what you had to do to come into embodiment on a planet like earth: take on the illusions down to the 48th level. Now, you are in the process of rising above these illusions one at a time—and you can only rise above them one at a time. It is not that because you still have many illusions left you have not yet overcome, that now you are imperfect.

No, my beloved, you are not imperfect! You are simply at a certain level of your path. There is nothing wrong with this. Stop chasing the rainbow of perfectionism—there is no pot of gold there. The fallen beings do not have anything you want, they have nothing to offer. Accept yourself at your present level of the spiritual path. Accept that you can express Christhood at a certain level and then dare to express it. The level you are at right now is much, much higher than most people on earth. You can express something that is of a much higher level, but you can also express something that can help many, many people come up higher. Accept that this is good enough.

Jesus himself said that you should look at each day and let the evil thereof be sufficient unto itself. You can take that one step further and say: Let the good thereof be sufficient unto itself. In other words, look at the level you are at, focus on that. Do not worry about the levels above you, do not worry about living up to some standard of perfection. Just focus on where you are at, be at peace with being where you are at and expressing Christhood as you can do it at this level.

I know, my beloved, that your linear mind wants to say: "But there are 144 levels of consciousness. You overcome all these illusions, you overcome all your attachments, you reach the level of Christhood, the level of Buddhahood and until you're there, you're not where you should be." My beloved, you are *exactly* where you should be right now, as long as you are willing to look at the illusion you are dealing with right now, transcend that illusion and then express your Christhood in challenging that illusion. Then, you are exactly where you should be.

Shedding the snake skin of perfectionism

You should not be at the 144th level of consciousness right now because that is not the path you have chosen. You have chosen to demonstrate how you rise to higher and higher levels of consciousness. You are not here to demonstrate how you jump from the 48th to the 144th level. Nobody can see an example in that. This is what the fallen beings have tried to do with Jesus: to make people believe that he did not walk a path but that he was just born at that level and therefore nobody can see him as an example. Look at the many Christians who cannot see him as an example. That is why we need *you* to serve as an example so that people can see someone who is like themselves, who started out like themselves but who has risen higher. Therefore, people can believe that what one has done, I can do too.

Perfectionism, my beloved, is truly one of the most insidious plots of the fallen beings. It can be difficult to overcome but at your present level it is not so difficult to overcome. There are, of course, people who are affected by perfectionism at the 48th level but at that level it is very difficult to overcome it. At your present level, it is only one more step, one small, doable step to overcome it, to see the spirit, to see it for what it is, to see it as an alien element in your four lower bodies, to look at it and say: "Get thee behind me Satan, you are no part of me anymore."

My beloved, it is a great joy for me when I have students who get this in their identity bodies. It is an even greater joy for me when I have students who allow it to filter down to where they get it at the conscious level. You see the spirit, see this perfectionism and you do not go into the reaction of blaming yourself for having been affected by perfectionism. You get off the treadmill and you simply say: "Oh, well, that is just one more spirit that has to go. So many have gone already, what is one more?"

I know this one claims to be the ultimate spirit because you have to be *perfect* to be accepted by God, but it is not true, my beloved. God accepts you for who you are right now. In fact, you could say that when it comes to God, acceptance and non-acceptance are simply meaningless concepts. You are an expression of God's Being. How could God *not* accept you?

My beloved, contemplate this carefully with your conscious mind. Go through this lesson a number of times. If you feel you need to take more than the nine days to overcome this perfectionism, by all means do so. It is not a race, my beloved, to complete this course. There is no competition on completing this course as quickly as possible.

As I have said before, you can race through the course with your outer mind but it does not mean you actually passed the initiations because you do not integrate them and therefore you have not risen to a higher level of consciousness. Take the time it takes. Perfectionism has tripped up so many spiritual students over the millennia and delayed their progress, sometimes even for lifetimes. I do not want to see you be among them. I want to see you pass this initiation, shed this snake skin of perfectionism, leave it behind and move forward to what is a new day of enjoying being who you are, knowing that you will be more tomorrow.

11 | INVOKING FREEDOM FROM PERFECTIONISM

In the name I AM THAT I AM, Jesus Christ, I call to my I AM Presence to flow through the I Will Be Presence that I AM and give this invocation with full power. I call to beloved Elohim Peace and Aloha and Purity and Astrea, Archangel Uriel and Aurora and Gabriel and Hope, Nada and Serapis Bey to help me overcome perfectionism. Help me see and surrender all patterns that block my oneness with Nada and with my I AM Presence, including ...

[Make personal calls]

Part 1

1. One of the more subtle ways that the fallen beings have attempted to manipulate human beings is by them defining the standard for what is right and wrong.

O Elohim Peace, in Unity's Flame,
there is no more room for duality's game,
we know that all form is from the same source,
empowering us to plot a new course.

O Elohim Peace, through your tranquility,
we are free from the chaos of duality,
in oneness with God a new identity,
we are raising the earth into Infinity.

2. In many cultures the fallen beings have managed to make people believe that God has defined a standard for what is right and wrong.

O Elohim Peace, the bell now you ring,
causing all atoms to vibrate and sing,
we give up the sense of a separate "me,"
we're crossing Samsara's turbulent sea.

O Elohim Peace, through your tranquility,
we are free from the chaos of duality,
in oneness with God a new identity,
we are raising the earth into Infinity.

3. If I have had a sense that I did something wrong but that sense was based on the standard defined by the fallen beings, then I may not have done something wrong at all.

O Elohim Peace, you help us to know,
that Jesus has come your Flame to bestow,
upon all who are ready to give up the strife,
by following Christ into infinite life.

11 | Invoking Freedom from Perfectionism

**O Elohim Peace, through your tranquility,
we are free from the chaos of duality,
in oneness with God a new identity,
we are raising the earth into Infinity.**

4. It is not constructive for me to continue the pattern of seeking to compensate for what I did wrong—if in fact I did not do anything wrong.

O Elohim Peace, through your eyes we see,
that only in oneness will we ever be free,
we now see that there is no separate thing,
to the ego-based self we no longer cling.

**O Elohim Peace, through your tranquility,
we are free from the chaos of duality,
in oneness with God a new identity,
we are raising the earth into Infinity.**

5. There is a difference between balancing karma from a neutral state of mind and balancing karma from an obsessive-compulsive desire to compensate.

O Elohim Peace, you show us the way,
for clearing the mind from duality's fray,
you pierce the illusions of both time and space,
separation consumed by your Infinite Grace.

**O Elohim Peace, through your tranquility,
we are free from the chaos of duality,
in oneness with God a new identity,
we are raising the earth into Infinity.**

6. First of all, balancing my karma is a matter of raising my consciousness, letting go of the internal spirits that caused me to create the karma.

> O Elohim Peace, what beauty your name,
> consuming within us duality's shame,
> the earth is set free from burden of fear,
> accepting your peace is now manifest here.

> **O Elohim Peace, through your tranquility,**
> **we are free from the chaos of duality,**
> **in oneness with God a new identity,**
> **we are raising the earth into Infinity.**

7. I will look at myself and see if stopping my spiritual practice would cause a reaction in me. If so, this is a compensatory pattern, this is obsessive-compulsive.

> O Elohim Peace, with Christ at our side,
> no force of duality can evermore hide,
> It was through the vibration of your Golden Flame,
> that Christ the illusion of death overcame.

> **O Elohim Peace, through your tranquility,**
> **we are free from the chaos of duality,**
> **in oneness with God a new identity,**
> **we are raising the earth into Infinity.**

8. If I am driven by an obsessive-compulsive desire to compensate for what I have done wrong in the past, I am not fully in control of my reactions. I am reacting to the fallen beings rather than the ascended masters.

11 | Invoking Freedom from Perfectionism

O Elohim Peace, you bring now to earth,
the unstoppable flame of Cosmic Rebirth,
we give up the sense that something is "mine,"
allowing your Light through our beings to shine.

**O Elohim Peace, through your tranquility,
we are free from the chaos of duality,
in oneness with God a new identity,
we are raising the earth into Infinity.**

9. The ascended masters want me to balance my karma and when I have done that, they want me to move on to something else instead of continuing to do the same thing.

O Elohim Peace, as peace now we feel,
all records of war you totally heal,
the earth is now free from forces of war,
restoring her purity known from before.

**O Elohim Peace, through your tranquility,
we are free from the chaos of duality,
in oneness with God a new identity,
we are raising the earth into Infinity.**

Part 2

1. I will tune in to what is the challenge I face at my present level of consciousness and how I move on from here. I will not continue to act on a decision made with the state of consciousness I had in the past.

Beloved Astrea, your heart is so true,
your Circle and Sword of white and blue,
cut all life free from dramas unwise,
on wings of Purity our planet will rise.

**Beloved Astrea, in oneness with you,
your circle and sword of electric blue,
with Purity's Light cutting right through,
raising the earth into all that is true.**

2. I have a compensatory pattern, but if I did not do something wrong, then it is pointless to try to compensate for something that was not wrong.

Beloved Astrea, in God Purity,
accelerate all of our life energy,
we're rising beyond every impurity,
as Purity's Light forever we see.

**Beloved Astrea, in oneness with you,
your circle and sword of electric blue,
with Purity's Light cutting right through,
raising the earth into all that is true.**

3. I am willing to take a look at my concept of right and wrong. I am willing to open my mind to a new way of looking at this.

Beloved Astrea, from Purity's Ray,
send forth deliverance to all life today,
acceleration to Purity, we are now free
from all that is less than love's Purity.

11 | Invoking Freedom from Perfectionism

**Beloved Astrea, in oneness with you,
your circle and sword of electric blue,
with Purity's Light cutting right through,
raising the earth into all that is true.**

4. When I first hear about the concept of Christhood, I will look at it with my present level of consciousness. There are many levels of Christhood and I cannot take my first conception of Christhood and carry that with me as I raise my consciousness.

Beloved Astrea, accelerate us all,
as for your deliverance we fervently call,
set all life free from vision impure
beyond fear and doubt, we're rising for sure.

**Beloved Astrea, in oneness with you,
your circle and sword of electric blue,
with Purity's Light cutting right through,
raising the earth into all that is true.**

5. Christhood is challenging status quo. Status quo is based on an illusion. For each of the 144 levels of consciousness on earth, there is a certain illusion tied to that level of consciousness.

Beloved Astrea, we're willing to see,
all of the lies that keep us unfree,
we surrender all lies causing the fall,
forever affirming the oneness of All.

**Beloved Astrea, in oneness with you,
your circle and sword of electric blue,
with Purity's Light cutting right through,
raising the earth into all that is true.**

6. For each of the 144 levels, there is a sense of status quo based on a certain illusion. Christhood is challenging the illusion at each of the 144 levels of consciousness.

Beloved Astrea, accelerate life
beyond all duality's struggle and strife,
consume all division between God and man,
accelerate fulfillment of God's perfect plan.

**Beloved Astrea, in oneness with you,
your circle and sword of electric blue,
with Purity's Light cutting right through,
raising the earth into all that is true.**

7. There are 144 different expressions of Christhood. According to the fallen standard, many of the acts of Christhood that challenge the illusions at lower levels of consciousness will seem wrong.

Beloved Astrea, we lovingly call,
break down separation's invisible wall,
raising our minds into true unity
with the Masters of love in Infinity.

**Beloved Astrea, in oneness with you,
your circle and sword of electric blue,
with Purity's Light cutting right through,
raising the earth into all that is true.**

11 | Invoking Freedom from Perfectionism

8. The obsessive-compulsive disorder causes me to accept responsibility for what I have not done. It causes me to accept responsibility for something that is not my responsibility.

> Beloved Astrea, help all of us find,
> the secret that we create with the mind,
> and thus what in ignorance we decreate,
> in knowledge we easily can recreate.

> **Beloved Astrea, in oneness with you,**
> **your circle and sword of electric blue,**
> **with Purity's Light cutting right through,**
> **raising the earth into all that is true.**

9. In the past, I was at a lower level of consciousness. I rose because I came to see through the illusion of that particular level. When I saw through that illusion, this became a challenge to the fallen beings.

> Beloved Astrea, we all do aspire,
> to learning to use your purity's fire,
> to raise every form in infamy sown,
> as Saint Germain makes this planet his own.

> **Beloved Astrea, in oneness with you,**
> **your circle and sword of electric blue,**
> **with Purity's Light cutting right through,**
> **raising the earth into all that is true.**

Part 3

1. The fallen beings did everything they could to make me feel that I was wrong for challenging the illusion. They tried to find some aspect of my actions that was not perfect.

> Uriel Archangel, immense is the power,
> of angels of peace, all war to devour.
> The demons of war, no match for your light,
> consuming them all, with radiance so bright.

> **Uriel Archangel, use your great sword,**
> **Uriel Archangel, consume all discord,**
> **Uriel Archangel, we're of one accord,**
> **Uriel Archangel, we walk with the Lord.**

2. When I challenge an illusion at a low level, I am not doing so by expressing the highest possible truth. My challenge will not be "perfect" according to the fallen standard.

> Uriel Archangel, intense is the sound,
> when millions of angels, their voices compound.
> They build a crescendo, piercing the night,
> life's glorious oneness revealed to our sight.

> **Uriel Archangel, use your great sword,**
> **Uriel Archangel, consume all discord,**
> **Uriel Archangel, we're of one accord,**
> **Uriel Archangel, we walk with the Lord.**

11 | Invoking Freedom from Perfectionism

3. The fallen beings tried to find some little aspect of it that they said was not perfect according to their standard. I reacted to this based on the level of consciousness I had at the time.

> Uriel Archangel, from out the Great Throne,
> your millions of trumpets, sound the One Tone.
> Consuming all discord with your harmony,
> the sound of all sounds will set all life free.
>
> **Uriel Archangel, use your great sword,**
> **Uriel Archangel, consume all discord,**
> **Uriel Archangel, we're of one accord,**
> **Uriel Archangel, we walk with the Lord.**

4. At that level of consciousness, I felt I had to be perfect, I was still caught up in the entire concept of perfectionism that has been perpetrated on people by the fallen beings.

> Uriel Archangel, all war is now done,
> for you bring a message, from heart of the One.
> The hearts of all men, now singing in peace,
> the spirals of love, forever increase.
>
> **Uriel Archangel, use your great sword,**
> **Uriel Archangel, consume all discord,**
> **Uriel Archangel, we're of one accord,**
> **Uriel Archangel, we walk with the Lord.**

5. I used the accusations of the fallen beings to decide: "I was wrong. I was not perfect." This is one of the most common reasons ascended master students dare not express their Christhood. I think that in order to express Christhood, I have to be perfect.

Uriel Archangel, your infinite peace,
from all warring beings our planet release,
war is a prison from which we are free,
embracing the peace of true unity.

**Uriel Archangel, use your great sword,
Uriel Archangel, consume all discord,
Uriel Archangel, we're of one accord,
Uriel Archangel, we walk with the Lord.**

6. I think God or the ascended masters have defined the standard and I think I was wrong according to this standard in the past when I tried to express my Christhood. Therefore, I have decided that I am not going to express my Christhood again until I am sure I am perfect.

Uriel Archangel, we send forth the call,
reveal now the oneness that unifies all,
help us the vision of peace now to see,
so we from all conflicts and struggles are free.

**Uriel Archangel, use your great sword,
Uriel Archangel, consume all discord,
Uriel Archangel, we're of one accord,
Uriel Archangel, we walk with the Lord.**

7. I know the fallen beings laugh at this, but I am going to have the last laugh. I am going to rise above this. I realize that Christhood can and must be expressed at each of the 144 levels of consciousness. And at the lower levels, the expression of Christhood cannot in any way be said to be "perfect."

11 | Invoking Freedom from Perfectionism

> Uriel Archangel, in service to life,
> you give us release from struggle and strife,
> forgetting the self is truly the key,
> to living a life in true harmony.
>
> **Uriel Archangel, use your great sword,**
> **Uriel Archangel, consume all discord,**
> **Uriel Archangel, we're of one accord,**
> **Uriel Archangel, we walk with the Lord.**

8. I am not going to blame myself for having expressed Christhood in the past that was not the highest expression of Christhood possible on earth. I am going to accept that I expressed that Christhood at the level of consciousness I was at.

> Uriel Archangel, the earth now you raise,
> out of duality's death-bringing haze,
> we call now upon your great Flame of Peace,
> commanding that all petty squabbles do cease.
>
> **Uriel Archangel, use your great sword,**
> **Uriel Archangel, consume all discord,**
> **Uriel Archangel, we're of one accord,**
> **Uriel Archangel, we walk with the Lord.**

9. I expressed it to challenge a particular level of consciousness and therefore my expression of Christhood was good enough, was perfectly acceptable and it challenged a particular illusion.

> Uriel Archangel, as peace is the norm,
> to your higher vision the earth does conform,
> as people have found your peace from within,
> a Golden Age is the prize that we win.

**Uriel Archangel, use your great sword,
Uriel Archangel, consume all discord,
Uriel Archangel, we're of one accord,
Uriel Archangel, we walk with the Lord.**

Part 4

1. I don't have to be perfect in order to express Christhood today, I simply have to recognize what level of consciousness I am at, and then I have to dare to express my Christhood at this level of consciousness based on the vision I have.

Gabriel Archangel, your light we revere,
immersed in your Presence, nothing we fear.
Disciples of Christ, we do leave behind,
the ego's desire for responding in kind.

**Gabriel Archangel, of this we are sure,
Gabriel Archangel, Christ light is the cure.
Gabriel Archangel, intentions so pure,
Gabriel Archangel, in you we're secure.**

2. When I am contemplating expressing my Christhood at my present level, I cannot and I *should* not expect myself to be perfect. Naturally, my expression of Christhood will be colored by the illusions I have not yet shed, the illusions that are above my present level of consciousness. It cannot be any other way.

Gabriel Archangel, we fear not the light,
in purifications' fire, we delight.
With your hand in ours, each challenge we face,
we follow the spiral to infinite grace.

Gabriel Archangel, of this we are sure,
Gabriel Archangel, Christ light is the cure.
Gabriel Archangel, intentions so pure,
Gabriel Archangel, in you we're secure.

3. I give up the sense that if I am being the Christ in action, I should never be angry or have other intense feelings.

Gabriel Archangel, your fire burning white,
ascending with you, out of the night.
The ego has nowhere to run and to hide,
in ascension's bright spiral, with you we abide.

Gabriel Archangel, of this we are sure,
Gabriel Archangel, Christ light is the cure.
Gabriel Archangel, intentions so pure,
Gabriel Archangel, in you we're secure.

4. The fallen beings have tried to create a gap that I can never cross between where I am now and Christhood. It seems like there is such a distance between me and Christhood that I could not possibly cross it.

Gabriel Archangel, your trumpet we hear,
announcing the birth of Christ drawing near.
In lightness of being, we now are reborn,
rising with Christ on bright Easter morn.

> **Gabriel Archangel, of this we are sure,**
> **Gabriel Archangel, Christ light is the cure.**
> **Gabriel Archangel, intentions so pure,**
> **Gabriel Archangel, in you we're secure.**

5. In reality, the distance is much smaller. The distance is not the distance between the 48th and the 144th level of consciousness. It is the distance between my present level of consciousness and the next. *That* distance I can cross at any moment by shifting my consciousness.

> Gabriel Archangel, the earth is now free,
> embracing a nondual reality,
> the judgment of Christ upon forces so dark,
> who deny that all have a spiritual spark.

> **Gabriel Archangel, of this we are sure,**
> **Gabriel Archangel, Christ light is the cure.**
> **Gabriel Archangel, intentions so pure,**
> **Gabriel Archangel, in you we're secure.**

6. I do not have to be the Christ the way Jesus was the Christ just before his crucifixion. I dare to be the Christ that challenges the illusion at my present level of consciousness even if I am not perfect in doing so.

> Gabriel Archangel, with angels so white,
> raising our planet out of the dark night,
> as we now intone the Word of the Lord,
> the beings who fell are bound by your sword.

> Gabriel Archangel, of this we are sure,
> Gabriel Archangel, Christ light is the cure.
> Gabriel Archangel, intentions so pure,
> Gabriel Archangel, in you we're secure.

7. Nada, help me to shift my mind and get rid of this internal spirit, this separate self of perfectionism. I say: "I am actually perfect in expressing my Christhood at my current level of consciousness."

> Gabriel Archangel, we call now to you,
> the astral plane your light burning through,
> entities, demons, discarnates are bound,
> as you and we intone Sacred Sound.

> Gabriel Archangel, of this we are sure,
> Gabriel Archangel, Christ light is the cure.
> Gabriel Archangel, intentions so pure,
> Gabriel Archangel, in you we're secure.

8. True perfection is reaching one step higher than my present level. Perfection is not some ultimate level that does not exist, except in the minds of the fallen beings.

> Gabriel Archangel, what glorious day,
> your radiant angels have come here to stay,
> your purifications fire burning white,
> intentions so pure, our hearts taking flight.

> Gabriel Archangel, of this we are sure,
> Gabriel Archangel, Christ light is the cure.
> Gabriel Archangel, intentions so pure,
> Gabriel Archangel, in you we're secure.

9. Nada, help me overcome this sense of perfectionism, the sense that I have to be perfect in everything I do. Help me see if I have used ascended master teachings to build this elaborate sense of how I need to be.

> Gabriel Archangel, our planet so pure,
> in our bright new future we do feel secure,
> with your band of light encircling the earth,
> Saint Germain's Golden Age is now given birth.
>
> **Gabriel Archangel, of this we are sure,**
> **Gabriel Archangel, Christ light is the cure.**
> **Gabriel Archangel, intentions so pure,**
> **Gabriel Archangel, in you we're secure.**

Part 5

1. Help me see if I have used my outer mind to create a straitjacket and force myself into it so I can barely move. I realize that the ascended masters are not the ones who want me to do this. It is an internal spirit who is driving me to do it.

> Master Nada, beauty's power,
> unfolding like a sacred flower.
> Master Nada, so sublime,
> a will that conquers even time.
>
> **Master Nada, peace you give,**
> **forevermore in peace we live,**
> **our planet has a peaceful morn,**
> **the Golden Age is hereby born.**

11 | Invoking Freedom from Perfectionism

2. I am consciously separating myself from this spirit and I see that it is based on a completely impossible goal defined by the fallen beings. There is no state of perfection that is possible on earth or that is required by the ascended masters.

> Master Nada, you bestow,
> upon us wisdom's rushing flow.
> Master Nada, mind so strong
> rising on your wings of song.
>
> **Master Nada, peace you give,**
> **forevermore in peace we live,**
> **our planet has a peaceful morn,**
> **the Golden Age is hereby born.**

3. Nada, help me truly accept that you completely, fully and absolutely accept me as I am right now. You do not have a standard that requires me to be at the 144th level before you will teach me.

> Master Nada, precious scent,
> your love is truly heaven-sent.
> Master Nada, kind and soft
> on wings of love we rise aloft.
>
> **Master Nada, peace you give,**
> **forevermore in peace we live,**
> **our planet has a peaceful morn,**
> **the Golden Age is hereby born.**

4. You are not judging me as being imperfect at my present level. You are completely accepting me for who I am at my

present level and you are only focused on helping me see that illusion and take the next step up.

> Master Nada, mother light,
> our hearts are rising like a kite.
> Master Nada, from your view,
> all life is pure as morning dew.

> **Master Nada, peace you give,**
> **forevermore in peace we live,**
> **our planet has a peaceful morn,**
> **the Golden Age is hereby born.**

5. I will never feel at peace with myself if I am judging myself based on a standard of perfectionism that I can never reach. If I always judge myself as being imperfect, how will I feel at peace with myself?

> Master Nada, truth you bring,
> as morning birds in love do sing.
> Master Nada, we now feel,
> your love that all four bodies heal.

> **Master Nada, peace you give,**
> **forevermore in peace we live,**
> **our planet has a peaceful morn,**
> **the Golden Age is hereby born.**

6. If I have always judged that I have done something wrong on earth and that I can only do something wrong on earth, how will I ever feel at peace with being here? How will I feel at peace on the spiritual path if I think that expressing Christhood requires me to be perfect?

11 | Invoking Freedom from Perfectionism

Master Nada, serve in peace,
as all emotions we release.
Master Nada, life is fun,
the solar plexus is a sun.

**Master Nada, peace you give,
forevermore in peace we live,
our planet has a peaceful morn,
the Golden Age is hereby born.**

7. Deep within me, I have a drive that is driving me to walk the spiritual path. Then, I have certain mechanisms in my identity, mental and emotional body that are working against this drive and this is what makes me feel not at peace with myself.

Master Nada, love is free,
conditions we no longer see.
Master Nada, rise above,
all human forms of lesser love.

**Master Nada, peace you give,
forevermore in peace we live,
our planet has a peaceful morn,
the Golden Age is hereby born.**

8. Nada, help me go through the initiations that resolve all the mechanisms that are working against my natural drive so that I can be free to recognize the drive from my I AM Presence, the drive to transcend myself and be the open door.

Master Nada, balance all,
the seven rays upon our call.
Master Nada, rise and shine,
your radiant beauty most divine.

Master Nada, peace you give,
forevermore in peace we live,
our planet has a peaceful morn,
the Golden Age is hereby born.

9. Part of perfectionism is the sense that I did something wrong by coming into embodiment. Something should not have happened and therefore I will never feel at peace until I overcome it.

Nada Dear, your Presence here,
filling up the inner sphere.
Life is now a sacred flow,
God Peace we do on all bestow.

Master Nada, peace you give,
forevermore in peace we live,
our planet has a peaceful morn,
the Golden Age is hereby born.

Part 6

1. There was *nothing* wrong that I did by coming into embodiment. I just did what I had to do to come into embodiment on a planet like earth and I took on the illusions down to the 48th

11 | Invoking Freedom from Perfectionism

level. Now, I am in the process of rising above these illusions one at a time.

> Serapis Bey, what power lies,
> behind your purifying eyes.
> Serapis Bey, it is a treat,
> to enter your sublime retreat.

> **Serapis Bey, we call to you,**
> **to help us dual lies see through,**
> **come purify our inner sight,**
> **we see the earth in your great light.**

2. I am not imperfect! I am simply at a certain level of my path. There is nothing wrong with this. I hereby stop chasing the rainbow of perfectionism—there is no pot of gold there.

> Serapis Bey, what wisdom found,
> your words are always most profound.
> Serapis Bey, we tell you true,
> our minds have room for naught but you.

> **Serapis Bey, we call to you,**
> **to help us dual lies see through,**
> **come purify our inner sight,**
> **we see the earth in your great light.**

3. I accept myself at my present level of the spiritual path. I accept that I can express Christhood at a certain level and I will dare to express it. The level I am at right now is much higher than most people on earth. I can express something that can help many people come up higher. I accept that this is good enough.

> Serapis Bey, what love beyond,
> our hearts do leap, as we respond.
> Serapis Bey, your life a poem,
> that calls us to our starry home.
>
> **Serapis Bey, we call to you,**
> **to help us dual lies see through,**
> **come purify our inner sight,**
> **we see the earth in your great light.**

4. I look at the level I am at and focus on that. I do not worry about the levels above me, I do not worry about living up to some standard of perfection. I am at peace with being where I am at and expressing Christhood at this level.

> Serapis Bey, your guidance sure,
> our base is clear and white and pure.
> Serapis Bey, no longer trapped,
> by soul in which the self was wrapped.
>
> **Serapis Bey, we call to you,**
> **to help us dual lies see through,**
> **come purify our inner sight,**
> **we see the earth in your great light.**

5. I am exactly where I should be right now, and I am willing to look at the illusion I am dealing with right now, transcend that illusion and then express my Christhood in challenging that illusion.

11 | Invoking Freedom from Perfectionism

> Serapis Bey, what healing balm,
> in mind that is forever calm.
> Serapis Bey, our thoughts are pure,
> your discipline we shall endure.
>
> **Serapis Bey, we call to you,**
> **to help us dual lies see through,**
> **come purify our inner sight,**
> **we see the earth in your great light.**

6. I have chosen to demonstrate how to rise to higher and higher levels of consciousness. I am not here to demonstrate how to jump from the 48th to the 144th level because nobody can see an example in that.

> Serapis Bey, what secret test,
> for egos who want to be best.
> Serapis Bey, expose the "me,"
> that takes away our harmony.
>
> **Serapis Bey, we call to you,**
> **to help us dual lies see through,**
> **come purify our inner sight,**
> **we see the earth in your great light.**

7. I need to serve as an example so that people can see those who are like themselves, who started out like themselves but who have risen higher. Therefore, people can believe that what one has done, all can do.

Serapis Bey, what moving sight,
the self ascends to sacred height.
Serapis Bey, forever free,
in sacred synchronicity.

**Serapis Bey, we call to you,
to help us dual lies see through,
come purify our inner sight,
we see the earth in your great light.**

8. Perfectionism is one of the most insidious plots of the fallen beings. At my present level, it is only one more step to overcome it. I see the spirit, I see it for what it is, I see it as an alien element in my four lower bodies, I look at it and say: "Get thee behind me Satan, you are no part of me anymore."

Serapis Bey, you balance all,
the seven rays upon our call.
Serapis Bey, in space and time,
the pyramid of self, we climb.

**Serapis Bey, we call to you,
to help us dual lies see through,
come purify our inner sight,
we see the earth in your great light.**

9. I will allow this victory to filter down to the conscious level. I see the spirit, see this perfectionism and I do not go into the reaction of blaming myself for having been affected by perfectionism. I am getting off the treadmill and I simply say: "Oh, well, that's just one more spirit that has to go. So many have gone already, what is one more?"

Serapis Bey, your Presence here,
filling up the inner sphere.
Life is now a sacred flow,
God Purity we do bestow.

**Serapis Bey, we call to you,
to help us dual lies see through,
come purify our inner sight,
we see the earth in your great light.**

Sealing:

In the name of the Divine Mother, I fully accept that the power of these calls is used to set free the River of Life, so it can outpicture the perfect vision of Christ for my own life, for all people and for the planet. In the name I AM THAT I AM, it is done! Amen.

12 | OVERCOMING A FALSE SENSE OF RESPONSIBILITY

I AM the Ascended Master Nada. At the fifth level of the initiations you go through in my retreat, we are dealing with the combination of peace and vision. What I wish to open up with in this discourse is a concept known among worldly psychologists as "magical thinking." It can give rise to what has often been called various forms of superstition.

It is often described as people confusing cause and effect where they come up with an explanation that is centered around themselves, often making them feel that their own thoughts were responsible for certain events happening or not happening. It is often described in children as the sense that your thoughts are responsible for what happened in life, and an attempt to explain everything based on what you know right now, relating everything to yourself.

The desire to be invulnerable

Well, my beloved, there are various aspects of this form of magical thinking, some not even understood by psychologists. I would like to begin here by reaching back to what I talked about in my last lesson. There is a certain desire among spiritual students to come to a point where you feel that you can do nothing wrong and where nothing can really harm you. You may know that there are certain computer games where you can be in some kind of world where there are enemies shooting at you, but you can put on a shield so that you are invulnerable to their attacks, at least for a time.

When you look at what I talk about, how in the past you have expressed your Christhood and you have then been tricked by the fallen beings into thinking that doing this was wrong, then you can see that an aspect of magical thinking is the idea that you can come to a point where nothing you do will be wrong and you cannot really be hurt by anything in this world. This is in some ways an extension of a desire that children have where they fantasize about being invulnerable, but it is also something that runs deeply in the collective consciousness.

As I have said, when you grow up in any culture on earth, you will be affected by certain very subtle beliefs. Of course, you have, when you look at the long history of this planet, many, many people who have been exposed to traumatic events that have given them deep wounds. They have attempted to create some spirit that has grown to become a collective spirit, that can either explain why this happened or give them some hope that one day they can come to the point of being invulnerable to this ever happening again.

You see that part of magical thinking is actually the idea that you can control the universe, that you can control certain aspects of this world so that you can avoid bad things and magnetize good things to you. There are many people who are superstitious about gambling, for example, where they think that wearing a lucky charm makes you more lucky. There are many other aspects of this kind of superstitious behavior where people are trying to do something in order to control what *will* or *will not* happen to them. Many people believe that wearing a medal around their neck with a saint on it, will protect them from bad events.

My beloved, you need to recognize here that there is a very, very old tradition or movement in this world to explain why certain things happen and to try to protect people from other things happening. You want to avoid the bad, you want to attract the good. You think that by taking some kind of measure, you can achieve this. In other words, there is a spirit (that has been created over a very long period of time on earth), which makes people believe that it is possible for them to gain some kind of control over the world.

As ascended master students you have grown up in an environment where this spirit has affected most people in some way or another and you have naturally been affected by it. Again, this is not to blame you in any way. It is simply a statement of the fact that at this level of initiation in this course, you are ready to deal with this particular issue. You are ready to take a look at the elements of magical thinking that you have in your own mind and you are ready to rise above them and be free of them. My beloved, when you do let them go, you will feel more free than you had ever thought possible while you were affected by this collective spirit and perhaps even some internal spirits in your own higher bodies.

The illusion of an almighty God

Now my beloved, let us begin by looking at this desire to be invulnerable, to be invincible. You may very well in the past have encountered fallen beings who attacked you personally in a very vicious, very uncompromising way. Naturally, you want to avoid this kind of trauma, you want to avoid this kind of pain, and this can give rise to you creating an internal spirit that makes you think that one day you should be invincible. You should be able to defeat the fallen beings, to destroy the fallen beings, to destroy anyone who attacks you or who attacks those whom you feel responsible for protecting, such as the innocent.

I need you to ponder here what this spirit actually comes from. It is, as all spirits (at least the major ones) a creation of the fallen beings. In a sense, all spirits are creations of the fallen beings, meaning they are based on the attacks and illusions of the fallen beings. Of course, the individual spirits are created by people in their reaction to the fallen beings.

What the fallen beings want you to think is that there is some kind of benevolent entity, usually called God, who is ultimately in control of the universe. Once you believe this, you think that certain things should not happen. Over the millennia, many people have felt that the obvious existence of evil on the planet challenges the existence of God. If there really is a God and if this God is good and almighty, then why does he allow evil to be on the planet?

You see that the fallen beings have, first of all, created the illusion that there is an almighty God who is in control of the universe. Then, they themselves have perpetrated many evil actions upon people that challenge the existence of this benevolent all-powerful God. This then, has caused the fallen beings

12 | Overcoming a False Sense of Responsibility

to create this contradiction in most people's minds. You think there should be a way to control what happens to you in your life. You think there should be some benevolent entity who is in control of what happens. Therefore, you think that by appealing to this entity through some kind of magical thinking, you should be able to secure the favors of this entity so that only good things happen to you and no bad things happen to you.

Some people live an entire lifetimes in this belief and feel that nothing really challenges it because nothing really bad happens to them. Other people start out having this belief and then something bad happens to them, and all of a sudden they are in a crisis of faith, perhaps even rejecting all concept of religion and God. Either way, this is what the fallen beings want because they are keeping people in a reactionary pattern. Even the people who think they can control God or the universe by performing certain actions, they are also kept in an illusion by the fallen beings.

What have we attempted to do in this course? We have attempted to help you accept greater and greater responsibility for your situation. What is the advantage of accepting responsibility? It is that you now see that you can do something about your situation. In a sense, you could ask the question: "Well, isn't this magical thinking? You are first saying that the fallen beings have created the illusion that there is a benevolent God who is in control of the universe. On the other hand, you are saying that we need to overcome magical thinking but nevertheless, now you are saying that we need to take responsibility for ourselves and see that we are co-creating our own circumstances. So how do we put all this together?" Well, we do not actually put it together. We look at the components and see them for what they are.

Giving up the belief in a personal God

First of all, naturally there is a Creator who, in a certain sense, has ultimate control of the universe. The Creator created the world of form, including the sphere in which you live. As we have explained through this messenger, a sphere is created as an unascended sphere, meaning it has not attained permanence. The purpose for creating a sphere in this state is that it allows for the outplaying of free will. The self-aware beings who are sent into the sphere to take embodiment in that sphere can outplay their free will in a way where they do not create anything permanent. They do not create anything they cannot later uncreate or overcome. In other words, they cannot be trapped in their own creation.

Because the sphere in which you live is not permanent, you can outplay free will in any way you want. When I say "you," I do not mean just you personally. All of the self-aware beings in your unascended sphere have free will, unrestricted free will. You can do things that limit yourself, you can do things that hurt others and this is possible because your sphere is not permanent. However, in order for free will to outplay itself, this also means that the Creator has set aside its control over an unascended sphere. This does not mean that God could not interfere if the Creator wanted to. The Creator could wipe out the entire sphere in an instant if it wanted to. However, it does mean that the Creator has said: "I will give these self-aware beings a certain time to work out their free will and come to the conclusion, based on free-will experimentation, that what is best for the whole is also what is best for the individual."

The reality, of course, is that earth is one of the relatively few planets in the entire universe that is at a very, very low level of collective consciousness. You may look at what is happening on earth and say that God should not allow these evils to happen and therefore God should wipe out the entire unascended sphere. However, there are billions of planets with a much higher level of collective consciousness than earth. Why should God wipe out the entire sphere based on what is happening on this little planet?

You see that as an ascended master student at this level, you need to give up the illusion created by the fallen beings that there is a personal God who is intimately interested in your personal life and situation here on earth. You need to give up the idea that somewhere up in heaven is an old man with a white beard who is constantly watching everything you do, say, think or feel down here on earth and who takes some kind of special interest in you. This remote God in the sky is a fictional creation of the fallen beings. It is time to just let it go. It is time to recognize here that there is no such God.

The magical helper

Now, one of the aspects of magical thinking often found in children is the belief in a magical helper. If children are feeling unhappy, threatened or afraid, they think that there is some magical helper who perhaps one day will step in and change their outer situation for them. Again, this is an understandable belief at a certain level of consciousness. It is a belief that appeals primarily to people below the 48th level. Because it is so strong in the form of a collective spirit, you have grown up in it, you have been affected by it. It is simply that at this level, you need to look at it and finally let it go.

Magical thinking says, for example, that if I do not think certain thoughts, if I do not perform certain actions, if I do think positive thoughts or put on a St. Christopher medal, then bad things will not happen to me. The issue with this form of thinking is that you think there is a middle man. You think that you are in a situation that you cannot personally do anything about, but there is some entity outside of yourself who can do something about the situation—if only you can find the way to trigger that entity into doing it, into using its powers.

Do you see the psychological effect of this? You are feeling powerless, you are reacting based on this sense of being powerless by appealing to some imaginary entity that supposedly has the power you do not have. Again, understandable in children, understandable in people at a certain level of consciousness. You are now at a level of consciousness far above this. It is therefore time for you to look at this and to see that this is all based on an illusion.

You are never powerless

First of all, I want to address the sense that you are powerless. My beloved, you are *never* powerless. I could not tell you this at a lower level of consciousness because people below the 48th level will not believe it. Even people at lower levels of consciousness who are part of this course have a hard time fully believing it. That is why we have to bring this up several times, in different disguises.

The reality here is that you are never powerless. This is, of course, a statement that needs to be understood from a deeper level. As I have said, the fallen beings love to put you in a situation where you feel that nothing bad should happen to you, then they perpetrate a physical event that is bad and then they put you in this state of doubt. Naturally, as ascended master students, you need to look at this. You need to fully recognize what I said earlier, namely that free will reigns supreme in an unascended sphere. You also need to recognize that earth is one of the lowest planets in your sphere. This means that when you are in embodiment on earth, there are certain things that *can* happen to you because other people can use their free will to harm you. There are other people who can use their free will to open themselves up to the control of the fallen beings in the emotional, mental or identity realms. Thereby, they can do something that hurts you physically. They can take a physical action that harms you.

I need you to come to the realization that there is nothing you can do about this and the reason is, as I have said, that free will must be allowed to outplay itself. This can take some contemplation, and if you find a particular difficulty accepting that free will must be allowed to outplay itself, then I recommend you reading the book, *My Lives with Lucifer, Satan, Hitler and Jesus*. It explains in great depth the purpose of free will and the working-out of free will.

I need you to ponder this and come to the point where you accept that earth is a very low planet and, therefore, it is quite possible that certain events will happen to you. You *are* powerless to stop other people from abusing their free will. There is nothing you can do to influence the free will of other people. Now, I know that many, many people (including many ascended master students) have the sense that it *should* be possible to influence the free will of other people so they do not harm you. I need you to give up this belief because the simple fact is, you do not *want* to influence the free will of other people. This can be a very difficult realization to come to, even for ascended master students who know all that you know about duality, free will and the purpose of the universe. I need you to, perhaps, take a little time to ponder this.

The most severe form of karma

You need to realize here that if you take an action that harms another person, you are making a certain karma for doing this. However, no matter what that physical action would be, taking a physical action is not the most severe form of karma you can make. The most severe form of karma you can make is by interfering with the free will of other people. Now, you may say here: "But what if I am preventing someone from killing themselves. I may be interfering with their free will but isn't it good that they don't kill themselves. So wasn't it right for me to interfere with their free will?" No, my beloved, it was not right and you will make karma for doing so.

You may say: "If a fallen being is about to kill a child, isn't it right for me to interfere with the fallen being's free will and make them not do this?" Again, no my beloved, that is not right, you will make karma for doing so. This is the kind of karma that the fallen beings have been making since they first fell and I can assure you that, as an ascended master student on the path towards the ascension, you do not want to make this kind of karma. My beloved, it is time for you to recognize here that there are what we might call two levels of the dualistic state of consciousness. There is one level where you simply become self-centered, focused on yourself and you are always trying to do what you think is best for yourself. Then, there is the lower level, which is the level of the fallen beings, where you are deliberately trying to control other people. At the first level you may seek to get what you want and to get other people to give you what you want. You are not doing it from a malicious view of wanting to actually control or destroy those other people. The fallen beings are at a level where they are deliberately and maliciously seeking to control others. This is not just to get what they want but to actually destroy other

12 | Overcoming a False Sense of Responsibility

people by creating all kinds of divisions and contradictions in their four lower bodies, by making them houses divided against themselves.

There is a certain point where the difference between the two is subtle. I am talking here in order to help you see the contrast. What I am saying here is that the most severe form of karma you can make is when you interfere with the three higher bodies of another person and influence the choices that the person makes. Even if you think you are doing this for the person's own good, you are still making a very severe karma for doing so. It is time for you to recognize here that if you have a sincere intention about making your ascension, qualifying for your ascension, during this lifetime, you cannot afford to make this kind of karma. Therefore, you need to come to that total, absolute acceptance that people must be allowed to outplay their free will even if they hurt themselves by doing so or if they hurt you by doing so.

Naturally, this does not mean that you cannot make people aware of what they are doing or that you cannot try to make them see what they do not see. What you cannot do is manipulate and control others. That is why I need you to come to the realization here that it is not appropriate for you to hold on to the belief that God, some saint or some angel can make other people do something or not do something. It is not appropriate for you to pray to God to stop other people from doing something that will harm you or harm themselves.

You see, my beloved, there is no authority in heaven that has the right to interfere with the free-will choices of human beings in embodiment. Therefore, it is not only a waste of your breath to pray to God to change the minds of other people, it is against the Law of Free Will. You will actually make karma for doing so. Not as severe as if you directly try to influence and manipulate other people but you are still making karma.

Accepting free will fully

What I am asking you to realize here is that there is state where you can look at the earth in the condition it is in right now and you can come to a full uncompromising, unconditional acceptance of free will. You can recognize that this is a low planet and there are simply things that will happen on a planet like earth. I am asking you to come to this point where you say: "I have taken embodiment on earth and ultimately it was because I chose to be here. I knew what kind of planet this is before I came into this embodiment, before I even came into my first embodiment here. And now I realize that I had my reasons, I may not remember consciously what those reasons were but part of the reason was surely that I wanted to grow from experiencing life on a planet like this. So how do I grow? I grow by coming to the realization that because of free will, I cannot prevent other people from doing what they choose to do. Nor is it my role to try to do this."

You can therefore give up the desire to find some magical way to prevent other people from doing what harms themselves or others. You give up the desire to influence God or to even find a way to influence other people. You can therefore come to an acceptance that when you are in embodiment on this earth, there are certain physical events that you cannot prevent.

What does it mean to be powerless?

You can come to accept this and it is easier to accept this when you recognize that even though you may be facing an event that you cannot prevent, you cannot stop, you are still not powerless. This may require a little thinking. What does it

12 | Overcoming a False Sense of Responsibility

mean to be powerless? Naturally, you have a sense (which is again a very powerful collective spirit on earth) that bad things should not happen and therefore there should be some power who could stop them. If you are threatened by some event, you have a sense in you that either you should be able to stop it or God should stop it and if neither of those things are happening you think you are powerless. When you step back from this, you recognize that this is an incorrect understanding of what it means to have power; it is not based on a recognition of what kind of planet you are on.

You are in an unascended sphere where free will reigns supreme because the purpose of an unascended sphere is to allow free will to outplay itself. Furthermore, you are on one of the lowest planets in this sphere, which means that you are on a planet where many, many bad things can happen because people choose to use their free will in a very extreme manner, in an extremely selfish manner. When you recognize what kind of planet you are on, you recognize that it is not realistic to think that you can have power to stop these outer events from happening. It is not realistic to think that you can have the power to stop an outbreak of war that involves millions and millions of people who made a collective decision to go to war.

It simply is not realistic to think that you as a person in embodiment could have that power. Nor is it realistic to think that God or any other celestial entity could have such power. That power simply does not exist on earth. It is as naive to think so as to think that there is some power who could suddenly suspend gravity and you could float into the air. My beloved, when you truly recognize this, you see that even though you do not have the power to stop the outer event, this does not mean you are powerless and it does not mean you should *feel* powerless. The fallen beings have set up a mechanism where they make you think that there should be a power to stop these events and when you experience that there is not, then you feel completely powerless, you feel at the mercy of events beyond your control. What is it that feels this? It is an internal spirit that feels this way, not *you*. What I need you to do here is to step back, look at this, see that it is an internal spirit that feels powerless and then ask yourself: "Well, how do *I* then feel?" *You,* what we have called the Conscious You, do not feel powerless. The Conscious You, when it is conscious of who and what it is, can never feel powerless.

The Conscious You recognizes, when it is aware of who and what it is, that nothing on earth can define you. What happens in a certain situation where you are exposed to very dramatic physical events? Well, of course, there is a physical consequence. You might get killed, your family and friends might get killed, your society may be destroyed. This has happened to most of you in past lifetimes and to a few of you in this lifetime, but, my beloved, is it the outer situation that affects you?

I have said that the Conscious You cannot be defined or even affected by anything on earth. You are pure awareness, you can always go back into pure awareness and thereby separate yourself from the wounds in your three higher bodies. What is it that affects you in an outer situation? Well, it is the way you *react* to the situation. Your reaction creates an internal spirit and that internal spirit stays in your three higher bodies even in succeeding lifetimes. As we have now told you over and over again during this course and in other teachings, you *are not* that spirit. You may have, up until this point, looked at the world through that spirit and reacted to that spirit but nevertheless, you *are not* the spirit. You have, during this course, overcome many internal spirits already and therefore, of course, you can overcome many more. I am simply asking you to overcome one more spirit by realizing that no matter what trauma you may have been exposed to in this or previous lifetimes, the ongoing effect of these physical events are the internal spirits that you carry with you in your three higher bodies. It is these spirits that are affecting you.

Recognizing the grace of time

Now, my beloved, I need you to step back here and consider that time is actually a grace. Many of you have not looked at time this way because time is often something that you see as putting some kind of demand or restriction on you. In your daily life, you always have to be somewhere at a certain time, you have to be at work for a certain amount of time, you are not free to dispose of your time. Many of you feel that life is short and time is running out and so people have a somewhat difficult relationship to time. Let me try to give you a different view here.

Let us say that sometime in the past, whether in this life or a previous life, you were exposed to a very dramatic event, such as a war destroying your family and society. This was a physical event, yet the physical event happened at a certain point in time and now time has moved on. You are no longer living in that moment in time. This means that you may look at that event today and you may say: "But the event was undeniably a physical event that took place in the physical world. Yet where in the physical world is that event today?" It is not there in the physical world because time has moved on.

Now, there may be certain consequences, certain effects of that event that are still there in the physical world. Let us make this easier to contemplate by saying that thousands of years ago in a past lifetime, you were exposed to a dramatic event when the Roman Empire conquered and destroyed your home city. This happened over 2,000 years ago. Today, there is no record of that event in the physical, there is not even any consequence any more, at least not a direct consequence of it. Is the event still affecting you? You have to recognize that at the physical level, that event is no longer affecting you. This, for that matter, is true also for an event that took place five minutes ago.

The grace of time is that it constantly moves on, which means that as time moves on, it erases previous events. These were physical events that took place in the physical octave but time has now erased them. This means that even though, at the time the event happened, you were powerless to stop the event from influencing you, time has given you new opportunities to overcome the effect of the event. We may say: "Today, is the physical event that took place 2,000 years ago relevant to you at all?" At the physical level, it clearly is not.

However, when the event happened, you reacted based on the level of consciousness you had at the time. You created certain internal spirits. If those spirits are still in your three higher bodies, if you have carried them with you in all of the lifetimes since that event took place, then the event is still affecting you. However, it is not *physically* affecting you and this means that you are not powerless to overcome that event. It is not a matter of you stopping a physical event that you cannot stop because the event is no longer there. It is a matter of you overcoming the *effects* of that event, namely the internal spirits. You *do* have the power to dissolve those spirits and free yourself from them.

How karma cycles through the four levels

In your past (whether two minutes ago or 2,000 years ago) you were exposed to a certain event. You reacted based on the level of consciousness you had at the time. You created certain internal spirits that were based on your reaction to the event. There is no blame here. What else could you do but react based on the level of consciousness you had when you experienced the event?

Now you have come to a higher level of consciousness and therefore you have the power to go to the spirits that were created at a lower level of consciousness, to see them for what they are, to separate yourself from them and say: "Get the behind me Satan." You can make the calls for Archangel Michael, Astrea and other masters to bind, consume and dissolve the spirits. When you see the illusion that the spirit was based upon, you can let that illusion go and you are free!

I need you to recognize here another subtle aspect of karma that most spiritual students have not understood. You may think, my beloved, that karma is a physical thing. So many people (both in the East and even in the New Age Community) believe that if you take a physical action, you are creating a physical karma and that karma will one day come back and hit you and this means something bad will happen to you. This, however, is not how karma works. We have said it before: "Karma is not punishment."

We have said that another aspect of time is that when you send out a certain karmic impulse by taking action, it is not instantly returned to you. This is, again, a grace period where the impulse cycles through the four levels of the material universe. When they come back to the physical, if you have learned your lesson, if you have overcome the consciousness that caused you to make the original karma, then nothing bad will happen to you physically. You understand? It is not a matter of punishing you for what you have done.

This also explains in a deeper way why these compensatory mechanisms are completely useless. It is not the case that if you killed somebody in the past, but if you do enough good deeds without changing your consciousness, then you will not be killed in the future when the karma comes back. The karma, when it comes back, descends through your identity body, your mental body, your emotional body. If you have the same consciousness today, the same internal spirit today, that caused you to kill a person ten lifetimes ago, then as the karma enters your identity body, it is activated – it is magnified – by that internal spirit in your identity body. This spirit might believe it was justified to kill that person under certain circumstances.

The karma then moves on to the mental body. If you still have an internal spirit there that might explain why it was okay that you killed that person, it is magnified again and it then descends into your emotional body. If you still have certain feelings of anger that you have not dealt with, it is magnified again. *Then,* it will descend into the physical where it might precipitate as some dramatic event where you are either killed or something else happens to you. If you have removed the spirits in the three higher bodies, there is nothing to magnify the karmic impulse and therefore it will not descend into the physical. It will simply dissolve before it reaches the physical.

Karma is not punishment. It is an opportunity to take up the lesson you did not learn the first time. If you have learned the lesson in the meantime, then you do not need the karma to descend into the physical where you cannot ignore it. You do not need the karma and that is why it can either be dissolved completely in your three higher bodies or an ascended master may decide to take it upon him- or herself in order to spare you the physical events that could delay your progress.

Dragging along old spirits

I need you to recognize here that even if you are facing a very difficult situation now, a difficult physical situation that you cannot avoid, you are still not powerless. You may not be able to stop the physical situation. If other people's free will is involved, then you do not want to stop the physical outplaying of the situation. What you want to do instead is focus on controlling your reaction to the situation. This is an opportunity for you to see if there is still some internal spirit that was created in the past in similar situations that would then cause you to react to the situation today with the level of consciousness you had when those spirits were created. Do you see the mechanism?

If you were exposed to a dramatic situation 2,000 years ago when you were at, let us say the 48th level of consciousness, you would have created internal spirits by reacting at the 48th level. Now you are at a much higher level of consciousness. Why on earth would you want to react to a situation based on the 48th level of consciousness when you are fully capable of reacting to that situation with your present level of consciousness? However, in order to avoid reacting at the former level of consciousness, you need to dissolve the spirit that was created in the past.

Any situation is an opportunity to look at your reaction, see the spirit that caused you to react in the past (when you were at the lower level of consciousness) and then dissolve it, rise above that spirit, free yourself from the spirit. Again, I am not asking you to be perfect here. I am not asking you to be able to react to every situation you encounter with the 144th level of Buddhic non-attachment. I am asking you to recognize that you are at a certain level. It is perfectly okay that you react at the 84th or the 87th level of consciousness. There is nothing wrong with reacting at your current level of consciousness; you do not need to blame yourself for this. You do not need to allow the fallen beings to trick you into thinking that now because you are an ascended master student, you should be able to react at the highest possible level of consciousness. This is not the way it works, this is not what is required.

Again, the path is a gradual path. You take one step at a time. At any moment, you are at a certain level of consciousness and naturally you react to a situation based on that level. I can assure you that at your current level of consciousness, the reaction to any situation will not be as severe as it was at, say the 48th level or another lower level of consciousness. Therefore, you need to recognize here that you may be facing an unpleasant situation and you may have a certain fear of how that situation will evolve, but that fear is based on the lower spirit that you have not dissolved. If you dissolve that spirit, you can react at your current level of consciousness and your fear and your animosity will not be nearly as intense.

Why you are not powerless

You see, my beloved, you are *never* powerless. There is no such thing as being powerless. You may again say: "But I can't stop the physical event." No, my beloved but the physical event will not affect you. It is *your reaction* to it that affects you. If you can control your reaction, if you can dissolve the lower spirits that caused you to react to similar situations with a lower level of consciousness, then you can take power over your reaction to the situation.

My beloved, one element of magical thinking is that you feel responsible for what happens. Psychologists say that young children often feel that the world is an extension of themselves and their bodies and therefore they are responsible for whatever happens.

Many children, for example, receive trauma because they feel responsible for their parents arguing. This is an inappropriate level of responsibility. What have we said in this course? We want you to accept greater and greater responsibility for yourself and for your own reaction, but at the same time you need to stop accepting responsibility for what is *not* your responsibility.

What is the liberating aspect of recognizing how free will works? It is, my beloved, that you are responsible for your own exercise of free will but you are absolutely *not* responsible for how other beings exercise their free will. You need to especially be aware that you are not responsible for how the fallen beings exercise their free will. You need to again think back to this problem of evil that has confounded so many religious thinkers and even philosophers.

Evil as it is seen on earth is not a rule, it is a rare exception. There are billions of planets in your universe that are in an upward spiral where there is no such thing as warfare or the kind of violence and torture and evil you see on earth. Earth is one of the very, very few planets where this is still allowed. You need to simply recognize that this is the kind of planet that you are in embodiment on. Therefore, you need to recognize that the fact that the fallen beings have perpetrated these kinds of evil and are still doing so is not a reflection on God, it is a reflection on *them*. You also need to recognize here that the fact that the fallen beings are doing what they are doing is not a reflection on *you*.

You did not deserve everything that happened

There is a certain sense among spiritual students – and it is again based on a subtle aspect of magical thinking – that if something bad happens to you, you must have done something to deserve it. This is based on the dream that ultimately there must be some benevolent God who is in control of the universe. You even have a statement that we have used sometimes, which says: "There is no injustice in the universe." You can go into a somewhat high-level reasoning and say that because of free will and the way free will is allowed to outplay itself, there *is* no injustice in the universe because whatever fallen beings do with their free will, they will be held accountable for it in the end.

However, when you look at a planet like earth, you will say that based on an evaluation of events on earth, then there certainly *is* injustice on earth. However, many spiritual students have this sense that: "Oh, ultimately God is good and God is in control and therefore God has a plan for the universe and therefore God must have allowed what happens here on earth. This means that God has created a law so that bad things can only happen to me if I have done something to deserve them. So therefore, there must be some problem in my thinking, in my mind that has caused me to attract to me these events where I have been abused by the fallen beings."

This is an aspect of magical thinking where you think that if you have been violated by the fallen beings, you must have done something to deserve it. In a sense, you could say you *have* done something to deserve it because you have chosen to take embodiment on earth and your mere presence is a challenge to the fallen beings. Of course, this is not something that has anything to do with justice or injustice. It has to do with the outplaying of free will.

You see here, it is not a flaw in your being that caused the fallen beings to feel threatened by your spiritual light so that they attempted to destroy you. You cannot allow yourself to feel responsible for this. However, at a lower level of consciousness it is inevitable that you reacted to the attacks of the fallen beings by creating an internal spirit based on the illusions you had at that lower level. Again, there is no blame. There is simply a recognition of the fact that at one point, when you were at a lower level of consciousness, you were attacked by the fallen beings who attempted to destroy you. You reacted to this based on the vision you had, based on the illusions you had taken on in order to descend to that level of consciousness. Therefore, you created an internal spirit and that internal spirit is based on the belief that there is no injustice in the universe and therefore you must have done something so that God allowed the fallen beings to do what they did to you.

This is just an internal spirit—it is not *you*. At this level of the path, you are ready to see this. You are ready to come to one of the most liberating experiences you can have, namely that you see, you *experience:* "I am not responsible for what the fallen beings did to me, I have done nothing wrong, I have done nothing to deserve it. I do not need to look for some flaw in my being to explain why this was allowed to happen. There is no flaw in my being. There is, however, an internal spirit that I created at the level of consciousness I had when I was attacked by the fallen beings. I need to look at that spirit; I need to dissolve it and then *I will be free.*"

A great turning point

My beloved, it is truly one of the great turning points on the spiritual path when you come to the recognition that you are not responsible for what other people did to you. Of course, we need to again look at this more carefully. As I said, in past lives you have had a lower level of consciousness. You may have done something at that lower level of consciousness that violated other people. Therefore, you could say that you have created a certain karma and if you have not dissolved the spirits in the three higher bodies, then that karma comes back to you as an event where other people violate you. In that case, you could say: "Yes! I have done something to deserve this." It is not that you deserved it but that you have not dissolved the spirits that caused you to do something similar to other people in the past.

Again, there can be a certain pattern where you need to look at: "Why did this event happen to me? Is it because I still have a similar mechanism in my psychology as I see in the other people who violated me? Do I still have certain internal spirits that are the same kind of internal spirits that these people have so that I did to other people in the past what these people are doing to me now?" In that case, of course, you need to work on yourself and dissolve it.

There are two different things we are talking about here. What I am talking about now is just what we might call the daily business of making karma on a dense planet like earth. What I was talking about earlier was that when you were first deliberately violated by the fallen beings, that initial act of the fallen beings violating you was not a result of karma you had made. You had not done anything to deserve this. That is why you can come to the point of seeing this. Then, you can recognize that the fallen beings managed to manipulate you into creating an internal spirit where you feel guilty for your interactions with the fallen beings. You feel guilty for even being here on earth, carrying the light that challenges the fallen beings.

I said earlier that you had created spirits in reaction to the fallen beings where you feel you are imperfect—there is something wrong with you. This is simply another shading of this where you actually feel guilt. You feel guilty for being who you are, you feel that you should not be here, you should not challenge the fallen beings. Again, you can feel guilty for having expressed your Christhood in a previous lifetime because it was not at the ultimate level of Christhood.

When you come to see this, when you come to separate yourself from it, this can be one of the major turning points on your path. Now, all of a sudden, all sense of guilt associated with being on earth can fall away. How can you be at peace with yourself if you feel guilty for being who you are, at least being who you are in the environment you are in here on earth? How can you feel at peace with being on earth if you feel guilty for your mere presence here? You may feel guilty for having done certain things but behind that is even the sense of feeling guilty for just being here.

My beloved, when you see this, when you see that this is an internal spirit, when you say: "Get thee behind me Satan" and when you feel that release where you see the illusion and in seeing the illusion you are free from it, then you will truly feel a new level of freedom. It is my great joy to see students come to this at the identity level, but it is an even greater joy to see students come to it at the physical level. I truly hope that *you* will have that experience as a result of working with this lesson.

13 | INVOKING FREEDOM FROM FALSE RESPONSIBILITY

In the name I AM THAT I AM, Jesus Christ, I call to my I AM Presence to flow through the I Will Be Presence that I AM and give this invocation with full power. I call to beloved Elohim Peace and Aloha and Cyclopea and Virginia, Archangel Uriel and Aurora and Raphael and Mother Mary, Nada and Hilarion to help me overcome all tendency to feel responsible for what is not my responsibility. Help me see and surrender all patterns that block my oneness with Nada and with my I AM Presence, including …

[Make personal calls]

Part 1

1. Nada, help me see any aspect of magical thinking, expressed as a desire that nothing I do will be wrong and that I cannot be hurt by anything in this world.

> O Elohim Peace, in Unity's Flame,
> there is no more room for duality's game,
> we know that all form is from the same source,
> empowering us to plot a new course.
>
> **O Elohim Peace, through your tranquility,**
> **we are free from the chaos of duality,**
> **in oneness with God a new identity,**
> **we are raising the earth into Infinity.**

2. Part of magical thinking is the idea that we can control the universe, that we can control certain aspects of this world so that we can avoid bad things and magnetize good things.

> O Elohim Peace, the bell now you ring,
> causing all atoms to vibrate and sing,
> we give up the sense of a separate "me,"
> we're crossing Samsara's turbulent sea.
>
> **O Elohim Peace, through your tranquility,**
> **we are free from the chaos of duality,**
> **in oneness with God a new identity,**
> **we are raising the earth into Infinity.**

3. There is a very old movement in the world to explain why certain things happen and to try to protect people from other things happening. There is a spirit that makes people believe that it is possible for them to gain some kind of control over the world.

13 | Invoking Freedom from False Responsibility

> O Elohim Peace, you help us to know,
> that Jesus has come your Flame to bestow,
> upon all who are ready to give up the strife,
> by following Christ into infinite life.
>
> **O Elohim Peace, through your tranquility,**
> **we are free from the chaos of duality,**
> **in oneness with God a new identity,**
> **we are raising the earth into Infinity.**

4. Nada, help me see the elements of magical thinking that I have in my own mind. I am willing to rise above them and be free of them.

> O Elohim Peace, through your eyes we see,
> that only in oneness will we ever be free,
> we now see that there is no separate thing,
> to the ego-based self we no longer cling.
>
> **O Elohim Peace, through your tranquility,**
> **we are free from the chaos of duality,**
> **in oneness with God a new identity,**
> **we are raising the earth into Infinity.**

5. Nada, help me see if I, in response to the attacks of the fallen beings, have created an internal spirit that makes me think that one day I should be invincible and be able to defeat the fallen beings.

> O Elohim Peace, you show us the way,
> for clearing the mind from duality's fray,
> you pierce the illusions of both time and space,
> separation consumed by your Infinite Grace.

> O Elohim Peace, through your tranquility,
> we are free from the chaos of duality,
> in oneness with God a new identity,
> we are raising the earth into Infinity.

6. I see that the fallen beings want me to think that there is a benevolent entity who is ultimately in control of the universe. Therefore, certain things should not happen.

> O Elohim Peace, what beauty your name,
> consuming within us duality's shame,
> the earth is set free from burden of fear,
> accepting your peace is now manifest here.

> O Elohim Peace, through your tranquility,
> we are free from the chaos of duality,
> in oneness with God a new identity,
> we are raising the earth into Infinity.

7. The fallen beings have created the illusion that there is an almighty God who is in control of the universe. Then, they themselves have perpetrated many evil actions that challenge the existence of this benevolent all-powerful God.

> O Elohim Peace, with Christ at our side,
> no force of duality can evermore hide,
> It was through the vibration of your Golden Flame,
> that Christ the illusion of death overcame.

> O Elohim Peace, through your tranquility,
> we are free from the chaos of duality,
> in oneness with God a new identity,
> we are raising the earth into Infinity.

8. This has caused the fallen beings to create a contradiction in most people's minds. We think God should remove evil but can observe that he has not done so. In reality, I live in an unascended sphere where the Creator allows free will to outplay itself.

> O Elohim Peace, you bring now to earth,
> the unstoppable flame of Cosmic Rebirth,
> we give up the sense that something is "mine,"
> allowing your Light through our beings to shine.
>
> **O Elohim Peace, through your tranquility,**
> **we are free from the chaos of duality,**
> **in oneness with God a new identity,**
> **we are raising the earth into Infinity.**

9. The Creator has said: "I will give these self-aware beings a certain time to work out their free will and come to the conclusion, based on free-will experimentation, that what is best for the whole is also what is best for the individual."

> O Elohim Peace, as peace now we feel,
> all records of war you totally heal,
> the earth is now free from forces of war,
> restoring her purity known from before.
>
> **O Elohim Peace, through your tranquility,**
> **we are free from the chaos of duality,**
> **in oneness with God a new identity,**
> **we are raising the earth into Infinity.**

Part 2

1. Nada, help me give up the illusion created by the fallen beings that there is a personal God who is intimately interested in my personal life and situation here on earth.

> Cyclopea so dear, the truth you reveal,
> the truth that duality's ailments will heal,
> your Emerald Light is like a great balm,
> our emotional bodies are perfectly calm.

> **Cyclopea so dear, in Emerald Sphere,**
> **in raising perception we shall persevere,**
> **as deep in our hearts your truth we revere,**
> **to immaculate vision the earth does adhere.**

2. I give up the idea that up in heaven is an old man with a white beard who is constantly watching everything I do, say, think or feel and who takes special interest in me. This remote God in the sky is a fictional creation of the fallen beings and I recognize that there is no such God.

> Cyclopea so dear, with you we unwind,
> all negative spirals clouding the mind,
> we know pure awareness is truly our core,
> the key to becoming the wide-open door.

> **Cyclopea so dear, in Emerald Sphere,**
> **in raising perception we shall persevere,**
> **as deep in our hearts your truth we revere,**
> **to immaculate vision the earth does adhere.**

13 | Invoking Freedom from False Responsibility

3. The problem with magical thinking is that it makes me think there is a middle man. I think that I am in a situation that I cannot personally do anything about, but there is some entity outside of myself who can do something, if only I can find the way to trigger it to act.

> Cyclopea so dear, clear our inner sight,
> empowered, we pierce the soul's fearful night,
> we now see our life through your single eye,
> beyond all disease we're ready to fly.

> **Cyclopea so dear, in Emerald Sphere,**
> **in raising perception we shall persevere,**
> **as deep in our hearts your truth we revere,**
> **to immaculate vision the earth does adhere.**

4. The psychological effect is that I am feeling powerless, and I am reacting based on this sense of being powerless by appealing to some imaginary entity that supposedly has the power I do not have. I am willing to look at this and to see that this is all based on an illusion.

> Cyclopea so dear, life can only reflect,
> the images that the mind does project,
> the key to our healing is clearing the mind,
> from the images the ego is hiding behind.

> **Cyclopea so dear, in Emerald Sphere,**
> **in raising perception we shall persevere,**
> **as deep in our hearts your truth we revere,**
> **to immaculate vision the earth does adhere.**

5. I am *never* powerless. The fallen beings love to put me in a situation where I feel that nothing bad should happen to me, then they perpetrate a physical event that is bad and then they put me in this state of doubt.

> Cyclopea so dear, we want to aim high,
> to your healing flame we ever draw nigh,
> through veils of duality we now take flight,
> bathed in your penetrating Emerald Light.
>
> **Cyclopea so dear, in Emerald Sphere,**
> **in raising perception we shall persevere,**
> **as deep in our hearts your truth we revere,**
> **to immaculate vision the earth does adhere.**

6. I fully recognize that free will reigns supreme in an unascended sphere. I recognize that earth is one of the lowest planets in my sphere.

> Cyclopea so dear, your Emerald Flame,
> exposes every subtle, dualistic power game,
> including the game of wanting to say,
> that truth is defined in only one way.
>
> **Cyclopea so dear, in Emerald Sphere,**
> **in raising perception we shall persevere,**
> **as deep in our hearts your truth we revere,**
> **to immaculate vision the earth does adhere.**

7. When I am in embodiment on earth, there are certain things that *can* happen to me because other people can use their free will to harm me. They can take a physical action that harms

13 | *Invoking Freedom from False Responsibility*

me. I realize that there is nothing I can do about this and the reason is that free will must be allowed to outplay itself.

> Cyclopea so dear, we're feeling the flow,
> as your Living Truth upon us you bestow,
> from all dual vision we are now set free,
> planet earth in immaculate matrix will be.

> **Cyclopea so dear, in Emerald Sphere,**
> **in raising perception we shall persevere,**
> **as deep in our hearts your truth we revere,**
> **to immaculate vision the earth does adhere.**

8. I accept that earth is a very low planet and, therefore, it is quite possible that certain events will happen to me. I am powerless to stop other people from abusing their free will. There is nothing I can do to influence the free will of other people.

> Cyclopea so dear, the truth is now clear,
> we see higher purpose for which we are here
> we know truth transcends all systems below,
> immersed in your light, we continue to grow.

> **Cyclopea so dear, in Emerald Sphere,**
> **in raising perception we shall persevere,**
> **as deep in our hearts your truth we revere,**
> **to immaculate vision the earth does adhere.**

9. I give up the belief that I should be able to stop other people from harming me because I do not want to influence the free will of other people.

> Cyclopea so dear, we're feeling your joy,
> as creative vision we now do employ,
> in lifting earth out of serpentine cage,
> to manifest Saint Germain's Golden Age.
>
> **Cyclopea so dear, in Emerald Sphere,
> in raising perception we shall persevere,
> as deep in our hearts your truth we revere,
> to immaculate vision the earth does adhere.**

Part 3

1. The most severe form of karma I can make is by interfering with the free will of other people, even if it is seemingly for their own good.

> Uriel Archangel, immense is the power,
> of angels of peace, all war to devour.
> The demons of war, no match for your light,
> consuming them all, with radiance so bright.
>
> **Uriel Archangel, use your great sword,
> Uriel Archangel, consume all discord,
> Uriel Archangel, we're of one accord,
> Uriel Archangel, we walk with the Lord.**

2. This is the kind of karma that the fallen beings have been making since they first fell, and as an ascended master student on the path towards the ascension, I do not want to make this kind of karma.

Uriel Archangel, intense is the sound,
when millions of angels, their voices compound.
They build a crescendo, piercing the night,
life's glorious oneness revealed to our sight.

Uriel Archangel, use your great sword,
Uriel Archangel, consume all discord,
Uriel Archangel, we're of one accord,
Uriel Archangel, we walk with the Lord.

3. The most severe form of karma I can make is when I interfere with the three higher bodies of another person and influence the choices that the person makes. Even if I think I am doing this for the person's own good, I am still making a very severe karma for doing so.

Uriel Archangel, from out the Great Throne,
your millions of trumpets, sound the One Tone.
Consuming all discord with your harmony,
the sound of all sounds will set all life free.

Uriel Archangel, use your great sword,
Uriel Archangel, consume all discord,
Uriel Archangel, we're of one accord,
Uriel Archangel, we walk with the Lord.

4. I recognize that I have a sincere intention about making my ascension, and therefore I cannot afford to make this kind of karma.

> Uriel Archangel, all war is now done,
> for you bring a message, from heart of the One.
> The hearts of all men, now singing in peace,
> the spirals of love, forever increase.
>
> **Uriel Archangel, use your great sword,**
> **Uriel Archangel, consume all discord,**
> **Uriel Archangel, we're of one accord,**
> **Uriel Archangel, we walk with the Lord.**

5. Nada, help me come to a total, absolute acceptance that people must be allowed to outplay their free will even if they hurt themselves by doing so or if they hurt me by doing so.

> Uriel Archangel, your infinite peace,
> from all warring beings our planet release,
> war is a prison from which we are free,
> embracing the peace of true unity.
>
> **Uriel Archangel, use your great sword,**
> **Uriel Archangel, consume all discord,**
> **Uriel Archangel, we're of one accord,**
> **Uriel Archangel, we walk with the Lord.**

6. I realize that it is not appropriate for me to hold on to the belief that God, some saint or some angel can make other people do something or not do something. It is not appropriate for me to pray to God to stop other people from doing something that will harm me or themselves.

13 | Invoking Freedom from False Responsibility

> Uriel Archangel, we send forth the call,
> reveal now the oneness that unifies all,
> help us the vision of peace now to see,
> so we from all conflicts and struggles are free.
>
> **Uriel Archangel, use your great sword,**
> **Uriel Archangel, consume all discord,**
> **Uriel Archangel, we're of one accord,**
> **Uriel Archangel, we walk with the Lord.**

7. There is no authority in heaven that has the right to interfere with the free-will choices of human beings in embodiment. I will make karma for praying to God to change the minds of other people.

> Uriel Archangel, in service to life,
> you give us release from struggle and strife,
> forgetting the self is truly the key,
> to living a life in true harmony.
>
> **Uriel Archangel, use your great sword,**
> **Uriel Archangel, consume all discord,**
> **Uriel Archangel, we're of one accord,**
> **Uriel Archangel, we walk with the Lord.**

8. Nada, help me look at the earth and come to a full, uncompromising, unconditional acceptance of free will. I recognize that this is a low planet and I say: "I have taken embodiment on earth and ultimately it was because I chose to be here. I knew what kind of planet this is before I came into my first embodiment here."

Uriel Archangel, the earth now you raise,
out of duality's death-bringing haze,
we call now upon your great Flame of Peace,
commanding that all petty squabbles do cease.

Uriel Archangel, use your great sword,
Uriel Archangel, consume all discord,
Uriel Archangel, we're of one accord,
Uriel Archangel, we walk with the Lord.

9. "I realize that I had my reasons. Part of the reason was that I wanted to grow from experiencing life on a planet like this. I grow by coming to the realization that because of free will, I cannot prevent other people from doing what they choose to do. Nor is it my role to try to do this."

Uriel Archangel, as peace is the norm,
to your higher vision the earth does conform,
as people have found your peace from within,
a Golden Age is the prize that we win.

Uriel Archangel, use your great sword,
Uriel Archangel, consume all discord,
Uriel Archangel, we're of one accord,
Uriel Archangel, we walk with the Lord.

Part 4

1. I give up the desire to find some magical way to prevent other people from doing what harms themselves or others. I give up the desire to influence God or to even find a way to

influence other people. I accept that when I am in embodiment on this earth, there are certain physical events that I cannot prevent.

> Raphael Archangel, your light so intense,
> raise us beyond all human pretense.
> Mother Mary and you have a vision so bold,
> to see that our highest potential unfold.
>
> **Raphael Archangel, for vision we pray,**
> **Raphael Archangel, show us the way,**
> **Raphael Archangel, your emerald ray,**
> **Raphael Archangel, our lives a new day.**

2. Despite this, I am still not powerless. I recognize that even though I do not have the power to stop an outer event, this does not mean I am powerless and it does not mean I should feel powerless.

> Raphael Archangel, in emerald sphere,
> to immaculate vision we always adhere.
> Mother Mary enfolds us in her Sacred Heart,
> from Mother's true love, we're never apart.
>
> **Raphael Archangel, for vision we pray,**
> **Raphael Archangel, show us the way,**
> **Raphael Archangel, your emerald ray,**
> **Raphael Archangel, our lives a new day.**

3. The fallen beings have set up a mechanism where they make me think that there should be a power to stop these events and when I experience that there is not, then I feel completely powerless, I feel at the mercy of events beyond my control.

Raphael Archangel, all ailments you heal,
each cell in our bodies in light now you seal.
Mother Mary's immaculate concept we see,
perfection of health our new reality.

**Raphael Archangel, for vision we pray,
Raphael Archangel, show us the way,
Raphael Archangel, your emerald ray,
Raphael Archangel, our lives a new day.**

4. What feels this is an internal spirit, not me. I see that it is an internal spirit that feels powerless and then I ask myself: "Well, how do *I* then feel?" I, meaning the Conscious You, do not feel powerless. The Conscious You, when it is conscious of who and what it is, can never feel powerless.

Raphael Archangel, your light is so real,
the vision of Christ in us you reveal.
Mother Mary now helps us to truly transcend,
in emerald light with you we ascend.

**Raphael Archangel, for vision we pray,
Raphael Archangel, show us the way,
Raphael Archangel, your emerald ray,
Raphael Archangel, our lives a new day.**

5. I am aware of who and what I am, and thus I know that nothing on earth can define me. I am pure awareness, I can always go back into pure awareness and thereby separate myself from the wounds in my three higher bodies.

> Raphael Archangel, diseases are done,
> as you help us see that all life is One,
> we no longer do your true love reject,
> immaculate vision on all we project.

> **Raphael Archangel, for vision we pray,**
> **Raphael Archangel, show us the way,**
> **Raphael Archangel, your emerald ray,**
> **Raphael Archangel, our lives a new day.**

6. What affects me in an outer situation is the way I react to the situation. My reaction creates an internal spirit and that internal spirit stays in my three higher bodies even in succeeding lifetimes.

> Raphael Archangel, we're healing the earth,
> in immaculate vision we give her rebirth,
> a new era has on this day begun,
> your emerald light now shines like a sun.

> **Raphael Archangel, for vision we pray,**
> **Raphael Archangel, show us the way,**
> **Raphael Archangel, your emerald ray,**
> **Raphael Archangel, our lives a new day.**

7. I am *not* that spirit. I may have, up until this point, looked at the world through that spirit and reacted to that spirit but nevertheless, I am not the spirit. I have overcome many internal spirits already and therefore I can overcome many more.

Raphael Archangel, the fall is behind,
as all of earth's people the Christ path do find,
we call now to you all people to heal,
as four lower bodies in love you do seal.

Raphael Archangel, for vision we pray,
Raphael Archangel, show us the way,
Raphael Archangel, your emerald ray,
Raphael Archangel, our lives a new day.

8. I realize that no matter what trauma I may have been exposed to in this or previous lifetimes, the ongoing effect of these physical events are the internal spirits that I carry with me in my three higher bodies. It is these spirits that are affecting me.

Raphael Archangel, as you bring the light,
the forces of darkness swiftly take flight,
their day is now done as we claim the earth,
spreading to all an innocent mirth.

Raphael Archangel, for vision we pray,
Raphael Archangel, show us the way,
Raphael Archangel, your emerald ray,
Raphael Archangel, our lives a new day.

9. A physical event happened at a certain point in time and now time has moved on. I am no longer living in that moment in time and the event is not there in the physical world because time has moved on.

Raphael Archangel, our vision set free,
as we can now see God's reality,
as Saint Germain's vision is manifest here,
the earth is now sealed in immaculate sphere.

Raphael Archangel, for vision we pray,
Raphael Archangel, show us the way,
Raphael Archangel, your emerald ray,
Raphael Archangel, our lives a new day.

Part 5

1. The grace of time is that it constantly moves on, which means that as time moves on, it erases previous events. These were physical events that took place in the physical octave but time has now erased them.

Master Nada, beauty's power,
unfolding like a sacred flower.
Master Nada, so sublime,
a will that conquers even time.

Master Nada, peace you give,
forevermore in peace we live,
our planet has a peaceful morn,
the Golden Age is hereby born.

2. Even though, at the time the event happened, I was powerless to stop the event from influencing me, time has given me new opportunities to overcome the effect of the event. When the event happened, I reacted based on the level of

consciousness I had at the time and I created certain internal spirits.

> Master Nada, you bestow,
> upon us wisdom's rushing flow.
> Master Nada, mind so strong
> rising on your wings of song.
>
> **Master Nada, peace you give,**
> **forevermore in peace we live,**
> **our planet has a peaceful morn,**
> **the Golden Age is hereby born.**

3. I am not powerless to overcome the event. It is not a matter of me stopping a physical event that I cannot stop because the event is no longer there. It is a matter of me overcoming the effects of that event, namely the internal spirits. I *do* have the power to dissolve those spirits and free myself from them.

> Master Nada, precious scent,
> your love is truly heaven-sent.
> Master Nada, kind and soft
> on wings of love we rise aloft.
>
> **Master Nada, peace you give,**
> **forevermore in peace we live,**
> **our planet has a peaceful morn,**
> **the Golden Age is hereby born.**

4. I have come to a higher level of consciousness and therefore I have the power to go to the spirits that were created at a lower level of consciousness, to see them for what they are,

to separate myself from them and say: "Get the behind me Satan."

> Master Nada, mother light,
> our hearts are rising like a kite.
> Master Nada, from your view,
> all life is pure as morning dew.
>
> **Master Nada, peace you give,**
> **forevermore in peace we live,**
> **our planet has a peaceful morn,**
> **the Golden Age is hereby born.**

5. In any situation, I will focus on controlling my reaction to the situation. This is an opportunity for me to see if there is still some internal spirit that was created in past situations, causing me to react to the situation today with the level of consciousness I had back then.

> Master Nada, truth you bring,
> as morning birds in love do sing.
> Master Nada, we now feel,
> your love that all four bodies heal.
>
> **Master Nada, peace you give,**
> **forevermore in peace we live,**
> **our planet has a peaceful morn,**
> **the Golden Age is hereby born.**

6. Any situation is an opportunity to look at my reaction, see the spirit that caused me to react in the past and then free myself from the spirit.

> Master Nada, serve in peace,
> as all emotions we release.
> Master Nada, life is fun,
> the solar plexus is a sun.
>
> **Master Nada, peace you give,**
> **forevermore in peace we live,**
> **our planet has a peaceful morn,**
> **the Golden Age is hereby born.**

7. I am never powerless. If I can control my reaction, if I can dissolve the lower spirits that caused me to react to similar situations with a lower level of consciousness, then I can take power over my reaction to any situation.

> Master Nada, love is free,
> conditions we no longer see.
> Master Nada, rise above,
> all human forms of lesser love.
>
> **Master Nada, peace you give,**
> **forevermore in peace we live,**
> **our planet has a peaceful morn,**
> **the Golden Age is hereby born.**

8. The liberating aspect of recognizing how free will works is that I am responsible for my own exercise of free will but I am absolutely *not* responsible for how other beings exercise their free will.

Master Nada, balance all,
the seven rays upon our call.
Master Nada, rise and shine,
your radiant beauty most divine.

**Master Nada, peace you give,
forevermore in peace we live,
our planet has a peaceful morn,
the Golden Age is hereby born.**

9. I am *not* responsible for how the fallen beings exercise their free will. The fallen beings have perpetrated all kinds of evil, but this is not a reflection on God, it is a reflection on *them*. The fact that the fallen beings are doing what they are doing is not a reflection on *me*.

Nada Dear, your Presence here,
filling up the inner sphere.
Life is now a sacred flow,
God Peace we do on all bestow.

**Master Nada, peace you give,
forevermore in peace we live,
our planet has a peaceful morn,
the Golden Age is hereby born.**

Part 6

1. I give up the sense that if something bad happens to me, I must have done something to deserve it. I give up the sense that there must be some problem in my mind that has caused

me to attract these events where I have been abused by the fallen beings.

> Hilarion, on emerald shore,
> we're free from all that's gone before.
> Hilarion, we let all go,
> that keeps us out of sacred flow.

> **Hilarion, with light so green,**
> **we see behind the matter screen,**
> **immaculate our inner sight,**
> **we see the earth is taking flight.**

2. This is an aspect of magical thinking where I think that if I have been violated by the fallen beings, I must have done something to deserve it. It is not a flaw in my being that caused the fallen beings to feel threatened by my spiritual light so they attempted to destroy me. I will not allow myself to feel responsible for this.

> Hilarion, the secret key,
> is wisdom's own reality.
> Hilarion, all life is healed,
> the ego's face no more concealed.

> **Hilarion, with light so green,**
> **we see behind the matter screen,**
> **immaculate our inner sight,**
> **we see the earth is taking flight.**

3. As a result of being attacked by the fallen beings, I created an internal spirit based on the belief that there is no injustice in

the universe and therefore I must have done something so that God allowed the fallen beings to attack me.

> Hilarion, your love for life,
> helps us surrender inner strife.
> Hilarion, your loving words,
> thrill our hearts like song of birds.

> **Hilarion, with light so green,**
> **we see behind the matter screen,**
> **immaculate our inner sight,**
> **we see the earth is taking flight.**

4. Nada, help me come to the liberating experience of knowing: "I am not responsible for what the fallen beings did to me, I have done nothing wrong, I have done nothing to deserve it. I do not need to look for some flaw in my being to explain why this was allowed to happen. There is no flaw in my being. There is, however, an internal spirit that I created at the level of consciousness I had when I was attacked by the fallen beings. I need to look at that spirit; I need to dissolve it and then I will be free."

> Hilarion, invoke the light,
> your sacred formulas recite.
> Hilarion, your secret tone,
> philosopher's most sacred stone.

> **Hilarion, with light so green,**
> **we see behind the matter screen,**
> **immaculate our inner sight,**
> **we see the earth is taking flight.**

5. Nada, help me come to the turning point of recognizing that I am not responsible for what other people did to me.

> Hilarion, with love you greet,
> us in your temple over Crete.
> Hilarion, your emerald light,
> the third eye sees with Christic sight.

> **Hilarion, with light so green,**
> **we see behind the matter screen,**
> **immaculate our inner sight,**
> **we see the earth is taking flight.**

6. This does not mean I reject all responsibility. I am willing to look at: "Do I still have a similar mechanism in my psychology as I see in other people who violated me? Do I still have certain internal spirits that are the same kind of internal spirits that these people have so that I did to other people in the past what these people are doing to me now?"

> Hilarion, you give us fruit,
> of truth that is so absolute.
> Hilarion, all stress decrease,
> as our ambitions we release.

> **Hilarion, with light so green,**
> **we see behind the matter screen,**
> **immaculate our inner sight,**
> **we see the earth is taking flight.**

7. The initial act of the fallen beings violating me was not a result of karma I had made. I had not done anything to deserve this. I recognize that the fallen beings managed to manipulate

me into creating an internal spirit where I feel guilty for my interactions with the fallen beings. I feel guilty for even being here on earth, carrying the light that challenges the fallen beings.

> Hilarion, our chakras clear,
> as we let go of subtlest fear.
> Hilarion, we are sincere,
> as freedom's truth we do revere.
>
> **Hilarion, with light so green,**
> **we see behind the matter screen,**
> **immaculate our inner sight,**
> **we see the earth is taking flight.**

8. Nada, help me see this, and separate myself from it. I feel that all sense of guilt associated with being on earth falls away. I see that this is an internal spirit, and I say: "Get thee behind me Satan."

> Hilarion, you balance all,
> the seven rays upon our call.
> Hilarion, you keep us true,
> as we remain all one with you.
>
> **Hilarion, with light so green,**
> **we see behind the matter screen,**
> **immaculate our inner sight,**
> **we see the earth is taking flight.**

9. I feel the release where I see the illusion and in seeing the illusion I am free from it, feeling a new level of freedom.

Hilarion, your Presence here,
filling up the inner sphere.
Life is now a sacred flow,
God Vision we on all bestow.

**Hilarion, with light so green,
we see behind the matter screen,
immaculate our inner sight,
we see the earth is taking flight.**

Sealing:

In the name of the Divine Mother, I fully accept that the power of these calls is used to set free the River of Life, so it can outpicture the perfect vision of Christ for my own life, for all people and for the planet. In the name I AM THAT I AM, it is done! Amen.

14 | FINDING PEACE IN RELATIONSHIPS

I AM the Ascended Master Nada. At this sixth level of the initiations in my retreat, you are naturally facing a double dose of the Sixth Ray. I would like to begin by building on some of the things I told you in my previous discourses, specifically about karma. There is, of course, many superficial understandings, ideas and theories about karma floating around in the world. I need you to step beyond these and come to a deeper realization of how you make karma.

There are many, many people who believe in either an eastern philosophy or a New Age philosophy that talks about karma as the result of some action you take, which means they basically believe that karma is something physical. You do something physical to create the karma and when the karma comes back to you, it results in certain physical events happening to you. Now, as I have explained in my previous discourse, this is not a correct understanding. There is no karma, so to speak, at the physical level because the karmic impulse that you create (even by taking a physical action) is not an impulse in the physical, vibrational spectrum. It is an impulse that goes into the three higher bodies and then cycles through those until it may return to you in your personal energy field. Then, as I explained, it may or may *not* become a physical event based on whether you have changed your consciousness.

The reason it is important to contemplate this is that you actually recognize that nothing in the physical defines you. You also recognize, in a sense, that it is not really anything in the physical world that determines whether or not you make your ascension. Many of you have adopted a certain view that in order to qualify for your ascension, you have to balance all of your karma. This is not incorrect but the karma is not a physical karma. It is, first of all, purifying your emotional, mental and identity bodies of the internal spirits that you have there. Really, balancing karma is not a matter of compensating for something by doing something physical. It is, first of all, a matter of resolving the internal spirits so that the prince of this world comes and has nothing in your three higher bodies whereby he can cause you to go into a reactionary pattern. This is truly what it means to balance karma.

There is, of course, a certain energy impulse, but again that impulse is not physical. I am not denying that you need to do a certain amount of decrees and invocations in order to dissolve that energy impulse, but the most important aspect of balancing karma is truly to dissolve the spirits.

Interacting with people without making karma

However, there is also another aspect of balancing karma and that is to avoid making new karma and this is, so to speak, the Omega aspect. Naturally, if you keep making new karma, you will have to do more and more violet flame in order to balance everything. You need to follow the first principle of First Aid, which is to stop the accident. In other words, you need to stop the karma-making, stop these reactionary spirals that cause you to make karma. I have talked about, in my previous discourse, how to stop this in terms of reacting to the fallen beings, causing them to make you feel guilty, unworthy, imperfect or whatever.

I now want to focus on one of the absolutely most common ways that people make karma and it is in their interaction with other people. Naturally, you are an ascended master student and you have followed our teachings for a while in order to rise to this level of initiation. You have overcome some of the more physical, violent, aggressive ways of interacting with other people. Still, you are at a certain level where you have not totally freed yourself from these reactionary spirals with other people. For a person at your level, it is not that you are taking aggressive actions against others, but you still have a tendency to feel that other people are taking aggressive actions against you—and, of course, they *are*.

You can take a look at the life of Jesus and even when he was at the 143rd level of consciousness, the fallen beings took actions against him and nailed him to a cross. Nevertheless, what I am talking about here specifically is that at this level, you have the sense that other people may take aggressive actions against you and you often feel powerless to deal with this. I have talked about the need to develop respect for free will so if you have total respect for another persons' free will, then you cannot necessarily stop them from taking an aggressive action against you. Then, how do you avoid feeling powerless?

Well my beloved, the way to do this is to acquire a deeper understanding of how free will outplays itself, especially in relation to karma. Now, let us begin by again taking a look at what kind of planet you are on. I have said that there are many planets with a much higher level of consciousness where you do not find the aggression that you see on earth. Earth is one of the lowest planets in terms of the level of aggression that people take against other people. When you recognize this, you can then start to look at what are your expectations about life on earth.

There are some of you who are avatars who have come from natural planets where you have never been exposed to aggression. Therefore, you carry a certain subtle memory that there should not be aggression. It is not natural that people take aggressive actions against others. Some of you are the original inhabitants of the earth and you carry with you a subtle memory of how the earth was before the fallen beings were allowed to embody here. You also have a sense that it is not "natural" or "right" that people take aggressive actions against others.

Another unrealistic expectation

You see here that you have an expectation about how life *should be* on earth. However, this expectation is out of touch with the reality of how life *is* on earth. There is a gap between your expectation and reality. You, therefore, need to perform a simple evaluation here. Is it possible for you to change the current situation on earth? Obviously, it is not. You cannot remove war and aggression from the planet by snapping your fingers.

What is the realistic course of action you can take? It is to let go of the expectation that was created either on a different planet or when the earth was a different planet. In other words, you need to recognize that you are carrying with you an unrealistic expectation and at this point you are ready to see that it is holding back your progress. It is creating a tension in you, a contradiction within you, that is pulling on you from different directions. It is causing you to be a house divided against itself, as all of these internal spirits do. As I already explained, the fallen beings love to create an expectation in you, for example that God should come and save you, and then see reality destroy that expectation, therefore leaving you in doubt about what is real and unreal.

You need to come to this point of recognizing that you are on a very dense, a very difficult, planet and therefore you need to simply look at your expectation and say: "But this does not apply on this planet. My expectation is not reasonable, it is not rational, it is not reality-based on this planet." Then, you simply need to let it go. You need to let it go—like you do any other internal spirit because your unrealistic expectation has become an internal spirit. You let it go, my beloved.

Then, you look at what kind of planet you are on and you say: "Based on what I now know about this planet, based on what I know about free will, is it realistic to have *any* expectation about what *should* or *should not* happen on earth?" The brutal answer is: "No." It will seem brutal at first, but when you accept it, it is liberating. You can now see that there is no reason to have any expectation and therefore there is no more resistance in you about life on earth. If you have no expectations about what should or should not happen, then you can meet life without this overlay. You can actually meet life, as Jesus said, with the innocent mind of a child.

When you adopt this childlike innocence of not having expectations about what should or should not happen, then you are now in the kingdom of God in your own mind. You now realize that there is no reason to expect what should or should not happen. You know that nothing that happens or does not happen defines you. Nothing in the physical defines you. Nothing in the physical hinders your ascension.

You can come to this point where you look at other people and you say: "Why should I then have any expectations about what other people should or should not do?" If you look at your life, you will see that for your entire lifetime (and I can assure you for many past lifetimes as well) you have had these (perhaps subtle, perhaps obvious) expectations about other people. You want them to do certain things, you do not want them to do other things and this puts you in a constant state of tension with other people. It also tends to make you feel powerless because on the one hand you have a desire to prevent other people from doing something that harms you or harms themselves, but on the other hand you feel you are not allowed to use any aggressive means to force them to do or not do this or that. You feel powerless once again.

The world does not revolve around you

Once you let go of the expectation that other people should do this or that, there is no need to feel powerless. You now realize that you can take another step towards peace of mind by reaching back to what I said about magical thinking. There is a certain collective spirit in the world that is based on the experiences that children go through when they are lying in the womb. It has been added on to by all of the people that have been born physically throughout the history of this planet.

When a mother is carrying a child in the womb, she realizes that this is another being, another body, growing inside her body. She realizes this because she very well remembers that there was a time when she was not pregnant and where she was in somewhat control of her own body. Now, there is another being growing inside of it and she clearly identifies this as another being inside her body. It is *her* child, she may have a connection to it but she knows this is another being that one day will be born and have a separate existence. However, how does the situation look for the child?

Well, most people do not remember their pre-birth memories but if you did, you would realize that the child in the womb has not experienced having a separate body because the child experiences that the mothers body is its body. The child does not realize that there is another separate being who is inhabiting the mothers' body. It actually feels that the mothers' body is *its* body, and as the body of the child grows inside the womb, it gradually starts having a little bit of confusion about why there is this body inside the bigger body. As a result of this, most children are born with a sense of awareness that the world is an extension of their body. They are used to their mothers' body being an extension of themselves. Now they are born into a world where, in the beginning, they have a sense that this world is an extension of their body. They do not yet have this sense of being a separate being in a separate body. This is not the case for all children, but for most.

The result of this is that many children go through this period, which psychologists have identified, where they feel: "The world is an extension of me, I am the center of the world. Therefore, I am responsible for everything that happens. Everything that happens revolves around me and relates to me."

I need you to come to recognize that in your three higher bodies, especially in the emotional body, there is an internal spirit that still feels that it is the center of your world. It may not feel responsible for everything that happens in the world and it does realize that there are other people that are separate beings. Nevertheless, this spirit feels that everything that happens in your life revolves around it. Everything that other people do relates to it.

As long as you have not seen through this spirit, there is a certain level, perhaps subconscious, where you tend to feel that the people around you do what they do in relation to you. In other words, you may feel responsible for it, you may feel hurt by it, you may feel that they are doing this to you. Now, I need you to ponder this because it is important that you come to recognize that it is an internal spirit that feels this way. The Conscious You does not feel this way. The Conscious You actually knows that it is a separate being, that other people are separate beings and they have their free will as you have your free will. Once you separate yourself from the spirit, you can realize something very, very important.

Feeling you caused the behavior of others

You may have a family member or another close associate who becomes very angry at you. It may be that the other person is accusing you of having done something you should not have done or not having done something you should have done according to the other person's evaluation. The person comes at you with a very aggressive, accusatory energy and your most likely reaction is to think that the person is doing this because of what you did or did not do. In other words, you feel responsible, you feel you are the cause of the other persons' behavior.

Now, we have talked about his before but you need to again look at this and come to the realization that the other person did not do or say what it did or said because of you. You are *not* responsible for the other persons' choices. You are responsible for *your own* choices but not for the *other person's* choices. Yes, you are responsible for your actions, what you did, what you said, but you are not responsible for how the other person reacted to it.

Most ascended master students who come to this level find it relatively easy to pass the initiation I talked about in my last discourse where I said that you need to come to recognize that you are responsible for your own reactions. They often find it more difficult to simply look at the other side of the coin and say: "If I am one hundred percent responsible for *my* reactions, then I am one hundred percent *not* responsible for the reactions of other people." You need to step back here and say: "Why did the other person do what that person did to me? I may have done something that triggered a reaction in the other person, and it is this reaction that caused them to then accuse me. However, whereas I *am* responsible for my action, I *am not* responsible for the other person's reaction."

Therefore, you can depersonalize the situation by realizing that the other person did not do this *to you*. The other person did it in response to you but the other person did not do it *to you*. You can now begin to create a distinction in your mind.

It is important here for you to realize that there is a difference between the duality consciousness and the Christ consciousness that can be subtle to understand. The duality consciousness we have called the consciousness of separation because it separates everything into different categories. It separates you from God, from other people and the planet you are living on. The Christ consciousness does not *separate* but it does *discern*—it makes distinctions.

There is a distinction to be made here where you recognize that you have a tendency to feel that when other people are doing something that affects you, they are doing it *to* you, they are doing it against you personally. If they are angry, you think they are angry with you and you feel responsible. As the person you are, who is open to changing yourself, you are always looking at: "How can I change myself so that this person is not angry with me?" As an aspect of growing in

Christ consciousness, you come to make this distinction where you say: "What the other person is doing is not directly done against me. It is not a personal attack on me. It is something that is caused by the persons' internal reactions."

Endless karmic spirals

You understand, my beloved, that the biggest challenge for most people on earth is dealing with the people who are closest to them, such as in a family. You feel you cannot get away from these people. Therefore, you feel that you have to react to them and you have to take seriously what they are doing or saying—you have to take it *personally*. As a result of this, most people have built these reactionary patterns with each other. If a family member is angry at you, you feel responsible, you feel you have to take this personally, you have to look at how you can change to avoid the person being angry.

This causes most people on earth to be involved in what we have sometimes called karmic spirals or karmic groups where they have such strong reactionary patterns to each other that they continue them lifetime after lifetime after lifetime. You see this everywhere. What I need you to recognize here is that these people are not doing this to you personally. They are maybe your family members and you may have a personal relationship to them, but they are not angry with you personally. This may be difficult to see so let us just perform a simple thought experiment. Say you have a family member who is angry with you over something you did. Now imagine that this family member had another person who did the same thing to them that you did. Would the person be angry with that person as well? The answer is: "Most likely."

This is not always the case because there are times where people feel that they can allow themselves to be angry with their family members but not with a stranger. You will see there is a certain tendency where people feel that they can actually treat their family members, their so-called "loved ones," worse than they can treat a complete stranger.

In most cases, you will see that if another person did the same thing to them (and at least that person had done this before), then your family member would be as angry at the third person as he or she is at you. This allows you to see that the other person's anger is not tied to you personally. It could just as well be directed at another person than you. If the other person's anger is not personal towards you, *where* is it personal? It is personal inside that person's consciousness. The anger is inside that person's emotional, mental and identity bodies. You may have triggered the anger but you are not the cause of it. The cause is an internal mechanism in that person's psychology, just as your own anger is an internal mechanism in your psychology.

Feeling responsible for other people's psychology

Now my beloved, you have been willing to look at your own psychology or you would not have been able to go through this course to this point. The other person in your family may not have been willing to do this. What you can do is to realize that your willingness to look at your own psychology should be exercised with caution. You should not be so willing to look at your own psychology that you take on the responsibility for the psychological mechanism that is in the minds of other people. The other person's anger is a psychological mechanism in his or her four lower bodies, *not* in *your* mind, not in your four lower bodies. Therefore, you cannot take responsibility for it and try to change yourself to avoid the anger in the other person. You *cannot* avoid it, the anger is still there in the other and it is just waiting for another trigger.

What you and most people do in these situations is that they try to build up in their mind a certain idea of what behavior they should avoid or what they should do or say in order to avoid the other person's anger. This now means that you have created an unbalanced action in yourself, caused by the other person's imbalance. What I am trying to show you here is that in order to step out of these reactionary patterns with other people, in order to attain peace in your relationship with other people, you need to look at yourself and you need to make this discernment that: "I am not going to feel responsible for other people's psychological issues and I'm not going to allow myself to continue to carry these internal spirits that I created in order to compensate for or avoid their emotional issues."

You are going to have to look at yourself in relation to other people and see where you have built this reactionary pattern. Then, you see that there is a spirit behind it and then you let go of that spirit. You have a right to let this spirit go. My beloved, when you can look at your relationship to a specific other person and use it to see your own reactionary patterns, your internal spirits, then you can free yourself from any pattern with that person.

Changing the dynamic of relationships

Now, this means two things. First of all, it means that when you are free of any reactionary patterns, you can meet that person with the innocent mind of the child and that means you can now avoid reacting to the person. You can avoid reacting like you did in the past. You will see that when you stop reacting the way people expect you to react, they might sometimes be surprised. There are many examples of how this alone can change the dynamic of a relationship. It may very well be that the person is also able to change.

There will, of course, be examples also where the person is not willing to change, even though *you* have changed. The person is too wrapped up in its own spiral, in its own psychology, and it is not willing to change. Now, in that case there are certain things that can happen. When you respond to another person's aggression with the childlike mind, with a completely neutral, love-based state of mind, that person receives the judgment of Christ. The judgment of Christ is an opportunity to look at something in themselves. If they do not take it, then this will, in a very real sense (we might say in a karmic sense) set you free from any obligation to that person. You can therefore choose freely whether or not you want to be around that person.

Many times you will see, my beloved, that when you free yourself from a certain reactionary pattern with other people, suddenly you no longer find those people in your life. There are, of course, cases where you are talking about close family members that you do not necessarily get away from physically. You come to a point where you have no reactionary pattern with them so whatever they do or do not do, you are not reacting to it. It is not disturbing you, it is not bothering you. You are just letting it go in one ear and out the other, as they say.

You see that this is a different way to relate to people and it is really the only way that you can attain peace in your relationship with other people. You are not about to take aggressive action. As I have taught you in my last discourse, you are not about to manipulate or influence the free will of other people.

All you can do is free yourself from the reactionary patterns and be yourself, my beloved. Express yourself at your present level of consciousness and thereby give the other person an opportunity to rise above his or her patterns. If they do not take it, then it does not really make any difference to you because you are not disturbed by it.

In other words, you need to come to a point where you can say about a close relationship: "If the other person does not change, can I live with that." Then, you can say: "Is this a person I can walk away from or not?" If you decide: "No, this is too close of a relationship, I don't want to walk away from the other person," then you can live with the person and not be disturbed by the other person's psychology. In some cases, you will come from the point of feeling: "Yes, I *can* live with the other person not changing but I don't actually want to." Then, you have a right to walk away from that person and say: "I do not want those kind of people in my life anymore." This is not because you are trying to avoid a reactionary pattern in yourself, it is simply because you feel and you realize that you have risen above the consciousness that these people have. Therefore, you have a right to decide that you prefer to associate with people at your level of consciousness or above.

Making karma with fallen beings

Now, we need to go even further with this and ask ourselves some other questions. I have said that you live on a dense planet with a lot of aggression. There are fallen beings here. There are fallen beings in embodiment who might take aggressive actions against you. There are also people who are not fallen beings but who might temporarily have their minds taken over by fallen beings. They might be compelled by the fallen beings at higher levels to take aggressive actions against you. You recognize here that the question then is: "If someone else takes aggressive action against you, what are the karmic implications of this?"

Here, we need to recognize that there is a collective spirit that is designed to try to make you feel responsible for things that are not your responsibility. The fallen beings, for example, love to violate you, cause you to go into a certain reaction to them and then make you feel that because your reaction to the fallen beings was not the highest possible, you must have made karma with the fallen beings. Is this the case, my beloved?

Well, let us take a more extreme position. Jesus told you to turn the other cheek. He demonstrated that for those who took aggressive action against him, he turned the other cheek and allowed them to crucify him. Jesus was at that point at a very high level of consciousness and therefore he had overcome most of the illusions that I said you take on in order to descend to the 48th level. He was not reacting to the fallen beings based on fear but based on love. In that case, when you are completely non-attached, then it is easy to see that Jesus did not make karma because the fallen beings crucified him. I trust that this is easy for you to see.

The fallen beings took aggressive action against a being with free will. They, of course, made karma for doing this but Jesus (because he did not react in a fear-based way) did not make karma. What about you? Say you descended to earth for the first time at the 48th level of consciousness. You were attacked by the fallen beings and you naturally (because you could not do anything else) reacted to them based on the 48th level of consciousness.

Well, here we need to make a distinction. If you took a physical action, for example fighting back and killing the fallen beings, then you *did* make karma for that action. If you could avoid taking the physical action (as many of you have been able to do even when you were exposed to very severe aggression), then you did not make karma. You may say to yourself: "But didn't we make karma by responding with anger?" I would say that this will depend on your level of anger.

When you descend to the 48th level of consciousness, you take on illusion after illusion until you are at the 48th level. At the 48th level, you are seeing through a veil, through a glass darkly, through a filter. Based on how you see the world through that filter, you react to what you are exposed to. At the 48th level, it is unavoidable that you react with a certain amount of anger when you are violated by others. If you react with that level of anger, you do not make karma for that reaction. You are at the 48th level; you are not expected to be at a higher level. You do not make karma for responding at the level of consciousness you are at.

Now, if your anger was more severe than is normal for the 48th level, you would make karma for that additional anger. We could also say that even though you are at the 48th level and seeing through a certain filter, there will always be a high reaction and a low reaction. In other words, a reaction that reinforces the 48th level of consciousness, perhaps even causes you to slip down to the 47th level or a higher reaction that transcends the 48th level and allows you to rise to the 49th level.

If you take the low road, then you can make karma for that. If you take the high road, you do not make karma even if your reaction was not total Buddhic non-attachment. You see my beloved, karma is not as simple, as linear as the fallen beings want you to believe. I can assure you that the fallen beings have attempted to influence all of the teachings on karma that are out there, such as the Hindu and Buddhist teachings, the Taoist teachings and many New Age teachings.

14 | Finding Peace in Relationships

Depersonalizing your relationships

What you begin to realize here is that you are now at the point where you can take a very important step that is as liberating as the step I had you take in my last discourse. It is the step where you can depersonalize your relationship to other people. You can say: "Whatever they do to me, it is not personal against me because they're acting based on their level of consciousness, based on their illusions, perhaps based on being possessed by dark forces. But at any level, it is not me exclusively they are acting against. In fact, if I wasn't here, they would just find someone else to act against, they would just find someone else to be their excuse for the aggression that is inside of them and that they need to take out on somebody because they can't stand having it inside themselves."

You can realize that when people commit any kind of aggression against others, it is not against those others. It is simply that they have such tension inside themselves that it suddenly boils over, they lose control and now they have to direct it outwards in order to be able to even stand being in their own auras. This is the mechanism that is behind virtually all aggression seen on this planet.

A person has some kind of division in its psyche. The fallen beings are exploiting this division to gradually build tension and then it comes to this breaking point where the person can no longer stand the internal chaos and tension. The fallen beings have then also managed to make the person set up this belief system, these internal spirits, that it is acceptable to direct that anger against someone else because *they* are the cause of it. The person is so blinded by the internal spirit that it does not see that this is an internal mechanism. It actually thinks that it only becomes angry because of what the other people did, and it is fully justified in being angry because these people should not have done this. You see here that when other people take aggressive actions, they are temporarily possessed by a dark spirit, they are not in control of their actions, they are not acting rationally. This is why you can say: "But I recognize what kind of planet I am on. I recognize there are fallen beings and dark spirits, that they are always seeking to create chaos and disharmony and that they will direct this at anybody who has any kind of harmony and peace." You can recognize that this is simply a force.

Now, my beloved, you may be in a thunder storm and the thunder claps are right over your head and they are very, very loud and there may be a lightning that strikes the ground not far from where you are. Do you feel that the thunder clouds are angry with you or are trying to hit you personally? I assume you do not at this level but you recognize that there are people in the world (and certainly in the past) who feel that there were aggressive spirits in nature who were out to get them personally. Therefore, they feel that there is an evil spirit trying to direct the lightning to hit them, instead of what you today tend to see as an impersonal natural force.

What I am trying to tell you here is that, surely, there are fallen beings who are targeting you because they want to stop your Christhood but they would target anybody with that level of Christhood. That is why I am saying that it is actually healthy for you to step back and look at this as simply a neutral, impersonal force. Therefore, you can avoid reacting personally to it. I am simply seeking to create a shift in your mind where you look at this and say: "I don't need to take this personally. I don't need to feel that I caused it, that I am responsible for it, that I need to react to it, that I need to change my behavior or my outlook on life in order to avoid this. I can simply look at this and then I can do the other aspect of turning the other cheek. I can look at it and let it pass right through me without having it create any reaction in me."

When other people cannot take your peace

It is an important initiation on the path to Christhood to be confronted with another human being who is angry at you, who is yelling all kinds of accusations at you, and yet you can stand there and have absolutely no reaction in you. When you can do this to the fallen beings and the dark forces and all other people, you can come to the point where you realize that you are not powerless. You have the power to take control over your own reactions, to root out the internal spirits that cause you to go into a reactionary pattern. When you exercise that power, you can come to the point where you have complete peace within yourself because you do not have an expectation of what other people should or should not do.

You know that whatever other people do, it will not create a reaction in you. Therefore, you do not need to expect because you do not need to be afraid that they are going to do something that creates a reaction in you. If you step back and take an honest look at your life up until this point, you will see that there are many, many times where you have been concerned about what other people might do. You knew that if they did certain things, it would create a reaction in you. The reaction in you was unpleasant and it might even cause you to blame yourself because you thought that a "spiritual person" should not react that way.

Just take an honest look at yourself and see how you may still have these mechanisms of avoidance. You are not seeking to compensate, you are seeking to avoid. You may also have a compensatory pattern where you are trying to be extra nice to people so they will not get mad at you. More often, it is a desire to avoid other people or other people's behavior because you want to avoid the reaction in yourself.

Naturally, you are now at the point where you can look at this and say: "But hey, the reaction is in *me*. That means I have power to change it. I don't need to change the other people anymore. I just need to change myself. I need to actually separate myself so I can see that this reaction is just an internal spirit. It is just *another* internal spirit like the many others that I have disposed of during this course so naturally I can dispose of this one too." You take the necessary steps that we have taught you. You let go of that spirit, you consume the energy, you see the illusion and then you are free.

Honestly, my beloved, you want at this point on the path to have peace in your relationship with other people. Are you ever going to attain that peace by changing other people? Obviously not, so the only way to attain it is to change yourself by letting go of the spirits and adopting the attitude that you do not need to change other people because your Christhood does not depend on the behavior of other people. It depends exclusively on what is going on inside your own four lower bodies, inside your own aura and mind.

A word about true service

Now, you will think, my beloved, that I have not so far said much about service. I will comment on this in connection with what I have said here. If you look at your life, you will see that there may be some expectations about what kind of service you should give to life as part of qualifying for your ascension, as part of your Divine plan. You may, in fact, have used the teachings of the ascended masters to build a certain expectation that makes you feel a certain tension in yourself.

You may feel that: "There must be a service I have to do but I'm not doing it or I'm not doing it enough. I'm just so busy with my everyday life that I don't have time to do this." You feel bad about this, you feel guilty, you feel like you are behind, you feel tense.

Now my beloved, I am in no way denying that you have a Divine plan or that you have a service to perform, but that service is not defined in your outer mind. It was defined by you before you came into embodiment and it was defined based on a higher awareness than you had when you came into embodiment.

Again, there was a point where you found a spiritual teaching, you learned about the concept of a Divine plan and giving service to life. This happened sometime in the past where you were at a lower level of consciousness than you are at right now. This means that in your outer mind, you formed an expectation based on the level of consciousness you had at the time and you have carried that expectation with you ever since. You think, therefore, that the way you looked at your Divine plan back then is the right way to look at it and you need to fulfill those expectations in a linear way.

What I am telling you is that you have now risen to a much higher level of consciousness. Therefore, it is time to look at this expectation and say: "It was simply unrealistic because it was based on a level of consciousness that was below where I am at right now. So I need to let go of this expectation, I need to step back and I need to allow the emergence of a new view of my Divine plan to come from within." In order to achieve this, you again need to have that openness, the innocent mind of the child. You can more easily adopt this if you will go with me on what I am telling you now.

I Nada, who is your primary initiator at this level of your path, hereby give you permission to let go of all expectations regarding your Divine plan and your service on earth. I give you permission to let it all drop; to put it all aside and to stop worrying about what you should do as part of your Divine plan or your service. I am giving you permission to set aside the entire sense that there is something you *should* do as a spiritual person.

If you are willing to go with me on this, it can create that silence, that lack of tension, in your mind where you can actually begin to listen within. You can hear what your I AM Presence wants you to know about your Divine plan instead of what some internal spirit (that you created at a lower level of consciousness) wants you to know about your Divine plan. Your Divine plan is *not* a source of stress. Your Divine plan is your greatest joy.

It is not something that is a duty or an obligation. It is not something that you feel you *have* to do. When there is a sense of obligation, duty or that you *have* to do this, it is because there is an internal spirit that is interfering with the process of your service to life. You need to then recognize this, neutralize it, step beyond it and listen. Listen with the open, innocent mind of the child, with a neutral mind and then you may receive the aspects of your Divine plan that are appropriate for your present level of consciousness. It will be a joy to receive it, not a burden.

My beloved I have given you many things to ponder here. I do not wish this lesson to be a burden to you. Therefore, I will then simply accept that I have given you enough to take you to the final level of initiation in my retreat. Here, I will help you attain greater freedom from the many pressures that you feel as an ascended master student on the path to the ascension.

15 | INVOKING PEACE IN RELATIONSHIPS

In the name I AM THAT I AM, Jesus Christ, I call to my I AM Presence to flow through the I Will Be Presence that I AM and give this invocation with full power. I call to beloved Elohim Peace and Aloha, Archangel Uriel and Aurora and Nada to help me attain peace in my relationships. Help me see and surrender all patterns that block my oneness with Nada and with my I AM Presence, including …

[Make personal calls]

Part 1

1. Nada, help me see my reactionary spirals with other people and my tendency to feel that when other people are taking aggressive actions against me, I am powerless to deal with this.

> O Elohim Peace, in Unity's Flame,
> there is no more room for duality's game,
> we know that all form is from the same source,
> empowering us to plot a new course.
>
> **O Elohim Peace, through your tranquility,**
> **we are free from the chaos of duality,**
> **in oneness with God a new identity,**
> **we are raising the earth into Infinity.**

2. Nada, help me see that I have an expectation about how life *should be* on earth, but it is out of touch with the reality of how life *is* on earth. There is a gap between my expectation and reality.

> O Elohim Peace, the bell now you ring,
> causing all atoms to vibrate and sing,
> we give up the sense of a separate "me,"
> we're crossing Samsara's turbulent sea.
>
> **O Elohim Peace, through your tranquility,**
> **we are free from the chaos of duality,**
> **in oneness with God a new identity,**
> **we are raising the earth into Infinity.**

3. I see that it is not possible for me to change the current situation on earth. The realistic course of action is to let go of the expectation that was created either on a different planet or when the earth was a different planet.

15 | Invoking Peace in Relationships

O Elohim Peace, you help us to know,
that Jesus has come your Flame to bestow,
upon all who are ready to give up the strife,
by following Christ into infinite life.

O Elohim Peace, through your tranquility,
we are free from the chaos of duality,
in oneness with God a new identity,
we are raising the earth into Infinity.

4. I recognize that I am carrying with me an unrealistic expectation and it is holding back my progress. It is creating a tension in me, causing me to be a house divided against itself, as all internal spirits do.

O Elohim Peace, through your eyes we see,
that only in oneness will we ever be free,
we now see that there is no separate thing,
to the ego-based self we no longer cling.

O Elohim Peace, through your tranquility,
we are free from the chaos of duality,
in oneness with God a new identity,
we are raising the earth into Infinity.

5. I let my expectation go, as I do with any other internal spirit. I look at what kind of planet I am on and I say: "Based on what I now know about this planet, based on what I know about free will, it is not realistic to have any expectation about what should or should not happen on earth."

O Elohim Peace, you show us the way,
for clearing the mind from duality's fray,
you pierce the illusions of both time and space,
separation consumed by your Infinite Grace.

**O Elohim Peace, through your tranquility,
we are free from the chaos of duality,
in oneness with God a new identity,
we are raising the earth into Infinity.**

6. I see that there is no reason to have any expectation and therefore there is no more resistance in me about life on earth. When I have no expectations about what should or should not happen, then I can meet life with the innocent mind of a child.

O Elohim Peace, what beauty your name,
consuming within us duality's shame,
the earth is set free from burden of fear,
accepting your peace is now manifest here.

**O Elohim Peace, through your tranquility,
we are free from the chaos of duality,
in oneness with God a new identity,
we are raising the earth into Infinity.**

7. When I adopt this childlike innocence of not having expectations about what should or should not happen, then I am in the kingdom of God in my own mind.

O Elohim Peace, with Christ at our side,
no force of duality can evermore hide,
It was through the vibration of your Golden Flame,
that Christ the illusion of death overcame.

> **O Elohim Peace, through your tranquility,**
> **we are free from the chaos of duality,**
> **in oneness with God a new identity,**
> **we are raising the earth into Infinity.**

8. There is no reason to expect what should or should not happen because nothing that happens or does not happen defines me. Nothing in the physical defines me. Nothing in the physical hinders my ascension.

> O Elohim Peace, you bring now to earth,
> the unstoppable flame of Cosmic Rebirth,
> we give up the sense that something is "mine,"
> allowing your Light through our beings to shine.

> **O Elohim Peace, through your tranquility,**
> **we are free from the chaos of duality,**
> **in oneness with God a new identity,**
> **we are raising the earth into Infinity.**

9. I look at other people and say: "Why should I have any expectations about what other people should or should not do?" I let go of the expectations that have put me in a constant state of tension with other people.

> O Elohim Peace, as peace now we feel,
> all records of war you totally heal,
> the earth is now free from forces of war,
> restoring her purity known from before.

**O Elohim Peace, through your tranquility,
we are free from the chaos of duality,
in oneness with God a new identity,
we are raising the earth into Infinity.**

Part 2

1. I see that my expectations have made me feel powerless because I have a desire to prevent other people from doing something harmful, but I feel I am not allowed to use any aggressive means to force them.

> O Elohim Peace, in Unity's Flame,
> there is no more room for duality's game,
> we know that all form is from the same source,
> empowering us to plot a new course.

**O Elohim Peace, through your tranquility,
we are free from the chaos of duality,
in oneness with God a new identity,
we are raising the earth into Infinity.**

2. Nada, help me see how, as an infant, I felt: "The world is an extension of me, I am the center of the world. Therefore, I am responsible for everything that happens. Everything that happens revolves around me and relates to me."

> O Elohim Peace, the bell now you ring,
> causing all atoms to vibrate and sing,
> we give up the sense of a separate "me,"
> we're crossing Samsara's turbulent sea.

15 | Invoking Peace in Relationships

**O Elohim Peace, through your tranquility,
we are free from the chaos of duality,
in oneness with God a new identity,
we are raising the earth into Infinity.**

3. I recognize that in my three higher bodies, especially in the emotional body, there is an internal spirit that still feels that it is the center of my world. This spirit feels that everything that happens in my life revolves around it. Everything that other people do relates to it.

O Elohim Peace, you help us to know,
that Jesus has come your Flame to bestow,
upon all who are ready to give up the strife,
by following Christ into infinite life.

**O Elohim Peace, through your tranquility,
we are free from the chaos of duality,
in oneness with God a new identity,
we are raising the earth into Infinity.**

4. This spirit causes me to feel that the people around me do what they do in relation to me. I feel responsible for it, I feel hurt by it, I feel that they are doing this to me.

O Elohim Peace, through your eyes we see,
that only in oneness will we ever be free,
we now see that there is no separate thing,
to the ego-based self we no longer cling.

**O Elohim Peace, through your tranquility,
we are free from the chaos of duality,
in oneness with God a new identity,
we are raising the earth into Infinity.**

5. I recognize that it is an internal spirit that feels this way. The Conscious You does not feel this way. The Conscious You knows that it is a separate being, that other people are separate beings and they have their free will, as I have my free will.

O Elohim Peace, you show us the way,
for clearing the mind from duality's fray,
you pierce the illusions of both time and space,
separation consumed by your Infinite Grace.

**O Elohim Peace, through your tranquility,
we are free from the chaos of duality,
in oneness with God a new identity,
we are raising the earth into Infinity.**

6. This spirit makes me feel that when other people are aggressive towards me, the person is doing this because of something I did. I feel responsible, I feel I am the cause of the other persons' behavior.

O Elohim Peace, what beauty your name,
consuming within us duality's shame,
the earth is set free from burden of fear,
accepting your peace is now manifest here.

> **O Elohim Peace, through your tranquility,**
> **we are free from the chaos of duality,**
> **in oneness with God a new identity,**
> **we are raising the earth into Infinity.**

7. The other person did not do what it did because of me. I am not responsible for the other persons' choices. I am responsible for my own choices but not for the other person's choices. I am responsible for my actions, but I am not responsible for how the other person reacted to it.

> O Elohim Peace, with Christ at our side,
> no force of duality can evermore hide,
> It was through the vibration of your Golden Flame,
> that Christ the illusion of death overcame.

> **O Elohim Peace, through your tranquility,**
> **we are free from the chaos of duality,**
> **in oneness with God a new identity,**
> **we are raising the earth into Infinity.**

8. Nada, help me say: "If I *am* one hundred percent responsible for my reactions, then I am one hundred percent *not* responsible for the reactions of other people. I may have done something that triggered a reaction in the other person, and it is this reaction that caused them to accuse me. I am responsible for my action, but I am not responsible for the other person's reaction."

> O Elohim Peace, you bring now to earth,
> the unstoppable flame of Cosmic Rebirth,
> we give up the sense that something is "mine,"
> allowing your Light through our beings to shine.

> **O Elohim Peace, through your tranquility,**
> **we are free from the chaos of duality,**
> **in oneness with God a new identity,**
> **we are raising the earth into Infinity.**

9. I can depersonalize any situation by realizing that the other person did not do this to me. The other person did it in response to me but the other person did not do it to me. I see the distinction in my mind.

> O Elohim Peace, as peace now we feel,
> all records of war you totally heal,
> the earth is now free from forces of war,
> restoring her purity known from before.

> **O Elohim Peace, through your tranquility,**
> **we are free from the chaos of duality,**
> **in oneness with God a new identity,**
> **we are raising the earth into Infinity.**

Part 3

1. As an aspect of growing in Christ consciousness, I make this distinction: "What the other person is doing is not directly done against me. It is not a personal attack on me. It is something that is caused by the persons' internal reactions."

> Uriel Archangel, immense is the power,
> of angels of peace, all war to devour.
> The demons of war, no match for your light,
> consuming them all, with radiance so bright.

15 | Invoking Peace in Relationships

> **Uriel Archangel, use your great sword,**
> **Uriel Archangel, consume all discord,**
> **Uriel Archangel, we're of one accord,**
> **Uriel Archangel, we walk with the Lord.**

2. The biggest challenge for me on earth is dealing with family members. I feel I have to react to them and I have to take them seriously, I have to take what they do personally.

> Uriel Archangel, intense is the sound,
> when millions of angels, their voices compound.
> They build a crescendo, piercing the night,
> life's glorious oneness revealed to our sight.

> **Uriel Archangel, use your great sword,**
> **Uriel Archangel, consume all discord,**
> **Uriel Archangel, we're of one accord,**
> **Uriel Archangel, we walk with the Lord.**

3. I have built these reactionary patterns, and if a family member is angry at me, I feel responsible, I feel I have to take this personally, I have to look at how I can change to avoid the person being angry.

> Uriel Archangel, from out the Great Throne,
> your millions of trumpets, sound the One Tone.
> Consuming all discord with your harmony,
> the sound of all sounds will set all life free.

> **Uriel Archangel, use your great sword,**
> **Uriel Archangel, consume all discord,**
> **Uriel Archangel, we're of one accord,**
> **Uriel Archangel, we walk with the Lord.**

4. Nada, help me recognize that these people are not doing this to me personally. The other person's anger is not tied to me personally. It could just as well be directed at another person than me.

> Uriel Archangel, all war is now done,
> for you bring a message, from heart of the One.
> The hearts of all men, now singing in peace,
> the spirals of love, forever increase.

> **Uriel Archangel, use your great sword,**
> **Uriel Archangel, consume all discord,**
> **Uriel Archangel, we're of one accord,**
> **Uriel Archangel, we walk with the Lord.**

5. The other person's anger is not personal towards me, it is personal inside that person's consciousness. The anger is inside that person's emotional, mental and identity bodies. I may have triggered the anger but I am not the cause of it. The cause is an internal mechanism in that person's psychology.

> Uriel Archangel, your infinite peace,
> from all warring beings our planet release,
> war is a prison from which we are free,
> embracing the peace of true unity.

> **Uriel Archangel, use your great sword,**
> **Uriel Archangel, consume all discord,**
> **Uriel Archangel, we're of one accord,**
> **Uriel Archangel, we walk with the Lord.**

6. Nada, help me see that my willingness to look at my own psychology should not cause me to take on the responsibility

for the psychological mechanism that is in the minds of other people.

> Uriel Archangel, we send forth the call,
> reveal now the oneness that unifies all,
> help us the vision of peace now to see,
> so we from all conflicts and struggles are free.

> **Uriel Archangel, use your great sword,**
> **Uriel Archangel, consume all discord,**
> **Uriel Archangel, we're of one accord,**
> **Uriel Archangel, we walk with the Lord.**

7. The other person's anger is a psychological mechanism in his or her four lower bodies, not in *my* mind, not in *my* four lower bodies. Therefore, I will not take responsibility for it and try to change myself to avoid the anger in the other person. The anger is there and it is just waiting for another trigger.

> Uriel Archangel, in service to life,
> you give us release from struggle and strife,
> forgetting the self is truly the key,
> to living a life in true harmony.

> **Uriel Archangel, use your great sword,**
> **Uriel Archangel, consume all discord,**
> **Uriel Archangel, we're of one accord,**
> **Uriel Archangel, we walk with the Lord.**

8. Nada, help me see if, in order to avoid another person's anger, I have created an unbalanced action in myself, a reactionary pattern. Help me make the discernment that: "I'm not going to feel responsible for other people's psychological

issues and I'm not going to allow myself to continue to carry these internal spirits that I created in order to compensate for or avoid their emotional issues."

> Uriel Archangel, the earth now you raise,
> out of duality's death-bringing haze,
> we call now upon your great Flame of Peace,
> commanding that all petty squabbles do cease.
>
> **Uriel Archangel, use your great sword,**
> **Uriel Archangel, consume all discord,**
> **Uriel Archangel, we're of one accord,**
> **Uriel Archangel, we walk with the Lord.**

9. Nada, help me look at myself in relation to other people and see where I have built this reactionary pattern. Help me see that there is a spirit behind it and let go of that spirit. I have a right to let this spirit go.

> Uriel Archangel, as peace is the norm,
> to your higher vision the earth does conform,
> as people have found your peace from within,
> a Golden Age is the prize that we win.
>
> **Uriel Archangel, use your great sword,**
> **Uriel Archangel, consume all discord,**
> **Uriel Archangel, we're of one accord,**
> **Uriel Archangel, we walk with the Lord.**

15 | Invoking Peace in Relationships

Part 4

1. Nada, help me find a different way to relate to people so I can attain peace in my relationship with other people. Help me free myself from the reactionary patterns and be myself.

> Uriel Archangel, immense is the power,
> of angels of peace, all war to devour.
> The demons of war, no match for your light,
> consuming them all, with radiance so bright.
>
> **Uriel Archangel, use your great sword,**
> **Uriel Archangel, consume all discord,**
> **Uriel Archangel, we're of one accord,**
> **Uriel Archangel, we walk with the Lord.**

2. I will express myself at my present level of consciousness and thereby give the other person an opportunity to rise above his or her patterns. If they do not take it, then it does not really make any difference to me because I am not disturbed by it.

> Uriel Archangel, intense is the sound,
> when millions of angels, their voices compound.
> They build a crescendo, piercing the night,
> life's glorious oneness revealed to our sight.
>
> **Uriel Archangel, use your great sword,**
> **Uriel Archangel, consume all discord,**
> **Uriel Archangel, we're of one accord,**
> **Uriel Archangel, we walk with the Lord.**

3. Nada, help me say about a close relationship: "If the other person does not change, I can live with that." Then, I also have the right to decide that I may not want to live with the other person and I am free to walk away.

> Uriel Archangel, from out the Great Throne,
> your millions of trumpets, sound the One Tone.
> Consuming all discord with your harmony,
> the sound of all sounds will set all life free.
>
> **Uriel Archangel, use your great sword,**
> **Uriel Archangel, consume all discord,**
> **Uriel Archangel, we're of one accord,**
> **Uriel Archangel, we walk with the Lord.**

4. When I have risen above the consciousness that other people have, I have a right to decide that I prefer to associate with people at my level of consciousness or above.

> Uriel Archangel, all war is now done,
> for you bring a message, from heart of the One.
> The hearts of all men, now singing in peace,
> the spirals of love, forever increase.
>
> **Uriel Archangel, use your great sword,**
> **Uriel Archangel, consume all discord,**
> **Uriel Archangel, we're of one accord,**
> **Uriel Archangel, we walk with the Lord.**

5. The fallen beings love to violate me, cause me to go into a certain reaction to them and then make me feel that because my reaction was not the highest possible, I must have made karma with the fallen beings.

> Uriel Archangel, your infinite peace,
> from all warring beings our planet release,
> war is a prison from which we are free,
> embracing the peace of true unity.
>
> **Uriel Archangel, use your great sword,**
> **Uriel Archangel, consume all discord,**
> **Uriel Archangel, we're of one accord,**
> **Uriel Archangel, we walk with the Lord.**

6. If I took a physical action, for example fighting back and killing the fallen beings, then I did make karma for that action. If I could avoid taking the physical action, then I did not make karma. I do not make karma for responding at the level of consciousness I am at.

> Uriel Archangel, we send forth the call,
> reveal now the oneness that unifies all,
> help us the vision of peace now to see,
> so we from all conflicts and struggles are free.
>
> **Uriel Archangel, use your great sword,**
> **Uriel Archangel, consume all discord,**
> **Uriel Archangel, we're of one accord,**
> **Uriel Archangel, we walk with the Lord.**

7. Nada, help me take the liberating step of depersonalizing my relationship to other people by saying: "Whatever they do to me, it is not personal against me because they're acting based on their level of consciousness, based on their illusions, perhaps based on being possessed by dark forces."

Uriel Archangel, in service to life,
you give us release from struggle and strife,
forgetting the self is truly the key,
to living a life in true harmony.

Uriel Archangel, use your great sword,
Uriel Archangel, consume all discord,
Uriel Archangel, we're of one accord,
Uriel Archangel, we walk with the Lord.

8. "It is not me exclusively they are acting against. If I wasn't here, they would just find someone else to act against, they would just find someone else to be their excuse for their aggression that is inside of them and that they need to take out on somebody because they can't stand having it inside themselves."

Uriel Archangel, the earth now you raise,
out of duality's death-bringing haze,
we call now upon your great Flame of Peace,
commanding that all petty squabbles do cease.

Uriel Archangel, use your great sword,
Uriel Archangel, consume all discord,
Uriel Archangel, we're of one accord,
Uriel Archangel, we walk with the Lord.

9. When people commit any kind of aggression against others, it is not against those others. It is simply that they have such tension inside themselves that they have to direct it outwards in order to be able to stand being in their own auras.

15 | Invoking Peace in Relationships

Uriel Archangel, as peace is the norm,
to your higher vision the earth does conform,
as people have found your peace from within,
a Golden Age is the prize that we win.

**Uriel Archangel, use your great sword,
Uriel Archangel, consume all discord,
Uriel Archangel, we're of one accord,
Uriel Archangel, we walk with the Lord.**

Part 5

1. When other people take aggressive actions, they are temporarily possessed by a dark spirit, they are not in control of their actions, they are not acting rationally. Therefore, I say: "I recognize what kind of planet I am on. I recognize there are fallen beings and dark spirits, that they are always seeking to create chaos and disharmony and that they will direct this at anybody who has any kind of harmony and peace. I recognize this as an impersonal force."

Master Nada, beauty's power,
unfolding like a sacred flower.
Master Nada, so sublime,
a will that conquers even time.

**Master Nada, peace you give,
forevermore in peace we live,
our planet has a peaceful morn,
the Golden Age is hereby born.**

2. Nada, help me to step back, look at this as a neutral, impersonal force and therefore avoid reacting personally to it. I am willing to shift my mind and say: "I don't need to take this personally. I don't need to feel that I caused it, that I am responsible for it, that I need to react to it, that I need to change my behavior or my outlook on life in order to avoid this. I can simply look at this and then I can do the other aspect of turning the other cheek. I can look at it and let it pass right through me without having it create any reaction in me."

> Master Nada, you bestow,
> upon us wisdom's rushing flow.
> Master Nada, mind so strong
> rising on your wings of song.

> **Master Nada, peace you give,**
> **forevermore in peace we live,**
> **our planet has a peaceful morn,**
> **the Golden Age is hereby born.**

3. When other people cannot force a reaction in me, I am not powerless. I have the power to take control over my own reactions, to root out the internal spirits that cause me to go into a reactionary pattern.

> Master Nada, precious scent,
> your love is truly heaven-sent.
> Master Nada, kind and soft
> on wings of love we rise aloft.

15 | Invoking Peace in Relationships

> **Master Nada, peace you give,**
> **forevermore in peace we live,**
> **our planet has a peaceful morn,**
> **the Golden Age is hereby born.**

4. When I exercise that power, I can come to the point where I have complete peace within myself because I do not have an expectation of what other people should or should not do.

> Master Nada, mother light,
> our hearts are rising like a kite.
> Master Nada, from your view,
> all life is pure as morning dew.

> **Master Nada, peace you give,**
> **forevermore in peace we live,**
> **our planet has a peaceful morn,**
> **the Golden Age is hereby born.**

5. I know that whatever other people do, it will not create a reaction in me. Therefore, I do not need to expect because I do not need to be afraid that they are going to do something that creates a reaction in me.

> Master Nada, truth you bring,
> as morning birds in love do sing.
> Master Nada, we now feel,
> your love that all four bodies heal.

> **Master Nada, peace you give,**
> **forevermore in peace we live,**
> **our planet has a peaceful morn,**
> **the Golden Age is hereby born.**

6. Nada, help me see where I have been concerned about what other people might do. I knew that if they did certain things, it would create a reaction in me. The reaction was unpleasant and it caused me to blame myself.

> Master Nada, serve in peace,
> as all emotions we release.
> Master Nada, life is fun,
> the solar plexus is a sun.
>
> **Master Nada, peace you give,**
> **forevermore in peace we live,**
> **our planet has a peaceful morn,**
> **the Golden Age is hereby born.**

7. Nada, help me see any mechanisms of avoidance where I am not seeking to compensate, I am seeking to avoid. Help me see any compensatory pattern where I am trying to be nice to people so they will not get mad at me.

> Master Nada, love is free,
> conditions we no longer see.
> Master Nada, rise above,
> all human forms of lesser love.
>
> **Master Nada, peace you give,**
> **forevermore in peace we live,**
> **our planet has a peaceful morn,**
> **the Golden Age is hereby born.**

8. Nada, help me see any desire to avoid other people or other people's behavior because I want to avoid the reaction in myself.

15 | Invoking Peace in Relationships

> Master Nada, balance all,
> the seven rays upon our call.
> Master Nada, rise and shine,
> your radiant beauty most divine.
>
> **Master Nada, peace you give,**
> **forevermore in peace we live,**
> **our planet has a peaceful morn,**
> **the Golden Age is hereby born.**

9. Nada, help me look at this and say: "But the reaction is in me. That means I have power to change it. I don't need to change the other people anymore. I just need to change myself."

> Nada Dear, your Presence here,
> filling up the inner sphere.
> Life is now a sacred flow,
> God Peace we do on all bestow.
>
> **Master Nada, peace you give,**
> **forevermore in peace we live,**
> **our planet has a peaceful morn,**
> **the Golden Age is hereby born.**

Part 6

1. "I need to separate myself so I can see that this reaction is just an internal spirit. It is just another internal spirit like the many others that I have disposed of during this course so naturally I can dispose of this one too."

> Master Nada, beauty's power,
> unfolding like a sacred flower.
> Master Nada, so sublime,
> a will that conquers even time.
>
> **Master Nada, peace you give,
> forevermore in peace we live,
> our planet has a peaceful morn,
> the Golden Age is hereby born.**

2. I want to have peace in my relationship with other people. I am never going to attain that peace by changing other people. The only way to attain it is to change myself by letting go of the spirits and adopting the attitude that I do not need to change other people.

> Master Nada, you bestow,
> upon us wisdom's rushing flow.
> Master Nada, mind so strong
> rising on your wings of song.
>
> **Master Nada, peace you give,
> forevermore in peace we live,
> our planet has a peaceful morn,
> the Golden Age is hereby born.**

3. My Christhood does not depend on the behavior of other people. It depends exclusively on what is going on inside my own four lower bodies, inside my own aura and mind.

15 | Invoking Peace in Relationships

Master Nada, precious scent,
your love is truly heaven-sent.
Master Nada, kind and soft
on wings of love we rise aloft.

**Master Nada, peace you give,
forevermore in peace we live,
our planet has a peaceful morn,
the Golden Age is hereby born.**

4. Nada, help me overcome any unrealistic expectations about what kind of service I should give as part of qualifying for my ascension, as part of my Divine plan. Help me see if I have used the teachings of the ascended masters to build an expectation that makes me feel a tension in myself.

Master Nada, mother light,
our hearts are rising like a kite.
Master Nada, from your view,
all life is pure as morning dew.

**Master Nada, peace you give,
forevermore in peace we live,
our planet has a peaceful morn,
the Golden Age is hereby born.**

5. When I learned about the concept of a Divine plan, I was at a lower level of consciousness. In my outer mind, I formed an expectation based on that level of consciousness and I have carried it ever since.

> Master Nada, truth you bring,
> as morning birds in love do sing.
> Master Nada, we now feel,
> your love that all four bodies heal.
>
> **Master Nada, peace you give,**
> **forevermore in peace we live,**
> **our planet has a peaceful morn,**
> **the Golden Age is hereby born.**

6. I have now risen to a much higher level of consciousness and I am willing to look at this expectation and say: "It was simply unrealistic because it was based on a level of consciousness that was below where I am at right now. So I need to let go of this expectation, I need to step back and I need to allow the emergence of a new view of my Divine plan to come from within."

> Master Nada, serve in peace,
> as all emotions we release.
> Master Nada, life is fun,
> the solar plexus is a sun.
>
> **Master Nada, peace you give,**
> **forevermore in peace we live,**
> **our planet has a peaceful morn,**
> **the Golden Age is hereby born.**

7. Nada, I accept that you give me permission to let go of all expectations regarding my Divine plan and my service on earth. You give me permission to let it all drop; to put it all aside and to stop worrying about what I should do as part of my Divine plan or my service. You give me permission to set

aside the entire sense that there is something I *should* do as a spiritual person.

> Master Nada, love is free,
> conditions we no longer see.
> Master Nada, rise above,
> all human forms of lesser love.
>
> **Master Nada, peace you give,**
> **forevermore in peace we live,**
> **our planet has a peaceful morn,**
> **the Golden Age is hereby born.**

8. I now accept the silence, the lack of tension, in my mind where I can begin to listen within. I can hear what my I AM Presence wants me to know about my Divine plan instead of what some internal spirit wants me to know.

> Master Nada, balance all,
> the seven rays upon our call.
> Master Nada, rise and shine,
> your radiant beauty most divine.
>
> **Master Nada, peace you give,**
> **forevermore in peace we live,**
> **our planet has a peaceful morn,**
> **the Golden Age is hereby born.**

9. My Divine plan is not a source of stress. My Divine plan is my greatest joy. It is not something that is a duty or an obligation. It is not something that I feel I *have* to do. I listen with the open, innocent mind of the child and I receive the aspects

of my Divine plan that are appropriate for my present level of consciousness.

> Nada Dear, your Presence here,
> filling up the inner sphere.
> Life is now a sacred flow,
> God Peace we do on all bestow.
>
> **Master Nada, peace you give,**
> **forevermore in peace we live,**
> **our planet has a peaceful morn,**
> **the Golden Age is hereby born.**

Sealing:

In the name of the Divine Mother, I fully accept that the power of these calls is used to set free the River of Life, so it can outpicture the perfect vision of Christ for my own life, for all people and for the planet. In the name I AM THAT I AM, it is done! Amen.

16 | AN ESCAPE FROM ESCAPISM

I AM the Ascended Master Nada, and I welcome you with great joy to this final level of the initiations in my retreat. I would like to begin by looking at what I said about human relationships in my last lesson. You recognize, when you step back from this, that the vast majority (and I am talking over ninety-nine percent) of human relationships are based on, driven by, controlled by internal spirits in all of the people involved in the relationship. You can look at many families and you can see that their interaction is completely driven by these internal spirits that they have built, perhaps even over several lifetimes. There is very rarely, if ever, in the course of one lifetime this moment of clarity where the people are relating to each other directly, openly, without these filters.

You will see in many love relationships that when two people first meet and fall in love, they may have a period where they are able to be open with each other. Then, as the relationship moves into a more settled pattern, the internal spirits begin to take over. Naturally, as an ascended master student, you can look at this and you can say: "I do not want the rest of my life to be driven by these internal spirits, where I'm constantly reacting to the internal spirits of other people through the internal spirits in my own being." Naturally, you want to make an effort and use the tools we have given you to rise above these internal spirits that you have regarding your relationship to other people.

Freedom from internal pressure

You can then take this one step further and look at: "What is my relationship to the ascended masters, to the spiritual path? Is the way I have approached the spiritual path so far also affected by internal spirits?" Of course, it *is* to some degree. I said in my last discourse that I would like to set you free from all pressures you have regarding being an ascended master student on the path to the ascension. If you will step back and look at yourself honestly, you will see that you have certain tensions about what you *should* or *should not* do as an ascended master student.

We have seen examples in the past where an organization sponsored by the ascended masters had built a collective culture that was very much based on a set of outer rules for what one *should* or *should not* do as a member of that organization. This resulted in the entire organization being enveloped in a collective spirit of judging each other where people were constantly judging each other based on these outer criteria. You see the same thing in many religious organizations but you see it also in political organizations and other types of settings, including, of course, families. You see that there is this tendency in the world to set up a standard for how one should behave as a member of a particular group and then to judge those who do not fall in line with the collective expectation or standard.

My beloved, you have free will and I respect your free will. You are, of course, allowed to continue your present pattern of relating to the ascended masters in a certain way through a certain internal spirit that is created based on a collective spirit. However, if you want to continue basing your relationship to spiritual teachers on such internal spirits and collective spirits, I have a request for you. Please leave *us,* the ascended masters, out of your little mind games. Please find some other teacher with whom you can play these games because we are not interested in playing these games with you.

We have now reached a point in this course where we collectively are confronting you with the need to step beyond these games. Stop relating to us through any and all of these human games that are often inspired by the fallen beings. Build a more direct personal relationship where you approach us with the open and innocent mind of a child and do not look at us through these filters. There are, of course, many such collective spirits and internal spirits that people have created in relation to the teacher, to authority figures and to other people. We have given you the tools in this course to come to see them, to identify them, to rise above them.

I am asking you, as a result of completing this level of the course, to take some time before you start the seventh level under Saint Germain to look at your relationship to ascended masters, look at the internal spirits you have relating to us and be willing to make an effort to dismiss those spirits. I am doing this because it is the goal of these first six of the Chohans to prepare you for the initiations you will receive from Saint Germain. These initiations will relate very much to how you can exercise your co-creative abilities. In order to fully exercise your co-creative abilities, you naturally need to have overcome these illusions at the lower levels of consciousness that prevent you from being fully creative because you think that the only way to be creative is to express yourself through some internal spirit.

You cannot – obviously – be truly creative if you are trying to be creative through an internal spirit. You are truly creative only when you are so free of internal spirits that there is an opening for the Light of your I AM Presence to shine through you and drive your creative efforts. As Jesus said: "I can of my own self (the lower self, the four lower bodies) do nothing. It is the Father (the I AM Presence) within me who is doing the work."

A special version of the flight response

As my final step on your path, I will talk about another mechanism that has been identified by psychologists. I have already talked about the mechanism of how you want to avoid certain things, the magical thinking where you think you are the center of the universe and you take everything personally. What I want to talk about now is the mechanism that psychologists have called the fight-or-flight response.

Now, if you look at many people today in the world, you can see that their interactions with other human beings is very much based on the fight response. People are very, very sensitive and they take everything personally so it takes very little for them to feel attacked by others. When they feel attacked by others, then they feel fully justified in going into a defense response where they fight back. They are defending themselves by attacking the other person. You will see many, many times in arguments where one person says something that makes the other person feel attacked. Now, the second person attacks back and the argument keeps rolling until both of them run out of energy (for the time being) and they go their separate ways. Many times, they come back later and continue the argument when they have gathered enough energy to do so.

My beloved, this is, of course, driven by internal spirits and by some very powerful collective spirits. What I need you to recognize here is that you are a spiritual person, you have been a spiritual person for many lifetimes. Many of you who are following this course have been on a spiritual path for most of the 2,000-year period in which Jesus gave his teachings about turning the other cheek, loving your enemies, doing unto others what you want them to do onto you. You have followed the outer teachings of Christianity to the best of your ability and you have attempted to overcome this fight response that is so built into the psychology of many people on earth. This fight response, of course, is caused by an external spirit that goes very, very far back in the history of this planet and therefore has grown very strong. It has been reinforced over and over again and is being reinforced today by the many people who act this way.

Many of you have, over the past 2,000 years, made an effort to free yourself from this tendency. However, because the teachings of Jesus were distorted and perverted and because so many things were left out, you have not necessarily always been able to do this in the way Jesus intended. Jesus, of course, intended you to walk the path of Christhood under him directly during these past 2,000 years. Many of you have not been able to find such a path because the outer teachings of Jesus were so distorted and because mystical esoteric movements were suppressed by Christianity.

You need to recognize here that it is a sort of instinctual response that when you are faced with aggression from other people, you either go into a fight mode or a flight mode. Now, there is, of course, a Christhood-based alternative to both of these, but when you do not have the path to Christhood, you often cannot see how you can, so to speak, respond in a more direct way to aggression. Therefore, most of you have gone into this tendency to feel that you should never show aggression, you should always turn the other cheek, do unto others and avoid being aggressive when you are exposed to aggression.

Now, based on your outer knowledge, the outer knowledge that was available after the creation of the distorted Christian churches, this was a reasonable and practical response. You could do little else. It has been constructive for you to, so to speak, discipline yourself not to react with aggression, not to respond in kind. However, you need to recognize that when you cannot be direct in response to aggression, it is almost inevitable that you switch and go into the flight response. The flight response is, of course, where you seek to get away from the condition that is difficult or unbearable to you. You seek to get away from the aggressor. This has partly set up the avoidance patterns I talked about in my last discourse but there is more to it.

An escape offered by fallen beings

Now my beloved, if you look at the 144 levels of consciousness, then you can say that the teachings that Jesus gave 2,000 years ago, the outer teachings that are recorded in the scriptures, were truly given for people who were not too far below the 48th level. They were given in order to help people quickly rise to the 48th level and then begin the path of rising towards the 96th level. What you realize here is that for each of the steps from the 48th level of consciousness to the 96th level of consciousness, there is a certain illusion that needs to be overcome. There is a certain collective spirit that needs to be overcome and in your being there is an internal spirit that needs to be overcome.

For each of these levels this presents you with a certain challenge. When you are at, say the 48th level of consciousness, you are looking at life through a certain filter. This means that when you are exposed to a certain action from another person, you might tend to look at this as an aggressive action. This means that at the 48th level, there is a certain fight-or-flight response that is normal for this level. At the 48th level, if you go into the fight response, you might take a certain aggressive action based on you feeling a certain anger. You are very likely to defend yourself even against physical attack.

When you now have adopted the outlook of Jesus that you should avoid physical aggression (you should turn the other cheek, you should be non-aggressive) what do you then do? You go into the flight response that is normal at the 48th level. There is nothing else you *can* do. This is not said to blame you; this is what we all did. What you need to recognize here is that the fallen beings are very clever. I have said that they like to create a certain division in your psyche. They like to get people to a point where they are out of control of their lives, where their minds are completely chaotic. Therefore, the fallen beings, at any moment, can stir them into being angry or reacting in other unbalanced ways. There are people who come to a point where they simply refuse to play this game, at least in its extreme forms. What do the fallen beings do for such people? Well, if they cannot get people to go into the *fight* response, then they are very clever at getting people to go into the *flight* response.

This means that the fallen beings on the one hand present you with an unpleasant aggressive condition that you seemingly cannot escape on the physical. Since they cannot get you to fight back, they offer you an escape from the condition, they offer you some form of escape from the condition that they have created. As I said, some people tend to go into the fight response. They are trapped by the fallen beings in this pattern of aggression in response to aggression. Those who break this pattern, who transcend this pattern and refuse to respond to aggression with aggression, they then are (very often without realizing it) going into the escape that the fallen beings offer them at their level of consciousness. What I am telling you here is that if you look at the levels of consciousness from the 48th to the 96th level (and for that matter the levels of consciousness below the 48th level), you will see that for each level there is a certain escape mechanism whereby you can escape what you at that level feel you cannot stand, you cannot deal with.

You cannot fight it; you cannot live with being exposed to it all the time so you are looking for a way out, a way to get away from it. Now, where are these escape mechanisms? Well, many of them are in the physical. You can see, for example (which I trust should be easy) that drugs and alcohol are some of the primary physical escape mechanisms. There are also other physical escape mechanisms where people, for example, as you saw in the Middle Ages, build stone castles and fortifications so they can sit behind these thick walls and feel they are protected against aggression. There are many ways that people seek to get away from potential danger by moving to remote locations. There are many people, for example, who have been involved in war and conflict in a past lifetime and in this lifetime they have chosen to live as farmers in a very remote location where they are not likely to ever encounter war in this lifetime.

Of course, nothing that the fallen beings do in the physical is just physical so there also is an escape mechanism, or a realm of escape, in the astral plane, in the emotional realm, in the mental realm and even some in the lower identity realm. What you will see is that many people have found a way to somewhat protect themselves against the worst forms of human aggression in this lifetime. You can see in many of the more evolved countries where there is not such a risk of war that people live a very comfortable, protected life. You can even see some very rich people who live in so-called gated communities where people cannot simply walk in but they need some kind of permission to enter. There are many examples where people have sought to physically isolate themselves. However, nothing you do is just physical so there is a parallel to your physical actions in consciousness. Or rather, we might say that your physical actions are caused by a reaction in consciousness.

Escapism in the mind

How is that reaction formed? It is formed by you having a desire. You are making a decision: "I never want to experience this again." Since you cannot take aggressive actions against it, then you go into the escape mechanism, the flight mechanism, where you seek to escape it in the mind. You accept a certain collective spirit, you create an internal spirit that offers you (in your mind) an escape or a relief from the condition in the physical that you no longer want to face.

You need to recognize here that for each of the levels between the 48th to the 96th level, there is a certain escape mechanism that, if you take it, ties you to the astral plane, the mental realm or the identity realm. You are tied to that level of the fallen beings where you can go in and you can feel a relief and you can feel safe from certain conditions. You will see, for example, that in the emotional realm there is a certain realm where you are offered the sense that if you are rich enough, then you are protected. You will see many rich people who have a strong tie to this realm in their emotional bodies and they feel secure as long as they have enough money. It is not really, obviously, that the money makes them feel secure. It is a *feeling* and that feeling is in their emotional bodies but it is reinforced by this realm in the emotional body of the planet. There are fallen beings, entities and demons there who are actually making people feel secure because it lulls them asleep and prevents them from walking the path to Christhood where you find the Christic Way, the Christ-based way, to respond to the condition that people want to avoid.

I am not saying here that you need to go back and look at every step from the 48th through the 96th level and find your escape mechanism. Most likely, you do not have one left for each of these levels but you still have some escape mechanisms left. This, of course, ties in with what I started out talking about, of how you play certain games with the idea of a teacher. The simple reality is, my beloved, that many people have used a religious or spiritual teaching as the basis for their personal escape mechanism.

You can see in more extreme forms, for example, how certain Christian fundamentalist groups are absolutely sure that they have the only literal interpretation of the Bible. They feel that because of their beliefs, they are guaranteed to be saved. Many of them feel that this salvation is very close because just about any moment now Jesus is going to appear in the sky, take them to heaven, send all other people to hell and then roll up the world as a scroll. This is their escape mechanism. There are certain conditions in the world that they cannot deal with and in order to avoid dealing with them, they have created this sense that because they belong to this outer religion, they will be saved. This makes them feel secure.

You understand that the purpose of any escape mechanism is to make you feel secure. This also prevents you from transcending yourself because if you feel secure, why would you need to transcend yourself and walk the path of Christhood? You can just stay at your certain level and wait for the outer savior to come and save you.

You can see that members of other religions have done the same thing. If you then take a look at New Age teachings, you will see again that many people have come up with various teachings that are simply escape mechanisms. Take for example the hysteria generated before 2012 and the supposed end of the Mayan calendar. Look how many people felt that some major event would happen and they, of course, would be the ones who had anticipated it and then they would get some prominent position after the event because of this. This was an escape mechanism that made people feel secure, that made people feel they could deal with life on earth as it is because they had created this condition in their minds of what would happen in the near or distant future.

You no longer need these escape mechanisms

The reality here is that you are on a dark planet; you are on a very difficult planet. There are many conditions on this earth that are very difficult to deal with emotionally, mentally and in your identity body. In order to be able to live here, then it is almost unavoidable that you create this escape mechanism so you can still feel somewhat safe, somewhat secure. You can feel you have some kind of equilibrium in this very difficult world.

Again, I am not blaming you, my beloved. There is no blame for the fact that you created an escape mechanism. I am simply saying that at this level of the path, where you are preparing yourself to go into a direct relationship with Saint Germain and learn to use your co-creative abilities, it is time for you to look at your most obvious escape mechanisms and simply realize that you no longer need them at this level of consciousness. When you reach a certain level of Christhood, you no longer need the escape mechanism because now whatever condition in the world used to be unbearable to you 48 levels of consciousness lower, is no longer unbearable.

When you have a certain amount of Christ discernment, you can deal with a condition in a constructive manner without feeling that this is too much. My beloved, to be brutally honest with you, if you look at the New Age movement, ninety-eight percent of the activities in that movement are nothing but escape mechanisms. This may seem shocking and from a certain perspective it *is* shocking. Of course, when you look at formal religions, it is the same. When you look at political movements it is much the same. Many of the people who, throughout the last couple of hundred years, believed in Marxism in some form did so as an escape mechanism. Other people have done so in other ways by thinking there is an ideal society in the future and they are the avant-garde who are the only ones who can see it.

What I need you to do here, as an extension of these seven initiations you have received from me and those you have received from the other Chohans, is to be willing to step back and look at your personal escape mechanism. As a preparation for being ready to begin the initiations under Saint Germain, I need you to look at how you have used the teachings of the ascended masters to reinforce an already existing escape mechanism that you have carried with you for lifetimes.

One of the primary ways that religious people have created escape mechanisms is the idea that their religion has the *only* truth, the *absolute* truth or the *highest possible* truth. This has set them apart from those who are not members of their religion. It has made them feel that they are the ones who are guaranteed to be saved whereas all others may not be saved or for sure will not be saved.

Escape from looking at yourself

You see how this has given people an excuse for saying: "But I am in this outer movement, I believe in this outer teaching. I don't do what they tell me not to do and I do most of the things they tell me to do. I am therefore a good member of this outer religion and therefore I don't need to look at certain things in my own psychology. I don't need to look at the beam in my own eye."

This is the primary effect of escape mechanisms when it comes to religion especially. This particular collective spirit is very, very strong on this planet. It is impossible for you to have been in embodiment on this planet for any length of time without having been affected by it. I especially say to you, as I said before, that many of you have adopted the Christian ideal of non-aggression without having the full teachings on Christhood. Therefore, you have felt you were stuck, you have felt you were powerless. You were exposed to aggression but you could not take aggressive counter-measures and so you have felt that your religious ideals made you powerless.

As a result of this, you have had a need to escape that which you could not change and which you could not deal with. Now, what we have taught you in this course, all of us six Chohans, is that you are never powerless. There is never a situation on earth that you cannot deal with by overcoming the internal spirit that causes you to react to that condition with fight or flight. You see here that you need to look at: "What are the conditions here on earth that I feel I cannot deal with, I cannot live with?" When you recognize the condition that you feel you cannot live with, then you can begin to identify the escape mechanism you have created in order to bring yourself to the point where you know you are in physical embodiment, you know this condition exists on the planet, but still you have come to a point where you have used a mechanism to feel secure. You can feel that you have yourself somewhat together even though this condition is still on the planet.

I need you to be willing to look at this because, my beloved, as long as you are relating to the ascended masters or to your I AM Presence through the filter of these escape mechanisms, you cannot really begin to exercise your true role as a co-creator. The reality here is that some of you have, as part of your Divine plan, that you will deal with the very mechanism that you now feel is unbearable. How can you deal with that particular condition if the way you look at the condition is colored by an escape mechanism that just makes you want to get away from the condition? This is not that you have to experience war, for example, at the physical but it may be that you are meant to challenge a certain aspect of the consciousness behind war. *That* you cannot do as long as you have an escape mechanism that makes you not want to look at war because you do not want to again experience the trauma that you experienced in the past when you were exposed to war. You see the pattern, my beloved?

Escapism blocks your Divine plan

In order to fulfill your Divine plane and help raise this planet above a certain consciousness, you need to be willing to look at that consciousness and go into it at the identity level, at the mental level, at the emotional level. You need to go in and look at your own illusions about this and look at the collective illusions. Then, you overcome it in yourself and then challenge it collectively either by making the calls or by speaking out in some way. The first condition that needs to be fulfilled here is that you are no longer seeking to escape the condition that you are meant to help change. You cannot change something while running away from it because the only way to change something is to look at it and go into it. You cannot go into that from which you are seeking to run away in your emotional, mental or lower identity body. That is why it has been said from ancient times that the only way to overcome your fear is to face your fear.

We have given you the tools. We have brought you to a level of consciousness where you are no longer driven by your fears. You will find that when you look at them, they are not nearly as overwhelming as they were before you started this course. You are fully capable of doing this and you are fully capable of looking at how you have used the teachings of the ascended masters as a form of escape mechanism where you felt secure because you are in these teachings.

I need you to recognize here that some of you have gone into a state of mind where you feel that all you need to do is to look at your own personal psychology. If you overcome everything in your personal psychology, then you do not need to look at certain aspects of the collective psychology.

Many of you have in the past been exposed to war and you have felt that this is such a huge beast on this planet that you cannot do anything about it personally. You have created this escape mechanism whereby you do not really want to look at war or the consciousness behind war. You have used our teachings to make yourself believe that you do not have to look at it, you just have to look at your own consciousness. My beloved, as you rise to the higher levels of Christhood, you need to confront these collective beasts. This is what you saw Jesus do in his public mission. I am not saying that you need to begin to do this right now because this, quite frankly, comes after the 96th level—the outer actions you take. You need to begin right now to recognize the escape mechanism and how the escape mechanism influences the way you look at the path. You also need to recognize that you cannot be fully co-creative as long as you have an escape mechanism.

Being a co-creator

What does it mean to be a co-creator with your I AM Presence? It means you are an open door for the I AM Presence. What does it mean to be an open door? It means that you are not putting a restriction on where the Light from your I AM Presence is going to flow. If you have an escape mechanism that says you do not want to look at a certain condition, then how can the Light of your I AM Presence flow into that condition? The Light of your I AM Presence flows through your four lower bodies. It flows over the bridge of your conscious attention. If you are not willing to put your conscious attention on a certain condition, then the Light of your I AM Presence cannot flow into it because there is no connection between the condition and your mind. Therefore, there is no connection between the condition and your I AM Presence because your mind is the inter-mediator.

It is time, it is simply time in this course, to recognize that you have reached a level where you no longer need these escape mechanisms. My beloved, some of you may feel that I am once again pointing out a condition where you fall short, a condition you need to overcome, something where you are lacking, where you are not good enough. This is not what I am doing. I am actually pointing out to you that by following this course and being willing to rise from the 48th level to this level, you have made major progress. You have risen far beyond where most people on this planet are at.

Now, I know that many times in your outer mind you are not quite acknowledging this. We see often in spiritual students two tendencies. We see some students who are very eager to feel that they have accomplished something, that they have made progress on the path, and this makes them better than other people. These are the people who have not yet overcome the superiority complex. They can use the teachings of the ascended masters to build a certain spiritual pride, which also is an escape mechanism. You feel better than others. Most of our students do not fall into this category, they fall into the category of those who have not quite overcome the inferiority complex. You tend to not really look consciously at your own accomplishments and achievements.

My beloved, whether you are in this or that category, I need you come to this point where it is not a matter of inferiority or superiority, it is not a matter of over-inflating your achievements or under-inflating them. It is a matter of being realistic and seeing that you have now reached a high level on the spiritual path. This means there are certain things you just do not need anymore. You can look at them and you can see: "I don't need this."

When you know you are not powerless, when you know nothing on earth defines you, when you know that any reaction you have is an internal spirit and when you know how to overcome that internal spirit, why do you need to escape any condition on earth? You know that the condition can only affect you through your reaction, which is based on an internal spirit. If you dismiss the spirit, the condition cannot affect you in your higher bodies and therefore why do you need to be afraid to look at it? Why do you need to escape looking at it?

You can then go into a certain condition at the identity level, look at how it has affected your identity, how it affects the identity of other people. You can go into it at the mental level and see how this affected your own mental body and how other people have come up with elaborate justifications for the condition at the mental level. You can go into your own emotional body, see how this affected you and see how other people have built this fear and hatred that is so intense that they cannot deal with it, and how they have then gone into an escape from these conditions. You can see how other people are trapped in these aggressive fight responses to these conditions. Then, when you have freed yourself from it in your own mind, you can be free to challenge it wherever you get an opportunity to do so.

A unprecedented opportunity to help others

My beloved, do you not realize that you live in an age where every human being has unprecedented opportunities for expressing themselves on this phenomenon, that you may have heard about, called the Internet? You have opportunities, that were never there in previous times, for speaking your truth as you see it at your present level of consciousness. I am not going to tell you specifically what to do here, but just look at the Internet and what is available and how you can actually use the Internet to promote the insights that you have received as a result of taking this course, as a result of following ascended master teachings. If you look at Facebook, for example, you will see how there are many people (and some of you included) who repeat these very, very cute little statements or little movies or this or that, that are simply fluff, that are often an expression of an escape mechanism made to make people feel better for the moment.

Would it not be possible for ascended master students to use the Internet to share some of the real insights, the challenging insights, that you have received as a result of being ascended master students and following this course? Consider how this could be done. Again, I am not trying to make you feel bad here for what you have not done, but I am, on the other hand, trying to push you a little bit into seeing that you are now ready to speak your truth as you see it. You do not need to wait for outer conditions to fall in line. You just need to make a decision and accept that you have something that most people on this planet do not have. You have insights, you have an awareness, you have a greater freedom. Therefore, you can help other people and it may very well be part of your Divine plan to do so.

Again, once you get rid of your escape mechanism, you will realize that you have had an escape mechanism that made you feel that you did not need to, or it was not right, or it was too dangerous for you to challenge the illusions and lies of the fallen beings. Therefore, for whatever reason you came up with personally, your primary, your most difficult-to-get-rid-of, escape mechanism is the one that says: "Oh, I don't actually have to express my Christhood, at least not yet or at least not in this or that way or by challenging this or that condition." The primary escape mechanism is the one that makes you feel that it is OK, that you can be secure in not expressing your Christhood or not doing it just yet or not doing it in this way or that way.

If you are willing to look at this mechanism, my beloved, and rise above it, then you will be ready for the instructions of

Saint Germain. You recognize that when you give instructions, you need to give instructions at a certain level and therefore the only people who can take advantage of the instructions are those who have risen to that level. Saint Germain is not going to give instructions for the 48th level. His aim is to take you to the 96th level and put you firmly on the path of Christhood that will take you to the 144th level. He needs to assume that you come to his retreat ready for the initiations he has prepared for you.

If you are not ready, you can still take Saint Germain's book, you can read it with the outer mind, you can do the invocations and exercises, but you will not rise in consciousness. Therefore, you will not be able to express your co-creative abilities. You will not be able to be an alchemist. You will not be able to precipitate the changes that Saint Germain will teach you to precipitate. In a sense, you could say that the first six Chohans have simply prepared you for Saint Germain. Of course, we have also prepared you for each other because until you have completed the initiations presented by Master MORE, you are not ready for Lanto and so on and so forth.

Overcoming discouragement

A topic I would like to bring up in the ending here is that the fallen beings, as I have said, love to expose you to a certain condition and make you feel you cannot escape it. They also love to expose you to a condition where you feel you have some escape, you feel you have a possibility for creating a better life for yourself or creating a better planet—and then it just does not happen and you become discouraged. It has been said that discouragement is the sharpest tool in the devil's toolkit. If you look honestly at the history of religions on this planet,

16 | An Escape from Escapism

you will see many, many people who have been converted to a religion, had a great sense of optimism and hope and then, perhaps after several lifetimes of following that religion, they have been disappointed and gone into discouragement.

We have said before that there are many people in the western world today who are atheists or anti-Christians because for several lifetimes they believed in the promises and followed the practices of the Christian religion. After several lifetimes of realizing that they would not be saved after that lifetime but had to go back into embodiment, they gave up on the Christian religion, became discouraged and as a result went into atheism, materialism or some denial of religion. I desire to make some small effort here to help you come to the point where you do not fall prey to this form of discouragement that the fallen beings would like you to fall into.

My beloved, if you have followed this course (you have studied each dictation, given the invocations for at least nine days), you will have made significant progress on your spiritual path. You may not feel this, although the majority of you who have followed this course do feel that the trek upward has been worth the inconvenience. You do realize that your consciousness has shifted. Those of you who do not feel it, you can come to feel this by shifting your attitude to life on earth as I have outlined in my previous discourses, but I will comment on this topic again.

My beloved, you know the old saying: "Is the glass half full or half empty?" This signifies that on a planet like earth, it is always very, very easy to find some negative condition that makes you focus on how unbearable life is on this planet, how many problems there are and how little progress has been made. You will see many people who go into the negative prophecies and thinking that this or that calamity is likely to occur at any moment, and therefore there is no point in being the Christ in action. This is again an escape mechanism. My beloved, there is a poverty consciousness that is very strong on earth. You know, of course, that billions of people live in poverty. Why is that? Because they are trapped in this collective spirit of poverty and lack, what we might call a "deficit attitude." This is created by the fallen beings. They have, from the beginning created this deficit attitude because their life is based on a deficit. Why is this so? Because they do not receive Light from the ascended realm, from their I AM Presences. They are forced to do whatever they do by stealing light from the four levels of the material universe, and therefore they constantly experience that there is lack. There is a lack of energy, there is a lack of money, there is a lack of everything else. You need to recognize here that this is a very strong collective spirit and that you have most likely been affected by this in creating an internal spirit of a sense of lack, a sense of deficit, that something is missing, that something is not good enough either on the planet, in your own life or in your own consciousness.

Now, my beloved, I am not here concerned about you changing the planet. I am not even concerned about your outer situation. What I am concerned about is that you come to recognize that as long as you are looking through the filter of this internal spirit, you will only see the lack, you will only see the negative. You will be able to see all the justifications for why you are not good enough, why you have not made enough progress on the path, why you have not transcended this or that, why you have not gotten out of this course what you expected to get when you started. My beloved, what have I said previously? When you first heard of the concept of your Divine plan, you looked at your Divine plan based on the level of consciousness you had at the time and you formed an expectation for how you could fulfill your Divine plan. Likewise, when you started this course, you did so at a lower level of consciousness than today. You formed an expectation based on that level of consciousness about what this course would do for you.

Today, you have risen to a higher level of consciousness and it is simply a matter of being willing to look at your previous expectation and say: "I no longer need you because I have risen to a higher level of consciousness and I am willing to now look at the course, look at the spiritual path, look at myself based on my present level of consciousness." If you are willing to make this shift, my beloved, you can make the conscious decision – and it *will* require a conscious decision; it is not going to simply happen as a result of you following this course or doing anything else – that you will adopt a positive attitude, a positive approach, a positive outlook on yourself, your spiritual path and your spiritual attainment.

What have we said throughout this course? Any reaction you have that is not love-based, that is not positive, comes from an internal spirit. If you have a reaction to this course, to yourself, to your spiritual progress through your deficiencies, then that reaction is not *you*. It is not the Conscious You who is reacting this way because the Conscious You knows it is not defined by anything on earth. It is an internal spirit reacting so be willing to look at that internal spirit and use the tools and the procedure we have now given you to let go of it. Of course, you have free will. If you want to live the rest of your life on this planet with a negative attitude, with a sense of deficit, then I respect your free-will choice. Then, you are not ready for the initiations of Saint Germain and you will get nothing out of it if you still read the book and do the invocations.

You cannot be a co-creator from a state of deficit. You can only be a co-creator when you are in that state of mind of knowing: "I can of my own self do nothing, it is the Father within me who is doing the works and with God all things are possible." Jesus said it 2,000 years ago. If the path of

Christhood had been preserved, people would have come to not only believe or understand but to *experience* as a living reality that you can co-create better circumstances for yourself and you can make a contribution to co-creating better circumstances in the world. You have already contributed to creating better circumstances in the world by rising to the level of consciousness you have achieved today. Allow yourself to acknowledge this, allow yourself to feel, to *know,* to *experience* that you have made progress.

Therefore, my beloved I only have one task left. It is not a task that is based on the initiations you have received from me but based on what you have received from all of the Chohans. It is not truly I, Nada, who is saying this but all six of us: Master MORE, Lanto, Paul the Venetian, Serapis Bey, Hilarion and myself. We say to you: "Well done thou good and faithful servant. Thou hast been faithful over a few things, now be willing to let Saint Germain make you ruler over many things."

17 | INVOKING FREEDOM FROM ESCAPISM

In the name I AM THAT I AM, Jesus Christ, I call to my I AM Presence to flow through the I Will Be Presence that I AM and give this invocation with full power. I call to beloved Elohim Peace and Aloha and Arcturus and Victoria, Archangel Uriel and Aurora and Zadkiel and Amethyst, Nada and Saint Germain to help me overcome all of my escape mechanisms. Help me see and surrender all patterns that block my oneness with Nada and with my I AM Presence, including ...

[Make personal calls]

Part 1

1. I see that for many people, their lives are driven by the fight-or-flight response. This is driven by internal spirits and a very strong collective spirit.

> O Elohim Peace, in Unity's Flame,
> there is no more room for duality's game,
> we know that all form is from the same source,
> empowering us to plot a new course.
>
> **O Elohim Peace, through your tranquility,**
> **we are free from the chaos of duality,**
> **in oneness with God a new identity,**
> **we are raising the earth into Infinity.**

2. I have attempted to overcome the fight response based on the official teachings of Christianity. I have felt I should never show aggression, I should always turn the other cheek and avoid being aggressive when I am exposed to aggression.

> O Elohim Peace, the bell now you ring,
> causing all atoms to vibrate and sing,
> we give up the sense of a separate "me,"
> we're crossing Samsara's turbulent sea.
>
> **O Elohim Peace, through your tranquility,**
> **we are free from the chaos of duality,**
> **in oneness with God a new identity,**
> **we are raising the earth into Infinity.**

3. I recognize that when I cannot be direct in response to aggression, I switch and go into the flight response. If the fallen beings cannot get me to go into the fight response, they seek to get me to go into the flight response.

17 | Invoking Freedom from Escapism

O Elohim Peace, you help us to know,
that Jesus has come your Flame to bestow,
upon all who are ready to give up the strife,
by following Christ into infinite life.

**O Elohim Peace, through your tranquility,
we are free from the chaos of duality,
in oneness with God a new identity,
we are raising the earth into Infinity.**

4. The fallen beings present me with an unpleasant aggressive condition that I seemingly cannot escape in the physical realm. Since they cannot get me to fight back, they offer me an escape from the condition they have created.

O Elohim Peace, through your eyes we see,
that only in oneness will we ever be free,
we now see that there is no separate thing,
to the ego-based self we no longer cling.

**O Elohim Peace, through your tranquility,
we are free from the chaos of duality,
in oneness with God a new identity,
we are raising the earth into Infinity.**

5. For each level of consciousness from the 48th to the 96th level, there is a certain escape mechanism whereby I can escape what I feel I cannot stand. I cannot fight it; I cannot live with being exposed to it all the time so I am looking for a way out, a way to get away from it.

O Elohim Peace, you show us the way,
for clearing the mind from duality's fray,
you pierce the illusions of both time and space,
separation consumed by your Infinite Grace.

O Elohim Peace, through your tranquility,
we are free from the chaos of duality,
in oneness with God a new identity,
we are raising the earth into Infinity.

6. There are physical escape mechanisms but there is also an escape mechanism in the astral plane, in the emotional realm, in the mental realm and in the lower identity realm.

O Elohim Peace, what beauty your name,
consuming within us duality's shame,
the earth is set free from burden of fear,
accepting your peace is now manifest here.

O Elohim Peace, through your tranquility,
we are free from the chaos of duality,
in oneness with God a new identity,
we are raising the earth into Infinity.

7. The basis for escape is that I make a decision: "I never want to experience this again." Since I cannot take aggressive actions against it, then I go into the flight mechanism where I seek to escape it in the mind.

O Elohim Peace, with Christ at our side,
no force of duality can evermore hide,
It was through the vibration of your Golden Flame,
that Christ the illusion of death overcame.

17 | *Invoking Freedom from Escapism*

> **O Elohim Peace, through your tranquility,**
> **we are free from the chaos of duality,**
> **in oneness with God a new identity,**
> **we are raising the earth into Infinity.**

8. In order to escape, I accept a certain collective spirit, I create an internal spirit that offers me (in my mind) an escape or a relief from the condition in the physical that I no longer want to face.

> O Elohim Peace, you bring now to earth,
> the unstoppable flame of Cosmic Rebirth,
> we give up the sense that something is "mine,"
> allowing your Light through our beings to shine.

> **O Elohim Peace, through your tranquility,**
> **we are free from the chaos of duality,**
> **in oneness with God a new identity,**
> **we are raising the earth into Infinity.**

9. For each of the levels between the 48th to the 96th level, there is a certain escape mechanism that, if I take it, ties me to the astral plane, the mental realm or the identity realm. I am tied to that level of the fallen beings where I can feel a relief and I can feel safe from certain conditions.

> O Elohim Peace, as peace now we feel,
> all records of war you totally heal,
> the earth is now free from forces of war,
> restoring her purity known from before.

> **O Elohim Peace, through your tranquility,**
> **we are free from the chaos of duality,**
> **in oneness with God a new identity,**
> **we are raising the earth into Infinity.**

Part 2

1. There are fallen beings, entities and demons who are making people feel secure because it lulls them asleep and prevents them from walking the path to Christhood where I find the Christ-based Way to respond to the condition that people want to avoid.

> Beloved Arcturus, release now the flow,
> of Violet Flame to help all life grow,
> in ever-expanding circles of light,
> it pulses within every atom so bright.
>
> **Beloved Arcturus, your Violet Flame pure,**
> **is for every ailment the ultimate cure,**
> **against it no darkness could ever endure,**
> **earth's freedom it will forever ensure.**

2. Nada, help me see if I have used a religious or spiritual teaching as the basis for my personal escape mechanism.

> Beloved Arcturus, thou Elohim Free,
> we open our hearts to your reality,
> we have no attachments to life here on earth,
> we claim a new life in your Flame of Rebirth.

**Beloved Arcturus, your Violet Flame pure,
is for every ailment the ultimate cure,
against it no darkness could ever endure,
earth's freedom it will forever ensure.**

3. The purpose of any escape mechanism is to make me feel secure. This also prevents me from transcending myself because if I feel secure, why would I need to transcend myself and walk the path of Christhood?

Beloved Arcturus, be with us alway,
reborn, we are ready to face a new day,
expanding our hearts into Infinity,
your flame is the key to our God-victory.

**Beloved Arcturus, your Violet Flame pure,
is for every ailment the ultimate cure,
against it no darkness could ever endure,
earth's freedom it will forever ensure.**

4. I am on a very difficult planet. There are many conditions on earth that are difficult to deal with emotionally, mentally and in my identity body. In order to be able to live here, it is almost unavoidable that I create an escape mechanism so I can find an equilibrium.

Beloved Arcturus, your bright violet fire,
now fills every atom, raising them higher,
the space in each atom all filled with your light,
as matter itself is shining so bright.

> **Beloved Arcturus, your Violet Flame pure,
> is for every ailment the ultimate cure,
> against it no darkness could ever endure,
> earth's freedom it will forever ensure.**

5. Nada, help me look at my most obvious escape mechanisms and realize that I no longer need them at this level of consciousness. I have reached a level of Christhood where I no longer need the escape mechanism.

> Beloved Arcturus, your transforming Grace,
> empowers us now every challenge to face,
> with your Freedom's Song filling the ear,
> we know that to God we're ever so dear.

> **Beloved Arcturus, your Violet Flame pure,
> is for every ailment the ultimate cure,
> against it no darkness could ever endure,
> earth's freedom it will forever ensure.**

6. Nada, I am willing to step back and look at my personal escape mechanism. Help me see how I have used the teachings of the ascended masters to reinforce an already existing escape mechanism that I have carried with me for lifetimes.

> Beloved Arcturus, we surrender all fear,
> we're feeling your Presence so tangibly near,
> as your violet light floods our inner space,
> towards the ascension we willingly race.

17 | Invoking Freedom from Escapism

**Beloved Arcturus, your Violet Flame pure,
is for every ailment the ultimate cure,
against it no darkness could ever endure,
earth's freedom it will forever ensure.**

7. Nada, help me overcome any tendency to think that because I follow the teachings of the ascended masters, I don't need to look at certain things in my own psychology. I don't need to look at the beam in my own eye.

Beloved Arcturus, bring in a new age,
help earth and humanity turn a new page,
your transforming light gives us certainty,
Saint Germain's Golden Age is a reality.

**Beloved Arcturus, your Violet Flame pure,
is for every ailment the ultimate cure,
against it no darkness could ever endure,
earth's freedom it will forever ensure.**

8. Nada, help me see if I have adopted the Christian ideal of non-aggression without having the full teachings on Christhood, therefore feeling stuck and powerless, feeling that my religious ideals made me powerless. I had a need to escape that which I could not change and could not deal with.

Beloved Arcturus, illusions you pierce,
no serpent can stand against angels so fierce,
no forces of darkness can stop Violet Flame,
all discord on earth it will instantly tame.

> **Beloved Arcturus, your Violet Flame pure,**
> **is for every ailment the ultimate cure,**
> **against it no darkness could ever endure,**
> **earth's freedom it will forever ensure.**

9. There is never a situation on earth that I cannot deal with by overcoming the internal spirit that causes me to react to that condition with fight or flight.

> Beloved Arcturus, we love Saint Germain,
> and therefore we call forth again and again,
> your Violet Flame to flood all the earth,
> so Saint Germain's eyes are filling with mirth.

> **Beloved Arcturus, your Violet Flame pure,**
> **is for every ailment the ultimate cure,**
> **against it no darkness could ever endure,**
> **earth's freedom it will forever ensure.**

Part 3

1. Nada, help me see the conditions on earth that I feel I cannot deal with, I cannot live with. Help me recognize the condition and begin to identify the escape mechanism I have created in order to feel secure.

> Uriel Archangel, immense is the power,
> of angels of peace, all war to devour.
> The demons of war, no match for your light,
> consuming them all, with radiance so bright.

**Uriel Archangel, use your great sword,
Uriel Archangel, consume all discord,
Uriel Archangel, we're of one accord,
Uriel Archangel, we walk with the Lord.**

2. I realize that as long as I am relating to the ascended masters or to my I AM Presence through the filter of these escape mechanisms, I cannot exercise my true role as a co-creator.

Uriel Archangel, intense is the sound,
when millions of angels, their voices compound.
They build a crescendo, piercing the night,
life's glorious oneness revealed to our sight.

**Uriel Archangel, use your great sword,
Uriel Archangel, consume all discord,
Uriel Archangel, we're of one accord,
Uriel Archangel, we walk with the Lord.**

3. Nada, help me see if it is part of my Divine plan that I will deal with the very mechanism that I now feel is unbearable. I cannot deal with that condition if the way I look at the condition is colored by an escape mechanism that makes me want to get away from the condition.

Uriel Archangel, from out the Great Throne,
your millions of trumpets, sound the One Tone.
Consuming all discord with your harmony,
the sound of all sounds will set all life free.

> **Uriel Archangel, use your great sword,**
> **Uriel Archangel, consume all discord,**
> **Uriel Archangel, we're of one accord,**
> **Uriel Archangel, we walk with the Lord.**

4. I am meant to challenge a certain consciousness, but I cannot do that as long as I have an escape mechanism that makes me not want to look at the condition because I do not want to experience the trauma that I experienced in the past.

> Uriel Archangel, all war is now done,
> for you bring a message, from heart of the One.
> The hearts of all men, now singing in peace,
> the spirals of love, forever increase.

> **Uriel Archangel, use your great sword,**
> **Uriel Archangel, consume all discord,**
> **Uriel Archangel, we're of one accord,**
> **Uriel Archangel, we walk with the Lord.**

5. I am willing to look at that consciousness and go into it at the identity level, at the mental level, at the emotional level. I am willing to look at my own illusions about this and look at the collective illusions.

> Uriel Archangel, your infinite peace,
> from all warring beings our planet release,
> war is a prison from which we are free,
> embracing the peace of true unity.

**Uriel Archangel, use your great sword,
Uriel Archangel, consume all discord,
Uriel Archangel, we're of one accord,
Uriel Archangel, we walk with the Lord.**

6. I am no longer seeking to escape the condition that I am meant to help change. I cannot change something while running away from it because the only way to change something is to look at it and go into it. I cannot go into that from which I am seeking to run away in my emotional, mental or identity body.

Uriel Archangel, we send forth the call,
reveal now the oneness that unifies all,
help us the vision of peace now to see,
so we from all conflicts and struggles are free.

**Uriel Archangel, use your great sword,
Uriel Archangel, consume all discord,
Uriel Archangel, we're of one accord,
Uriel Archangel, we walk with the Lord.**

7. I realize that when I look at my fears, they are not nearly as overwhelming as they were before I started this course. I am fully capable of looking at how I have used the teachings of the ascended masters as a form of escape mechanism where I felt secure because I am in these teachings.

Uriel Archangel, in service to life,
you give us release from struggle and strife,
forgetting the self is truly the key,
to living a life in true harmony.

**Uriel Archangel, use your great sword,
Uriel Archangel, consume all discord,
Uriel Archangel, we're of one accord,
Uriel Archangel, we walk with the Lord.**

8. Nada, help me see if I have gone into a state of mind where I feel that all I need to do is to look at my own personal psychology. If I overcome everything in my personal psychology, then I do not need to look at certain aspects of the collective psychology.

> Uriel Archangel, the earth now you raise,
> out of duality's death-bringing haze,
> we call now upon your great Flame of Peace,
> commanding that all petty squabbles do cease.

**Uriel Archangel, use your great sword,
Uriel Archangel, consume all discord,
Uriel Archangel, we're of one accord,
Uriel Archangel, we walk with the Lord.**

9. Nada, help me see if I have used your teachings to make myself believe that I do not have to look at a certain condition, such as war, I just have to look at my own consciousness.

> Uriel Archangel, as peace is the norm,
> to your higher vision the earth does conform,
> as people have found your peace from within,
> a Golden Age is the prize that we win.

**Uriel Archangel, use your great sword,
Uriel Archangel, consume all discord,
Uriel Archangel, we're of one accord,
Uriel Archangel, we walk with the Lord.**

Part 4

1. Nada, help me recognize the escape mechanism and how the escape mechanism influences the way I look at the path. I recognize that I cannot be fully co-creative as long as I have an escape mechanism.

Zadkiel Archangel, your flow is so swift,
in your violet light, we instantly shift,
into a vibration in which we are free,
from all limitations of the lesser me.

**Zadkiel Archangel, encircle the earth,
Zadkiel Archangel, with your violet girth,
Zadkiel Archangel, unstoppable mirth,
Zadkiel Archangel, our planet's rebirth.**

2. If I have an escape mechanism that says I do not want to look at a certain condition, the Light of my I AM Presence cannot flow into that condition. The Light flows through my four lower bodies over the bridge of my conscious attention.

Zadkiel Archangel, we truly aspire,
to being the master of your violet fire,
wielding the power, of your alchemy,
we use Sacred Word, to set all life free.

> **Zadkiel Archangel, encircle the earth,**
> **Zadkiel Archangel, with your violet girth,**
> **Zadkiel Archangel, unstoppable mirth,**
> **Zadkiel Archangel, our planet's rebirth.**

3. I recognize that I have reached a level where I no longer need these escape mechanisms. By following this course and being willing to rise from the 48th level to this level, I have made major progress. I have risen far beyond the level where I created the escape mechanism.

> Zadkiel Archangel, your violet light,
> transforming the earth, with unstoppable might,
> so swiftly our planet, beginning to spin,
> with legions of angels, our victory we win.

> **Zadkiel Archangel, encircle the earth,**
> **Zadkiel Archangel, with your violet girth,**
> **Zadkiel Archangel, unstoppable mirth,**
> **Zadkiel Archangel, our planet's rebirth.**

4. I am being realistic and seeing that I have now reached a high level on the spiritual path. This means there are certain things I do not need anymore. I can look at them and I can see: "I don't need this."

> Zadkiel Archangel, the earth is now free,
> from burdens put on her by humanity,
> all people are free from their inner strife,
> embracing the freedom to start a new life.

17 | Invoking Freedom from Escapism

**Zadkiel Archangel, encircle the earth,
Zadkiel Archangel, with your violet girth,
Zadkiel Archangel, unstoppable mirth,
Zadkiel Archangel, our planet's rebirth.**

5. When I know I am not powerless, when I know nothing on earth defines me, when I know that any reaction I have is an internal spirit and when I know how to overcome that internal spirit, why do I need to escape any condition on earth?

Zadkiel Archangel, the earth will now spin,
much faster as we Christ victory win,
for in Christ the captives are truly set free,
bathed in Christ Light the earth now will be.

**Zadkiel Archangel, encircle the earth,
Zadkiel Archangel, with your violet girth,
Zadkiel Archangel, unstoppable mirth,
Zadkiel Archangel, our planet's rebirth.**

6. I know that a condition can only affect me through my reaction, which is based on an internal spirit. If I dismiss the spirit, the condition cannot affect me in my higher bodies and therefore I do not need to be afraid to look at it. Why do I need to escape looking at it?

Zadkiel Archangel, the forces of night,
are bound by your penetrating Freedom Light,
the earth is now cleared by forces so dark,
as your Violet Light provides a new spark.

> **Zadkiel Archangel, encircle the earth,**
> **Zadkiel Archangel, with your violet girth,**
> **Zadkiel Archangel, unstoppable mirth,**
> **Zadkiel Archangel, our planet's rebirth.**

7. Nada, help me go into a certain condition at the identity level, look at how it has affected my identity and how it affects the identity of other people.

> Zadkiel Archangel, we truly love you,
> and to Saint Germain we will always be true,
> help us now see our plans so Divine,
> so we on this planet our full light can shine.

> **Zadkiel Archangel, encircle the earth,**
> **Zadkiel Archangel, with your violet girth,**
> **Zadkiel Archangel, unstoppable mirth,**
> **Zadkiel Archangel, our planet's rebirth.**

8. Nada, help me go into it at the mental level and see how the condition affected my own mental body and how other people have come up with elaborate justifications for the condition at the mental level.

> Zadkiel Archangel, there is no more night,
> a new day is born from your great Violet Light,
> transforming all manifestations of fear,
> we know that the Golden Age is now here.

> **Zadkiel Archangel, encircle the earth,**
> **Zadkiel Archangel, with your violet girth,**
> **Zadkiel Archangel, unstoppable mirth,**
> **Zadkiel Archangel, our planet's rebirth.**

17 | Invoking Freedom from Escapism

9. Nada, help me go into my own emotional body, see how this affected me and see how other people have built this fear and hatred that is so intense that they cannot deal with it, and how they have then gone into an escape from these conditions.

Zadkiel Archangel, your violet flame,
the earth and humanity, never the same,
Saint Germain's Golden Age, is a reality,
what glorious wonder, we joyously see.

Zadkiel Archangel, encircle the earth,
Zadkiel Archangel, with your violet girth,
Zadkiel Archangel, unstoppable mirth,
Zadkiel Archangel, our planet's rebirth.

Part 5

1. Nada, help me see how other people are trapped in aggressive fight responses to these conditions. Help me free myself from it in my own mind so I am free to challenge it.

Master Nada, beauty's power,
unfolding like a sacred flower.
Master Nada, so sublime,
a will that conquers even time.

Master Nada, peace you give,
forevermore in peace we live,
our planet has a peaceful morn,
the Golden Age is hereby born.

2. Nada, help me see how I can personally use the Internet to share some of the real insights, the challenging insights, that I have received as a result of being an ascended master student and following this course.

> Master Nada, you bestow,
> upon us wisdom's rushing flow.
> Master Nada, mind so strong
> rising on your wings of song.

> **Master Nada, peace you give,**
> **forevermore in peace we live,**
> **our planet has a peaceful morn,**
> **the Golden Age is hereby born.**

3. I am making the decision and I accept that I have something that most people on this planet do not have. I have insights, I have an awareness, I have a greater freedom. Therefore, I can help other people and it is part of my Divine plan to do so.

> Master Nada, precious scent,
> your love is truly heaven-sent.
> Master Nada, kind and soft
> on wings of love we rise aloft.

> **Master Nada, peace you give,**
> **forevermore in peace we live,**
> **our planet has a peaceful morn,**
> **the Golden Age is hereby born.**

4. My escape mechanism made me feel that I did not need to challenge the illusions and lies of the fallen beings. Nada, help me see my primary escape mechanism that made me feel: "Oh,

17 | Invoking Freedom from Escapism

I don't actually have to express my Christhood, at least not yet or at least not in this or that way or by challenging this or that condition."

Master Nada, mother light,
our hearts are rising like a kite.
Master Nada, from your view,
all life is pure as morning dew.

**Master Nada, peace you give,
forevermore in peace we live,
our planet has a peaceful morn,
the Golden Age is hereby born.**

5. The primary escape mechanism is the one that makes me feel secure in not expressing my Christhood or not doing it just yet or not doing it in this way or that way.

Master Nada, truth you bring,
as morning birds in love do sing.
Master Nada, we now feel,
your love that all four bodies heal.

**Master Nada, peace you give,
forevermore in peace we live,
our planet has a peaceful morn,
the Golden Age is hereby born.**

6. I am willing to look at this mechanism and rise above it because I am determined to be ready for the instructions of Saint Germain. I will come to his retreat and be ready for the initiations he has prepared for me.

> Master Nada, serve in peace,
> as all emotions we release.
> Master Nada, life is fun,
> the solar plexus is a sun.
>
> **Master Nada, peace you give,**
> **forevermore in peace we live,**
> **our planet has a peaceful morn,**
> **the Golden Age is hereby born.**

7. The fallen beings love to expose me to a condition where I feel I have some escape, I feel I have a possibility for creating a better life for myself or creating a better planet and then it just does not happen and I become discouraged.

> Master Nada, love is free,
> conditions we no longer see.
> Master Nada, rise above,
> all human forms of lesser love.
>
> **Master Nada, peace you give,**
> **forevermore in peace we live,**
> **our planet has a peaceful morn,**
> **the Golden Age is hereby born.**

8. Discouragement is the sharpest tool in the devil's toolkit. Many people have been converted to a religion, had a great sense of optimism and hope and then they have been disappointed and gone into discouragement.

> Master Nada, balance all,
> the seven rays upon our call.
> Master Nada, rise and shine,
> your radiant beauty most divine.
>
> **Master Nada, peace you give,**
> **forevermore in peace we live,**
> **our planet has a peaceful morn,**
> **the Golden Age is hereby born.**

9. Nada, help me come to the point where I do not fall prey to the form of discouragement that the fallen beings want me to fall into.

> Nada Dear, your Presence here,
> filling up the inner sphere.
> Life is now a sacred flow,
> God Peace we do on all bestow.
>
> **Master Nada, peace you give,**
> **forevermore in peace we live,**
> **our planet has a peaceful morn,**
> **the Golden Age is hereby born.**

Part 6

1. As a result of following this course, I have made significant progress on my spiritual path. I realize that my consciousness has shifted.

Saint Germain, your alchemy,
with violet fire now sets us free.
Saint Germain, we ever grow,
in freedom's overpowering flow.

**O Saint Germain, your Golden Age,
sets people free from psychic cage,
the earth is raised to starry height,
as we project with Freedom's Sight.**

2. Nada, help me recognize that as long as I am looking through the filter of this internal spirit, I will only see the lack; I will only see the negative. I will be able to see all the justifications for why I am not good enough.

Saint Germain, your mastery,
of violet flame geometry.
Saint Germain, in you we see,
the formulas that set us free.

**O Saint Germain, your Golden Age,
sets people free from psychic cage,
the earth is raised to starry height,
as we project with Freedom's Sight.**

3. When I started this course, I did so at a lower level of consciousness and I formed an expectation about what this course would do for me. Today, I have risen to a higher level of consciousness and I am willing to look at my previous expectation and say: "I no longer need you because I have risen to a higher level of consciousness and I am willing to now look at the course, look at the spiritual path, look at myself based on my present level of consciousness."

Saint Germain, in Liberty,
you give the love that sets all free.
Saint Germain, we do adore,
the violet flame that makes all more.

**O Saint Germain, your Golden Age,
sets people free from psychic cage,
the earth is raised to starry height,
as we project with Freedom's Sight.**

4. I am willing to make this shift, and I make the conscious decision that I will adopt a positive attitude, a positive approach, a positive outlook on myself, my spiritual path and my spiritual attainment.

Saint Germain, in unity,
we will transcend duality.
Saint Germain, the self so pure,
your violet chemistry so sure.

**O Saint Germain, your Golden Age,
sets people free from psychic cage,
the earth is raised to starry height,
as we project with Freedom's Sight.**

5. Any reaction I have that is not love-based, that is not positive, comes from an internal spirit. Any negative reaction is not me. It is not the Conscious You who is reacting this way because the Conscious You knows it is not defined by anything on earth.

Saint Germain, reality,
in violet light we are carefree.
Saint Germain, our auras seal,
your violet flame our chakras heal.

**O Saint Germain, your Golden Age,
sets people free from psychic cage,
the earth is raised to starry height,
as we project with Freedom's Sight.**

6. It is an internal spirit reacting and I am willing to look at that internal spirit and use the tools to let go of it.

Saint Germain, your chemistry,
with violet fire set atoms free.
Saint Germain, from lead to gold,
transforming vision we behold.

**O Saint Germain, your Golden Age,
sets people free from psychic cage,
the earth is raised to starry height,
as we project with Freedom's Sight.**

7. I cannot be a co-creator from a state of deficit. I can only be a co-creator when I know: "I can of my own self do nothing, it is the Father within me who is doing the works and with God all things are possible."

Saint Germain, transcendency,
as we are always one with thee.
Saint Germain, from soul we're free,
we so delight in knowing thee.

**O Saint Germain, your Golden Age,
sets people free from psychic cage,
the earth is raised to starry height,
as we project with Freedom's Sight.**

8. I want to experience as a living reality that I can co-create better circumstances for myself and I can make a contribution to co-creating better circumstances in the world.

Saint Germain, nobility,
the key to sacred alchemy.
Saint Germain, you balance all,
the seven rays upon our call.

**O Saint Germain, your Golden Age,
sets people free from psychic cage,
the earth is raised to starry height,
as we project with Freedom's Sight.**

9. I have already contributed to creating better circumstances in the world by rising to the level of consciousness I have achieved today. I allow myself to acknowledge this, allow myself to feel, to know, to experience that I have made progress.

Saint Germain, your Presence here,
filling up the inner sphere.
Life is now a sacred flow,
God Freedom we on all bestow.

**O Saint Germain, your Golden Age,
sets people free from psychic cage,
the earth is raised to starry height,
as we project with Freedom's Sight.**

Sealing:

In the name of the Divine Mother, I fully accept that the power of these calls is used to set free the River of Life, so it can outpicture the perfect vision of Christ for my own life, for all people and for the planet. In the name I AM THAT I AM, it is done! Amen.

18 | SELF-ACTUALIZING BY SELF-EMPTYING

I AM the Ascended Master Saint Germain, Chohan of the Seventh Ray. It is not my intention here to in any way imply that what you have received from beloved Nada is not enough to prepare you for the course you will take under me and the Seventh Ray. However, I wish to give you some time to internalize not only what you have learned from Nada but a few additional ideas so that you can be prepared in the best possible way to receive the instructions I will give you.

My intention with the seven levels of initiation you will go through in my retreat is that I will prepare you to master what has sometimes been called the "Art of Precipitation," or even what some have called "Alchemy." It is the art of bringing into the physical what you desire to bring into the physical.

Now my beloved, there are books and teachings on this floating around in the world. There is a certain group of people out there in the world who are very focused on this idea that you can precipitate something. For many of them, this is based on a primitive vision where they think that precipitation means that you can manifest gold, jewels or money out of thin air, so to speak.

I know that not many of these people will be willing to go through the course that you have gone through under the previous six Chohans in order to prepare yourself to learn how to precipitate. Nevertheless, I do also know that among ascended master students most of you are still having some unrealistic expectations or ideas about what it means to perform alchemy or to precipitate. I wish to give you a few ideas here that can prepare you for the initiations you will go through as you join me in the Cave of Symbols for the final level of this course in self-mastery.

Monitor your waking dreams

Now my beloved, Nada has prepared you very well by giving you some of the teachings on the compensatory mechanisms and the escape mechanisms. I simply wish to direct what she has given you into focusing on a specific topic. It is my hope that you will use the time you have between completing Nada's course to when you begin my course, to contemplate these ideas so that you can begin to internalize not only what I am saying but what Nada has been saying. Therefore, you can overcome some of the illusions that will make it very difficult, if not impossible, for you to follow the instructions I will give you.

When you take what Nada has said about the compensatory mechanism and about the escape mechanism, I wish to direct this to the topic of dreams. I am not here talking about the dreams you have at night. This is not a Freudian course in interpreting your dreams. I am talking about the dreams you have in your waking consciousness. Some may call them daydreams others may call them higher visions or more long-term dreams. They may relate to what kind of life you would like to have, what kind of life you would like to manifest, what are your spiritual goals, what is the goal you see for society even in the Golden Age of Saint Germain? These are the kinds of dreams or visions that I am focusing on.

Naturally, it should not be difficult for you to see here that many of the people who have focused on precipitating the kind of life they want, have done this based on a certain daydream that they had. If you will bother to look out there at what people say about precipitation, many of them are focused about getting rich because they think that this will solve all of their problems. Well my beloved, there are indeed some psychologists who have done some very scientific studies that show that when people do get rich, they do not actually get happier, at least not after an initial period of euphoria. What you quickly realize, as an ascended master student, is that many of the people out there who engage in this process of precipitation, whether they are using treasure maps or other techniques, they come from a very self-focused level of seeking to overcome a sense of lack.

Consider what you really want

Now my beloved, it is impossible for you to precipitate what you truly want if you are coming from a sense of lack. This is a statement that needs to be qualified. I know very well that you can go out there and find books and courses from people who have set themselves up as experts on manifesting the life you want, manifesting riches. You can find examples of people who are saying: "Well, I became rich by adopting a positive mental attitude and so can you." If you have ever looked more closely, you will see that some of these authors who have written best-selling books about how to get rich, they have become rich by selling their books to those who are not rich but who are dreaming about becoming rich. Obviously my beloved, their scheme worked for them but it is not going to work for everybody because everybody cannot become rich by telling everybody else how to become rich. This I trust is obvious. It is in essence a kind of pyramid scheme and as all pyramid schemes, it can only keep rolling as long as enough people believe in it.

My beloved, the reality here is that many people begin the process of alchemy or precipitation with some very unrealistic dreams about what they want to manifest. I know you can find many people who have not set themselves up as experts, but are still saying that they created a treasure map, they put a picture on there with the exact house they wanted and within a certain amount of time that house manifested for them. I am not denying that this can take place but you need to recognize here that you are an ascended master student. You have followed this course for six levels, you have really made an effort to raise your consciousness.

Is what you really want to precipitate a fancy house and lots of money to travel or whatever most people dream about? I think not. What I am asking you to do here is that between you finishing the course under Nada and beginning the course under me, you consider your dreams, your visions. What is it you really want, what is it you really desire?

The hierarchy of human needs

Naturally, we have spoken before about the psychologist Maslow who came up with a pyramid, the hierarchy of human needs. You will know, I am sure, that at the very top level of the pyramid are the self-actualization needs. Many of the people that I talked about earlier (who have either written books or who have done treasure mapping), they will say that they are working on their self-actualization needs. In a sense, we could say that this is correct because there are lower self-actualization needs and higher self-actualization needs.

You understand, my beloved, that the physical universe is to some degree – to *some* degree – functioning as a realm of wish-fulfillment. What you see in some of the more affluent nations is that more and more people are acquiring a high degree of material affluence. If you could look back at these lifestreams, you would see that in many past lifetimes they had been very poor. Indeed, even a hundred years ago, the majority of the population even in these countries were very poor.

You could say that when you look at the evolution of a certain lifestream, you can see that if a soul has experienced being poor for many lifetimes, it actually needs to go through at least one embodiment (perhaps even more) where it has material affluence. You could say that this is a legitimate desire, a legitimate need of that lifestream and therefore it is part of the lifestream's process of self-actualization. You could say that some of the books that are out there, some of the techniques that are out there, are not necessarily invalid. It is possible for people to use some of these techniques to manifest what they want, such as material affluence.

I do not want to in any way go into some criticism about the offerings that are out there. I only want to put out to you that you are an ascended master student. You have risen quite high in consciousness compared to the average person. The question is: "Do you still need to manifest material affluence or some other physical desire or are you ready to step up to the higher self-actualization needs?" You see my beloved, as even

Maslow was well aware, self-actualization really is not about wish-fulfillment or getting everything you want in the physical world.

Self-actualization is about developing your "self," which means, first of all, raising your consciousness. Maslow was quite well aware of this. He, of course, would not have used the terminology that we use in terms of the path to Christhood or rising towards the 144th level of consciousness and making your ascension, but he was quite aware of the process of personal growth. Of course, if you are ready to start the initiations under me on the Seventh Ray, then you are also ready to begin your higher self-actualization needs. Therefore, what I am asking you to do is to spend some time, before you start the course under me, to consider what remnants you still have of these lower self-actualization needs.

Are you still having out-dated dreams?

I am asking you to look at your dreams about life and what you would like to precipitate, what you would like to manifest in life, and to consider whether this is what you *really* want. In other words, I am asking you to consider your expectations, your intention that you take with you as you begin the course in my retreat. Are you coming in with a desire that Saint Germain is going to teach me some kind of technique to manifest riches and a wonderful house and this or that or the next thing? Or are you coming with the expectation that Saint Germain is going to show me how to manifest my higher self-actualization needs, desires and dreams?

If the first is the case, then I can assure you, you *will* get what you want out of my course, but it will not be the highest potential of what you *could* get out of the course. If you are

18 | Self-Actualizing by Self-Emptying

willing to get the highest potential, then you can greatly benefit from using this time to step up.

I am asking you to go over again what Nada said about the compensatory mechanisms and about the escape mechanisms. You see, my beloved, you have all been experiencing traumatic events in past lives, perhaps even in this lifetime. As one who has been in embodiment, as the other Chohans, I am in no way trying to make you feel bad or blaming you for anything. I know very well that when we are "hammered down by the fallen beings," as Nada so eloquently put it, then we need to do something to compensate for this or to escape the pain.

We very easily create certain dreams. These are dreams that can have several levels. Now, on a very personal level, you will see (if you look at yourself) that many spiritual students have a tendency to go through certain scenarios in their minds. They, of course, take different outer forms, depending on the culture and the situation you grew up in. The basis of this is that you are either treated badly by other people or you are accused unjustly of having done something that you did not do. You outplay in your mind a scenario of how you are, often through some almost supernatural event, exonerated from this situation.

Now my beloved, we need to be careful here. I am not saying that these kind of mechanisms are completely wrong. When you have been through a trauma, there is a certain period where you can actually benefit from going through these scenarios in the mind. It can help you work through it, work through the pain, to a sufficient level where you are ready to move on. The problem is that most of you did not grow up with an understanding of psychology and the spiritual path.

It is very difficult to move on if you do not understand the whole process of raising your consciousness. Since you did not grow up with this, but came across it later in life, you may not have gone back and looked at these dreams that you might have had in your childhood and seen that you are actually now ready to leave these scenarios behind. You are ready to stop outplaying these scenarios in your mind because now you know that what caused the trauma was the creation of an internal spirit. What causes you to still feel pain relating to this trauma is that you carried this spirit with you.

We have, of course, given you the tools to let go, to overcome, to let die these spirits. It is a matter of looking at this and realizing that there is a spirit behind these kinds of daydreams, these kinds of scenarios. Once you see the spirit and let go of it, you can let go of the scenario, you no longer need to outplay this. In other words, I am asking you to look at these kinds of scenarios so that you can dissolve them before you come to my retreat. You do not come to my retreat with an expectation that you are going to learn how to finally precipitate the outer situation you have been dreaming about in your scenario.

A cost-benefit analysis

I can assure you that it is not part of your Divine plan, not part of your path to Christhood, that you outplay in the physical the scenarios you have been dreaming about. It is part of your Divine plan that you resolve this at the psychological level so you overcome it in your psychology, in your mind, by letting go of the spirit. This is what is in your Divine plan, this is part of your path to Christhood.

You understand what I am saying here? Many, many people have some daydreams, some visions, some scenarios but if you consider what it would take for you to outplay in the physical just one of these scenarios, you could see that this could be a rather complicated process that would require major changes in your life. It can take up a very long part of your lifespan and your energy and your attention.

Do you see what I am saying here? The question you need to ask yourself is: "If I was to outplay in the physical this scenario that I have in my mind, could I do this in the remainder of this lifetime and still have time left over to manifest my Divine plan?" You will see that the answer is a clear "No." You cannot outplay in the physical one or even a couple of such scenarios. It would eat up your life.

The same thing about manifesting great riches or a beautiful house or money to travel. If you look realistically at what this would take, how much of your time and energy would it eat up? I know, my beloved, that many of you have this idea that the money should just manifest out of thin air. Somehow, it should fall from the sky and now, from one moment to the next, by the snap of your fingers, you have all the money you want.

If you look realistically at the people in the world who have a lot of money, is that the way it has happened for most of them? Surely, some people have won the lottery but, nevertheless, most people who have acquired wealth have done so by going through a process and that process has caused them time, energy and attention.

Again, if you were to spend the time, energy and attention to manifest your goals of material affluence, would there be enough time, energy and attention left over to fulfill your Divine plan and reach the highest level of Christhood you have the potential to reach in this lifetime?

I think not, and I think you will see this by doing what they call a cost-benefit analysis. What are the costs in order to acquire my goals, my dreams? What would the benefit be? Is the benefit really the highest benefit I can see? Is it the highest benefit I want out of this life? If the benefit is not my first priority but the cost would be to eat up a considerable portion of my life, is this really my highest desire? Is this really what I desire? Is this really part of my self-actualization needs?

You see, my beloved, I talked about the people who are at a lower level, and it is part of *their* self-actualization process to experience material affluence. This is correct at a certain level of consciousness, but that level of consciousness is below where you are at as a result of following this course. Therefore, what I am saying here is that you are carrying with you in your outer minds (most likely in your mental and emotional bodies but perhaps even in your identity body) some of these old desires that were formed in the past.

Overcoming lower desires

They were legitimate desires at the time but the question is: "Are they still legitimate for your present level of consciousness?" If you find that they are not, then you have the option of overcoming these desires by letting go of the spirit behind them. This is something people cannot do at a lower level.

In other words, people who are, say at the 46th level of consciousness or even in the 50s of the levels of consciousness, they have to experience certain things before they can let go of the desire. When you rise higher, you do not have to experience it physically. You can look at this, you can see that there is a spirit behind it and you can say: "Well, I have let go of so many spirits already and I want to fulfill my Divine plan so I am willing to let go of this one also."

You see my beloved, some of these scenarios that we all created while we were in physical embodiment are a compensatory mechanism. We felt powerless to deal with the situations we were exposed to by the fallen beings (or even many conditions on earth, such as war). Then, in our minds we created these compensatory scenarios where we could either feel secure or we could outplay in our minds what we could not outplay in the physical.

Again, there is a certain legitimacy to outplaying in your mind what you cannot outplay in the physical. You can come to the point where you have worked through it enough that you can let go of the desire. However, you will not let go of the desire until you see that it is coming from a spirit.

Do you understand? You will never be able to outplay this in the physical and that is not the purpose for you creating these scenarios. The purpose was to work it out in your mind. You can come to a point where you have worked through it in your mind but you have not taken that last step of identifying that it comes from a spirit and letting go of that spirit. This is what you can do now.

Overcoming delusions of grandeur

Now, I also need you to look at some of the higher desires you have about your own personal growth and about what might happen as a result of your growth. There is a concept called "delusions of grandeur" and, indeed, many spiritual students, including many ascended master students, have a certain aspect of these delusions of grandeur. Again my beloved, there was a point where you were, to use Nada's expression, "hammered down by the fallen beings." Of course, this was traumatic and this very much made you feel not only powerless but inadequate.

You could not stand against what the fallen beings did to you or did to other people. You could not stop this in the physical so you felt inadequate. What did you do? You created a scenario in your mind that was a compensatory mechanism where now in your own mind, you were outplaying a certain scenario. Instead of being hammered down by the fallen beings, you rose up, you took up some kind of position, you filled the role of the prince on the white horse who came in and saved the day. Many of you have had various scenarios like this, perhaps mostly as children. Perhaps, you still have some ideas in your mind of how you will at some point be exonerated, elevated as a result of walking the spiritual path.

Many of you may think that you will come to fulfill some important role in the world, like you see Jesus doing. If you look at Jesus' lifetime, did he feel he was fulfilling an important role in the world? Did anybody else think so, for that matter, except the very small flock of disciples? You see that from a certain outer standpoint, you could say that Jesus' lifetime was a failure. On the other hand, he qualified for his ascension, he set the matrix for the Piscean Age so from a spiritual standpoint it was a success. I need you to recognize here that it is entirely possible that being elevated to some important position is not part of your Divine plan, is not part of your path to Christhood.

The success of your mission is much more a spiritual success that cannot really be seen from the physical level. Again, I need you to look at what kind of scenarios, what kind of daydreams, you have in your mind. Then, consider whether this is really what you want, whether this is really what is in your Divine plan. Again, you can do a cost-benefit analysis. What would be the cost of you having to go through such a scenario? In other words, how much of your time, attention and energy would it eat up? Then, if you find that it would eat up too much and not leave much room for anything else in your life, then perhaps you can consider whether it really is as important as you have so far thought it was.

What is it that thinks it is so important? Well, it is, of course, the spirit that was created back in the past. You have risen way above the level of consciousness you had when you created that spirit so it is really just a matter of looking at this and saying: "I don't want to have my life run by this desire anymore and therefore this spirit has to go." My beloved, we have given you the tools.

Dreams about the golden age

I also need you to take a look at your dreams and visions about what it means to manifest the Golden Age of Saint Germain. Now, I still see ascended master students who (admittedly based on some of the teachings we have given in a past age where the collective consciousness was much lower) who are thinking that the Golden Age means some very advanced vision where you have wonderful technology, incredibly beautiful cities with gold in the streets and gold-lined buildings.

Well my beloved, we only have 2,000 years as the Age of Aquarius. Do you really think, if you look at the evolutionary process, that this is a realistic scenario in the next 2,000 years? You might also consider that the Aquarian Age builds on the Piscean Age. What was the ideal Jesus set for the Piscean Age? "Love your neighbor as yourself."

In other words, do you really think that Saint Germain's Golden Age means that there will be cities with gold in the streets while two-thirds of the world's population are still living at the starvation level? Or do you think that the gold that could have been put in the streets would be used to create greater equality so that all people had an opportunity to live a life where they could see the fruit of their efforts? Therefore, they could see that by raising their level of consciousness, they could manifest a better life for themselves? Do you really think my vision is so limited that I want to create these elaborate scenarios or do you think my vision is based on the vision of Christ of wanting to raise up everybody to have a decent life, a life of opportunity for growth? You see here, my beloved, again it is a matter at looking at some of these visions, looking at what would it take to manifest them. You can see very clearly that if we are going to have golden cities manifest within the next 2,000 years, it will have to happen exactly the same way it happened for the kings and the emperors and the feudal lords of the past. They may have had golden palaces, but they were built by the labor of the majority of the population who lived as virtual slaves. This is not Saint Germain's vision for the golden age, my beloved. I trust you can see this. It is a matter of again looking at these daydreams and saying: "There is no reality here. This is not what is in my Divine plan, this is not the highest vision I am capable of acquiring."

Having no dreams left

My beloved, some of you, if you go through this process of dismissing these dreams and fantasies, you may end up coming to a point where you feel: "But what do I have now? I have no more dreams, I have no more visions—I have gotten rid of them all." Then, I will say, my beloved: "Well done, now you are ready to start the course under my guidance."

I am not asking you to build new dreams and new visions based on whatever. I am asking you to get rid of all dreams and visions so that you can start my course on a blank page, with an empty mind. Your emotional body, your mental body, your identity body is not filled with all these dreams and compensatory scenarios and delusions of grandeur.

18 | Self-Actualizing by Self-Emptying

I desire you to realize that the preparation for starting the initiations under me is not that you fill your mind with all kinds of things. Instead, the preparation is that you empty all four levels of your mind as much as possible.

You meet me with the innocent mind of the child who is ready to receive a higher vision from me and your I AM Presence, rather than from some internal spirit that is truly an offspring of the collective spirits generated by the fallen beings and humankind at large.

Again, your preparations for being ready to receive the initiations from me are to overcome these dreams that prevent you from meeting me with the open and innocent mind of a child. It is a self-emptying process because what Maslow did not quite realize is that the highest aspect of self-actualization is not to *elevate* the self but to *transcend* the self.

Self-actualization does not mean that you elevate the outer self to some ultimate status. This is what all of the false teachers in the world want you to believe, including, of course, the fallen beings in and out of embodiment. This is what many spiritual students out there in the world believe and that is why they fall for these "precipitation courses" where they can learn to manifest what the outer self wants. I am not one of these teachers. I AM the hierarch of the Age of Aquarius and I aim to take you to the point where you can fulfill what is in your Divine plan.

I can assure you that if you have followed the course up until this point, it is part of your Divine plan that you make a contribution to manifesting my Golden Age. I can also assure you that so far you have not had a realistic vision of what that means for you personally. It is my hope that as you go through the seven levels of initiation under me, you will bring the vision that is in your I AM Presence and your Divine plan down through the identity, mental and emotional bodies so that you can begin to see at least aspects of it with your conscious mind. For that to happen, I need your conscious mind to be a blank page, to be the childlike innocent mind. This is my challenge to you between now and when you start my course.

www.ingramcontent.com/pod-product-compliance
Lightning Source LLC
Chambersburg PA
CBHW030517230426
43665CB00010B/655